NURTURING WELLBEING DEVELOPMENT IN EDUCATION

At the core of education, the notion of wellbeing permeates both learner and educator wellbeing. This book explores the central role and responsibility of education in ensuring the wellbeing of children and young people. Vignettes are presented at the beginning of each chapter to identify particular wellbeing issues in education and provide proactive educational wellbeing initiatives to address the issues of learner and teacher wellbeing, alternative education, disabilities, cyber citizens, initial teacher education, rural education and leadership of community wellbeing. Theoretical approaches, including ecological systems theory and community practices across digital imagery, case studies, questionnaires and survey methodology are employed to explore the key message of wellbeing to educational success. This book provides a critical engagement with the educational discourse of wellbeing, whilst addressing issues impacting on wellbeing with worldwide implications. It offers a unique insight into both learner and teacher wellbeing and how education can contribute to enhancing wellbeing outcomes for society in general. *Nurturing Wellbeing Development in Education* discusses, among other issues:

- wellbeing in disability education;
- technology and wellbeing;
- teacher wellbeing; and
- leading and empowering community wellbeing.

This book includes national and international research that explores wellbeing issues in relation to the fields of education, disability, alternative education, rural, social media and teacher wellbeing, with implications for policy and practice that appeals to worldwide audiences.

Faye McCallum is Professor and Dean of Education at Southern Cross University, Gold Coast, Australia.

Deborah Price is Lecturer in Inclusive Education and Wellbeing; Program Director Master of Teaching; and Deputy Director of the Centre for Research in Education Wellbeing Research Group, at the Division of Education, Arts and Social Sciences, School of Education; University of South Australia, Adelaide, Australia.

NURTURING WELLBEING DEVELOPMENT IN EDUCATION

From little things, big things grow

Edited by Faye McCallum and Deborah Price

Routledge
Taylor & Francis Group

LONDON AND NEW YORK

First published 2016
by Routledge
2 Park Square, Milton Park, Abingdon, Oxon OX14 4RN

and by Routledge
711 Third Avenue, New York, NY 10017

Routledge is an imprint of the Taylor & Francis Group, an informa business

British Library Cataloguing in Publication Data
A catalogue record for this book is available from the British Library

Library of Congress Cataloging in Publication Data
A catalog record for this book has been requested

ISBN: 978-1-138-79382-8 (hbk)
ISBN: 978-1-138-79383-5 (pbk)
ISBN: 978-1-315-76083-4 (ebk)

Typeset in Bembo
by Cenveo Publisher Services

This book is dedicated to our supportive families who hold a strong belief in nurturing not only their own wellbeing, but contributing to the wellbeing of others.

Faye thanks her husband, Steve, whose support has been relentless, and her two children, Heath and Sophie, who have believed in their mum and lived their lives to the fullest, with an eye on their overall wellbeing and that of others. They have modelled wellbeing in all dimensions—physical, social, emotional, cognitive and spiritual—which helped to make the writing of this book a reality.

Deborah wishes to thank her husband, Jamie, and three amazing daughters, Alexandra, Isabelle and Bridgette, who have been the driving motivation and inspiration for this book.

We also dedicate this book to the children, young people, parents, caregivers, educators and broader educational sector in working collectively in attaining and sustaining wellbeing of all individuals and communities.

CONTENTS

PREFACE

This book is just what educators need. At last, a highly accessible, well-researched and comprehensive look at how wellbeing can be promoted in schools and education sites. While Faye McCallum and Deborah Price deliberately steer away from the usual documentation of health problems amongst children and young people, it is worth remembering that although children are the healthiest group in society, they nonetheless are not as well as we would want. In the context of Australia, for example, one in five young people experiences a serious mental health problem; body image is identified by youth as a significant problem; young Australians are becoming increasingly obese and, although a small minority, it is nonetheless significant that the age at which young people begin to use the drug known as 'ice' is getting younger. These developments place a responsibility on educators to ensure that children and young people are supported to be well. However, as McCallum and Price explain in this book, the meanings of wellbeing vary widely, with approaches to promoting wellbeing spanning the individualised focus on encouraging optimism and 'studying the positive' to more holistic approaches that encompass social environments through an ecological approach.

Although promoting wellbeing is increasingly seen to be relevant to schools and other education sites, so far there has not been a lot of progress in measuring how well students are (apart from broad measures of student satisfaction). It is timely for the authors of this book to point out that as well as developing indicators of risk, measures of the positive attributes of and contributors to wellbeing are needed. The increasing body of evidence that wellbeing is integral to learning may well provide the impetus for the development of such indicators in educational settings.

McCallum and Price opt for the overarching concept of 'positive school ecology' to frame their approach to promoting wellbeing in educational settings. This enables them to include the community and school/education site in promoting the social, emotional, physical, spiritual and cognitive dimensions of wellbeing. While this may seem a tall order, the chapters in this book effortlessly guide the reader to understand the conceptual, practical and pedagogical implications of these dimensions. The emphasis is on a proactive approach and educators will be pleased to find practical suggestions, tools and teaching tips at the end of each chapter for creating schools and sites where young people feel they belong and where learning thrives.

The chapter on wellbeing within disability education is a case in point. Here, Price demonstrates what a proactive, positive social ecology (or strength-based) approach looks like. The focus is on what young people (who also happen to have a disability) can be and do. As Price points out, the wellbeing of young people with a disability is not reducible to their disability. Her description of enabling pedagogies that give students a voice provides some very helpful clues for making all students feel 'at home' and valued in their classroom and school. In this chapter, as well as the chapters on alternative education sites, and wellbeing and technology, the book demonstrates how wellbeing offers a framework through which the relational aspects of learning environments can be taken seriously. Wellbeing is integrally related to the quality of relationships that children and young people experience. Whether due to the 'alternative' spaces provided by schools or through the connections that young people make via communication technologies, having a say, being heard, being respected and respecting others, experiencing learning that is meaningful, and expanding the capacity to be and do, are central aspects of wellbeing.

Today's youth will, in the future, have to navigate a world that we know will only be more complex and challenging than it is at present. While educators don't have a crystal ball to see into that future, they can play a significant role in preparing all young people to be able, responsive, creative and well individuals—and in so doing, contribute to a better society. I expect that McCallum and Price's book will indeed contribute to this project—and in so doing will enable 'big things to grow'.

Professor Johanna Wyn
Director, Youth Research Centre
The University of Melbourne

ACKNOWLEDGEMENTS

We wish to acknowledge Anne Morrison for her dedication and commitment to this book. Without her effort and hard work this book would not have sailed through as smoothly to publication.

In particular, we would like to acknowledge the research participants who have contributed to the foundational research underpinning each chapter. The voices of children, young people, pre-service teachers and educators are pivotal in fully exploring the field of wellbeing in education and we are particularly indebted for their willingness to share their individual perceptions and experiences. Aligned with this we acknowledge the contribution of research teams who have a vested interest in ascertaining evidence-based data to continually improve and advance educational initiatives, from a holistic wellbeing philosophy. These include Dr Brenton Fopp, Dr Deborah Green and Dr Greg Yates who supported Deborah Price in working on a University of South Australia Divisional Research Performance Fund Project titled *Place-based critical inquiry: exploring sense of place, school ecology and social inclusion for students with special needs*.

We also acknowledge the international blind peer reviewers who scrutinised each chapter and provided rigorous feedback and critique. And Professor Wyn for her fabulous feedback and willingness to write the Preface.

Faye also acknowledges the sterling effort, passion and friendship of her colleague, co-writer and co-researcher, Debbie. We have achieved milestones together, enjoyed the experience, and share a deep desire for wellbeing in all facets of our personal and professional lives.

1

WELLBEING IN EDUCATION

Deborah Price and Faye McCallum

Wellbeing is 'wishy washy stuff'

At a recent Research in Education conference, we presented a symposium on wellbeing education from various perspectives. Our presentation included research and practitioner examples that spanned the schooling sector, higher education, collective groups in education and wellbeing for individuals.

The session was well attended by academics and researchers from various sectors. They warmly applauded and recognised the existing research into wellbeing and acknowledged the difficulty of publishing in this area in high impact educational research journals. Nevertheless, a noteworthy professor concluded the discussion by stating: 'Well. It's just wishy washy stuff anyway, isn't it?'

On another occasion, we were presenting an international conference paper on wellbeing education in higher education. After keen discussion on the importance of wellbeing for learners and educators, we were challenged by the following statement: 'Wellbeing is absolutely crucial but where do you find time in your initial teacher education programme, given the importance of the core curriculum? And where do educators find time to teach wellbeing given the overcrowded core curriculum responsibilities?'

Needless to say these comments got us thinking. Given increasing evidence that wellbeing is the most important factor for young people's success, happiness, mental health and achievement, why is it that some key researchers and educators don't seem to 'get it'?

Our reflections on this attitude have taken us across the world. In places where violence, abuse, degradation, exploitation, poverty and neglect abounds, little ones grow up without love, safety, health and an education, despite the fact they have the right to do so. In more affluent places, children can also experience adversity but on a completely different level. And yet most children are happy and healthy and succeed at making a worthwhile contribution to society as adults. This analogy is reflected in our choice of book title taken from the original

---

(Continued)

> (Continued)
> *music track written by Paul Kelly and Kev Carmody (1991) 'From little things, big things grow'. Through education it is our belief that we can make a difference and that education has a true role to play in the wellbeing of all children to ensure they have the opportunity to grow up well, happy, healthy and safe. That is:*
>
> 1. *education has a role to play in the wellbeing of all children and young people; and*
> 2. *education about wellbeing has a role to play in the wellbeing of all children and young people.*
>
> *This book will explore different educational contexts in which the wellbeing of children and young people has a key role and will suggest strategies, tips and questions for us all to ponder.*

Wellbeing has emerged as something everyone seemingly aims for and arguably has a right to. *Nurturing wellbeing development in education: 'From little things, big things grow'* aims to engage educators, educational curriculum and policy developers, caregivers and broader stakeholders charged with the responsibility of children and young people's wellbeing in examining proactive wellbeing initiatives based on positive educational site/school ecology. Whilst predominantly Australian research underpins this book, the foundational approaches and models inform international wellbeing educational initiatives as the wellbeing of children and young people is of global importance. In particular, given the inextricable link between wellbeing and academic achievement, educators, policy and curriculum developers, caregivers and broader stakeholders are challenged with increasing responsibility in authentically placing wellbeing as foundational and integral to learning.

Chapter 1, *Wellbeing in education*, begins by critically analysing definitions of wellbeing, framing our own wellbeing definition and describing an overview of contemporary educational wellbeing initiatives. Chapter 2, *Wellbeing for all*, addresses how all learners require wellbeing if they are to be successful in not only education but their future happiness and positive societal participation. This notion of inclusive wellbeing is advanced in Chapter 3, *Wellbeing in disability education*, whereby the voice of students with disability conveys what is important to them in relation to the space and place of an educational setting and the interconnection with their own wellbeing. In advocating positive ecology, the emphasis of this chapter is on what students *can do* and *be*. Chapter 4, *Wellbeing in alternative education*, identifies the significant role of social interactions between learners, peers and educators in reconnecting learners verging on educational marginalisation. Proactive conceptualisation of alternative education supports the social, emotional, educational and behavioural needs of students. The increasing importance of technology and social media as a contributor to and enabler of young people's wellbeing is addressed in Chapter 5, *Technology and wellbeing*. In particular this chapter highlights the tension between positive and negative effects of technology and social media on social relationships. *Nurturing wellbeing development in education: 'From little things, big things grow'* situates learners' wellbeing as core business in education. Therefore Chapter 6, *Teacher wellbeing*, highlights how advancing teacher and educator wellbeing is imperative in advancing educator quality and sustainability in the profession, and also positively influences learner wellbeing and academic achievement. In supporting both teacher/educator and learner wellbeing, Chapter 7, *Leading and empowering lifelong wellbeing: Well educators, well learners, well communities* concludes by outlining the importance of proactive and supportive leadership which empowers and works collaboratively with the educational community by instilling a life-long wellbeing philosophy. As such, wellbeing education is everyone's responsibility.

What is wellbeing?

What exactly is wellbeing? How do individuals or groups across diverse experiences, backgrounds, culture, associations, beliefs and values understand the term wellbeing? Does wellbeing hold the same meaning for everyone? Does the definition of wellbeing hold constant across time and events? Does wellbeing depend on foundational requirements? How do individuals assess their own level of wellbeing? Can others accurately determine your level of wellbeing? And what is the role of education in the wellbeing of learners, staff and the wider community?

Whilst some may argue the field of wellbeing research is emergent, we suggest that varying constructs of wellbeing have been central within education, family, community, health, governance and political arenas throughout history. These constructs have encompassed a range of approaches including holistic, multidimensional, agency, ownership and responsibility, active participation, connectedness, community, positive attitude and lifelong learning (McCallum & Price 2010). At any one time, the prevailing social and environmental context (i.e. wars, Great Depression, Global Financial Crisis, terrorism, drought etc.) may emphasise particular wellbeing constructs. For example, over the last few decades the focus has been on health, financial status, women's rights and affirmative action, welfare, children and young people, safety, psychological states and community initiatives. All of these fall under the umbrella of the construct of wellbeing. So what specifically is understood by the term *wellbeing*?

The construct of wellbeing has emerged in tandem with positive approaches to health and psychology and counter to the predominant reactive medical approaches; that is, prioritising promotion of holistic wellbeing in contrast to solely attempting to reduce the effects of ill-health (White & Wyn 2013, p. 213). To date, differing views and definitions of wellbeing exist. For instance, over a considerable period, wellbeing has significantly been associated with health as shown in a word search for wellbeing in Figure 1.1. The authors canvassed approximately 150 final year Bachelor of Education student teachers and asked: *What does Wellbeing mean to you?* Their responses were collated and compiled into a wordle shown as Figure 1.1.

The link between wellbeing and health can be traced back to the World Health Organisation (WHO) which defined health holistically as 'a state of complete physical, social and mental well-being' (WHO 1947, p. 1). What was notable in this early definition was the focus on advocating for a positive approach to health rather than just the absence of disease (WHO 1947). Nevertheless, such early proactive and positive approaches to health, wellness and wellbeing, whilst experiencing some further advances, are still dominated by negative deficit approaches which focus on ill-health and lack of wellness and wellbeing. This is why currently there is a resurgence and naming up of wellbeing. Contemporary approaches have subsequently contributed to an increasing emphasis on holistic wellbeing, in contrast to a predominant health focus, which advance proactive and positive perspectives. WHO continues to advance its health agenda by identifying prerequisite conditions and resources that underpin health, such as peace, shelter, education, food, income, a stable ecosystem, sustainable resources, social justice and equity (WHO 1986). Similar fundamental conditions are identified in Maslow's Hierarchical Model of Needs (1943).

FIGURE 1.1 Brainstorm of key words that represent wellbeing

The term wellness has been used quite interchangeably with the term wellbeing. Dunn (1959, p. 3) defined wellness as maximising one's potential on the 'health axis', reinforcing the health focus of early approaches. In subsequent years, definitions of wellness have broadened to include 'wholeness in mind, body, spirit and community' (Witmer & Sweeney 1992, p. 1) and an individual's active decision-making process towards experiencing more success (Anspaugh, Hamrick & Rosato 2009, p. 2).

McCallum and Price (2012) advocate the importance of broadening definitions to include social, emotional, physical, spiritual and cognitive dimensions which promote an individual's holistic wellbeing. Globally, the terms health and wellbeing are used together as evidenced by the Public Health England report (2013) on how healthy behaviour supports children's wellbeing. This report describes how healthy childhood behaviours—including physical activity, healthy eating and limits on screen time—are associated with wellbeing outcomes in adulthood. They continue by defining wellbeing in terms of being more than absence of illness and moving beyond life satisfaction, thereby being linked with individual's health, health behaviours and resilience (Public Health England 2013, p. 5). Wellbeing is characterised as more than just the absence of illness and includes life satisfaction, healthy behaviours and resilience. In her definition of wellbeing, Ryff (1989) identifies six dimensions of wellbeing: self-acceptance, positive relations with others, autonomy, environmental mastery, purpose in life and personal growth. An international literature review for the Australian Department of Education, Employment and Workplace Relations (DEEWR) considered a range of definitions of wellbeing in order to identify shared characteristics. These characteristics included: the emotional component of positive affect, resilience, satisfaction with relationships and other dimensions of one's life, effective functioning and the maximising of one's potential (Noble, McGrath, Wyatt, Carbines & Robb 2008, p. 5). This literature review also specifically considered student wellbeing, which was defined as 'a sustainable state of positive mood and attitude, resilience, and satisfaction with self, relationships and experiences at school' (Noble et al. 2008, p. 5).

As can be noticed, an early emphasis on individual wellbeing has shifted to include social, relational, contextual and community wellbeing. That is, one's individual happiness, life satisfaction, resilience, self-esteem, optimism, quality of life and so forth, are strongly associated with one's circumstances in life. This view is supported by Van Petegem, Aelterman, Rosseel and Creemers (2007, p. 448) who describe wellbeing as situationally oriented, and feeding from experience, satisfaction and feelings. In particular, White and Wyn (2013) describe the social and relational notions of wellbeing whereby 'identities are experienced and actively produced by young people but these productions and experiences are contingent on social and institutional relationships' (2013, p 12). These broader constructs point to the subjectivity of wellbeing (Eid & Larsen 2008) and suggest that ecological systems can influence how wellbeing is defined for individuals and community groups (Price & McCallum 2014).

Ereaut and Whiting (2008) situate wellbeing within broader discourses, including the discourses of medicine (the health dimensions of wellbeing), operationalisation (measurement of wellbeing); sustainability (enabling the wellbeing of future societies); holism (mind, body, environmental and social wellbeing); philosophy (ideal state); and consumer culture and self-responsibility (resilience, independence). Wellbeing is different for each individual and the communities they occupy (McCallum & Price 2012). Ultimately, the definition of wellbeing has been highly debated due to the multiplicity of approaches (Forgeard, Jayawickreme, Kern & Seligman 2011), elusive nature of the construct (Pollard & Lee 2003), lack of specificity (Fraillon 2004) and complexity (Foresight Mental Capital and Wellbeing Project 2008). Wellbeing can be viewed as:

> a dynamic state, in which the individual is able to develop their potential, work productively and creatively, build strong and positive relationships with others, and contribute to their community. It is enhanced when an individual is able to fulfil their personal and social goals and achieve a sense of purpose in society.
>
> *(Foresight Mental Capital and Wellbeing Project 2008, p. 10)*

One might suggest that embedded in this definition is the necessity for people to feel connected and experience a sense of belonging within their community. In defining wellbeing it is important to recognise the fluidity of the notion and to exercise care if applying one's own preconceived notions of wellbeing to others. Wellbeing could be understood as an extremely personal construct and whilst there is general consensus that it takes on a more positive, optimal and desirable definition than narrow, generic and deficit constructs, one's perceptions are extremely personal and need to be respected. It has also been contested that efforts to define the construct of wellbeing 'must go beyond an account or description of wellbeing itself, and be able to make a clear and definite statement of the exact meaning of the term' (Dodge 2012, p. 222). However what we propose in this book is that in defining wellbeing, the exact meaning of wellbeing is not a fixed entity, it is dynamic and fluid, and until it is viewed as such efforts to promote wellbeing inclusive of all individuals may well fall short or potentially undermine one's wellbeing.

Therefore our definition of wellbeing for the purpose of the book is outlined as follows:

> Wellbeing is diverse and fluid respecting individual, family and community beliefs, values, experiences, culture, opportunities and contexts across time and change. It encompasses

intertwined individual, collective and environmental elements which continually inter-act across the lifespan. Wellbeing is something we all aim for, underpinned by positive notions, yet is unique to each of us and provides us with a sense of who we are which needs to be respected. Our role with wellbeing education is to provide the opportunity, access, choices, resources and capacities for individuals and communities to aspire to their unique sense of wellbeing, whilst contributing to a sense of community wellbeing.

Whilst the aim of advocating the term *wellbeing* as a positive and proactive approach rather than reactive and deficit is timely, there are still competing educational approaches. Some educators have begun to advance a capabilities approach, focusing on what individuals 'can do and be' (Nussbaum 2003; Sen 1985), particularly in relation to their own wellbeing (Price & McCallum 2014; Price in review), whilst others continue to focus on reducing perceived deficits in wellbeing, that is fixing perceived poor wellbeing. Additionally, across the globe, broader social contexts (such as poverty or war) and specific events (such as the Global Financial Crisis, tsunamis and drought) pose challenges to the wellbeing of individuals and communities. But it is important to recognise that everyone, including children and young people within educational settings have a right to experience, feel and sustain their wellbeing. Given this fundamental right, there has been a recent surge in 'wellbeing in education' initiatives which advocate the centrality of wellbeing for learner satisfaction, achievement and success. We now describe some of these initiatives.

What is wellbeing in education?

Take a moment to reflect on the vignette at the beginning of this chapter. In particular, focus on the comment that *Wellbeing is absolutely crucial but where do you find time in your initial teacher education programme, given the importance of the core curriculum? And where do educators find time to teach wellbeing given the overcrowded core curriculum responsibilities?* Whatever your own personal context may be, whether it is in early years, primary, middle, secondary, adult or higher education, academia, parent/caregiver, specialist professional support, and so forth, what is your understanding of the role of wellbeing within education?

The United Nations Convention on the Rights of the Child (1989) has provided significant emphasis on increasing the profile of child wellbeing, including the foundational entitlements of children. This has been complemented by the Organisation for Economic Cooperation and Development (OECD) who provide overarching approaches to enhancing the wellbeing of children and young people. The increased focus on child wellbeing within the global policy arena can be partly attributed to a revival of interest in social indicators to measure wellbeing and to provide evidence-based and comparative policy profiles of children (OECD 2009).

In recent decades, some educational bodies have become interested in the concept of wellbeing and have incorporated wellbeing discourses into their policies and practices. There have been various reasons for this, including increasing awareness of links between wellbeing and academic achievement and responsibility of the educational sector to promote both learner achievement and wellbeing.

Of note, official discourse within educational sites over the last 20 years, have included the term wellbeing (Wyn 2009, p. 7). Wellbeing has been seen as key within twenty-first century education (Waters 2011) and identified as a new area of relevance to education in addition to traditional educational agendas such as literacy and numeracy (Wyn 2007, p. 35). This has been evidenced within policy, educational curriculum and pedagogy, educational procedures and community educational partnerships. Increasing evidence of the bi-directional relationship between wellbeing and learner achievement (Durlak, Weissberg, Dymnicki, Taylor & Schellinger 2011; Noble et al. 2008) reinforces why a focus on wellbeing is important for successful educational outcomes. For example, the OECD's Programme for International Student Assessment (PISA) measures the progress of 15 year olds across reading, science and mathematics, and Australia's National Assessment Program—Literacy and Numeracy (NAPLAN) assesses students in Years 3, 5, 7 and 9 for reading, writing, language conventions (spelling, grammar and punctuation) and numeracy. The intended aim of these assessments is to map global and national data, compare data, monitor improvements, provide transparency and public access to data, to arguably improve educational outcomes of all learners. This is a highly contested field in relation to the equity, social justice and inclusion of all learners which significantly impacts on the wellbeing of learners, families, educators and communities. Given our fluid and diverse definition of wellbeing influenced by a range of contextual and individual factors, such generalised global academic assessments and comparisons potentially may further pose barriers to learner wellbeing, including underachievement, exclusion from assessments and/or educational opportunities, public visibility of results or further reinforcing negative stereotypical attitudes towards at risk/marginalised groups. Such factors may influence the learner's wellbeing, their family/caregiver sense of identity and wellbeing, the educators' wellbeing due to their responsibility and accountability with flow on effects to community status and productivity. Such ecological influences and interconnections of wellbeing across systems have been identified by Price and McCallum (2014).

Wyn (2007) contends that 'health and wellbeing are marginalised in school curricula not because of a 'crowded curriculum' but because not all elements are given equal value within our current policy frameworks' (p. 35). Whilst there has been prioritisation for the inclusion of all learners through broader educational policies, such as *Every Child Matters* in the United Kingdom (DfES 2003) and the *No Child Left Behind Act of 2001* in the United States, in addition to academic outcomes, wellbeing outcomes need to be embedded within these initiatives if wellbeing is to be genuinely addressed in education. Given the influence of wellbeing on achievement, then we contend that equitable emphasis should be placed on the wellbeing of all learners in both policy and educational practice. We contend that through a focus on wellbeing, individuals, groups and communities can experience access, opportunities, choices, capabilities and freedom in order to live life according to one's desires.

Holistic and multidimensional approaches to wellbeing in education

Historically, educational initiatives have focussed solely on 'the basics'. Today, the goals and directions of education are increasingly placing emphasis on producing successful and confident learners who develop into active and informed citizens (National Curriculum Board May 2009, p. 7). A more holistic approach to education is beginning to be adopted, as educational settings focus on wellbeing in order to support both the academic achievement and wellbeing of their learners. In order to achieve this, students are staying at school longer and are making stronger connections with their education and school community. However, we contend that academic achievement and wellbeing are not separate entities, but closely interconnected. Education and, in particular, educators and teachers are seen as being pivotal in shaping young people's lives. This is evidenced by the increasing inclusion of the term *wellbeing* within education, including overarching educational policy. For example, in Australia the *Melbourne Declaration on Educational Goals for Young Australians* advocates that schools play a vital role in promoting the intellectual, physical, social, emotional, moral, spiritual and aesthetic development and wellbeing of young Australians (MCEETYA 2008, p. 4). The interrelationships between these multidimensional elements of wellbeing have prioritised the need to promote not only an individual's cognitive wellbeing, that is intellectual/academic dimensions, but also address social, emotional, spiritual and physical wellbeing dimensions. This holistic focus on the child has been viewed as a way to advance academic achievement and contribute to quality of life. In educational settings, this has prompted the implementation of multidimensional programmes designed to nurture children and young people's wellbeing (Garrison Institute 2005; Tregenza 2008; Yager 2009).

Multidimensional approaches to wellbeing have included several initiatives. For example, in South Australia, the Department of Education and Child Development (DECD, previously DECS) introduced the *DECS Learner Wellbeing Framework for birth to year 12*. This framework adopted a whole care and educational site inquiry approach to the improvement of learner wellbeing across the five dimensions (i.e. cognitive, emotional, social, physical and spiritual), based on the strong and mutual interconnection between learning and wellbeing (DECS 2007, p. 3). This multidimensional approach has prompted extensive debate (amongst educators and broader stakeholders), for example, in relation to whether optimal wellbeing requires a balance across all dimensions or if individuals should be encouraged to emphasise those dimensions that are particularly salient to them. What is commonly agreed, however, is that these dimensions are interconnected. For example: social and emotional wellbeing influences one's cognitive wellbeing and vice versa; a sense of connectedness and belonging through spiritual wellbeing contributes to academic outcomes; physical wellbeing influences social, emotional and cognitive dimensions, and so on. Included within the *DECS Learner Wellbeing Framework* was the importance of addressing wellbeing across the entire care and education community, and across the domains of the learning environment, curriculum and pedagogy, policies and procedures and partnerships (DECS 2007). Whilst academic achievement remains a central goal of the framework, this holistic approach recognises that learners 'will engage readily with learning when in an optimum state of wellbeing' (DECS 2007, p. 4) and that the whole educational community plays a significant role in achieving this. This holistic approach takes on not just an individual notion of wellbeing, but rather considers wellbeing within a broader school ecology. The concept of school ecology will be addressed later in this chapter, but first we consider some of the specific educational approaches designed to promote individual wellbeing which have seen a surge in recent years. This includes the positive psychology movement.

Positive psychology and positive education

Contemporary education has increasingly incorporated student wellbeing as a focus to improve learning outcomes. Positive psychology is one such movement which seeks to 'cultivate positive emotions, resilience and positive character strengths' (Waters 2011, p. 75). Positive psychology programmes in schools are reportedly 'significantly related to student wellbeing, relationships and academic performance' (Waters 2011, p. 75). Ed Diener has been instrumental in the positive psychology approaches to wellbeing, not only within education but the broader spectrum, in particular subjective wellbeing (Diener 1984). Subjective wellbeing has been defined as 'an overarching domain that includes a broad collection of constructs that relate to individuals' subjective evaluation of the quality of their lives' (Lucas, in Eid & Larsen 2008, p. 171). Larson, Diener and Emmons (1985) identified that the best predictor of subjective wellbeing, in terms of affective experience, is the ratio of positive compared to negative states in a person's life over time. This has initiated a whole surge in research and educational initiatives within the positive psychology arena which focuses more on the positive characteristics rather than conventional psychology 'darker aspects of human nature' (Eid & Larsen 2008).

Positive psychologist Martin Seligman views wellbeing as more than an absence of illness. He emphasises the promotion of physical and mental health through early intervention, positive communities and positive workplaces. Some of his early work centred on promoting optimism in overcoming learned helplessness (Seligman 1998). According to Seligman and Csikszentmihalyi (2000), positive psychology promotes life's positives rather than purely repairing the negatives. Positive psychology advocates suggest that 'studying the positive can give us new knowledge about human flourishing, knowledge that would not be available to us if we simply studied the negative' (Wong 2011, p. 77). Seligman's introduction of the term 'flourishing' within education focuses on the strengths and character of the individual to help build wellbeing and to foster the resilience needed to overcome challenges. This wellbeing capacity is argued to create better, stronger and more positive relationships between individuals, families and institutions (Seligman, Ernst, Gillham, Reivich & Linkins 2009). Such a notion has arisen from Csikszentmihalyi's (1991) concept of 'flow', in which wellbeing is seen as a sense of immersion and engagement with the things we do in life. When we are in a state of flow we are energised by what we do. In advancing the notion of wellbeing as a central consideration before optimum learning can occur, Seligman (2012) has developed the *PERMA* model which encompasses Positive emotions, Engagement, Relationships, Meaning and Accomplishment. The PERMA model focuses on the positive factors that influence an individual's wellbeing. Positive psychology interventions prioritise strategies that increase or sustain wellbeing as opposed to strategies designed to react to or decrease misery. Thereby they have been suggested to advance a more holistic approach within educational programmes rather than a narrower focus, such as solely focusing on advancing an individual student's happiness.

Happiness and life satisfaction have been extensively researched, with a wide array of approaches applied within education. Fordyce (1988) introduced a measure which asked people to estimate the percentage of time they feel happy, neutral or unhappy over a given time period. This measure has been used extensively to capture the level of happiness within educational settings. Michalos (2008) provides the following profile of happiness:

> a happy person is likely to have low levels of fear, hostility, tension, anxiety, guilt and anger; high degrees of energy, vitality and activity; a high level of self-esteem and an emotionally stable personality; a strong social orientation; healthy, satisfying, warm love [sic] and social relationships; an active lifestyle with meaningful work; and to be relatively optimistic, worry-free, present-oriented and well-directed.
>
> *(Michalos 2008, p. 351)*

Scoffham and Barnes advance an ecological perspective of happiness as a state of flourishing involving personal fulfilment within a shared moral framework which is relative, occurring in various environments and arising from a variety of stimuli (Scoffham & Barnes 2011). They suggest that 'when people are happy they recognise it and appreciate its benefits' (p. 537). However critics of happiness initiatives question the influence of the context, environment, life events, genetics and personality on one's happiness. Such critics argue that an individual does not experience happiness 100 per cent of the time; wellbeing incorporates how one operates effectively in times of crisis, trauma, ill-health, loneliness or just within everyday busyness and routines. This critique has prompted the development of resilience programmes which are being prioritised within some educational initiatives.

Resilience initiatives in education focus on developing 'the process of, capacity for or outcome of successful adaptation despite challenging or threatening circumstances' (Masten, Best & Garmezy 1990, p. 426). Resilience includes being able to overcome life's hurdles as well as reaching out and seeking opportunities for growth (Reivich & Shatté 2002). Given the ever-changing, fast paced and challenging contemporary societal conditions, initiatives which support both learners and educators to identify risk and protective factors (McCallum & Price 2012) can provide an ecological buffer to potentially mitigate the negative effects of risk factors. These initiatives may include explicit resilience training through programmes such as *Bounce Back* (McGrath & Noble 2012), *Penn Resiliency Programme* (Gillham, Jaycox, Reivich, Seligman & Silver 1990) and *You Can Do It* (Bernard 2004). These approaches incorporate a wide range of skills and character strength training and activities including cognitive reframing, assertiveness, decision making, coping, relaxation, confidence, persistence, organisation and relationships. In general, such programmes 'have been shown to reduce distress, improve wellbeing and promote learning' (Waters 2011, p. 81).

Hope is another character strength which continues to be advanced through recent initiatives in futures thinking for young people. Educating young people in being optimistic about the future, advancing aspirations and being agentic in their wellbeing is a key emphasis in current wellbeing education initiatives (Wrench, Hammond, McCallum & Price 2013). As Snyder (1995) suggests, individuals with increased elements of hope tend to have more sense of agency, approaching goals with willpower, in a positive emotional state, a sense of challenge and a focus on success rather than failure (p. 355). Embedded within this is their ability to generate pathways to move towards and ultimately attain a goal (Snyder 1995). Such a positive approach within wellbeing education provides foundation for a lifelong learning attitude, sense of agency and empowerment incorporating self-regulation and self-control of possible pathways and futures. However, it is suggested that to be resilient and hopeful, one also needs to be aware and mindful of one's own being.

As part of the positive psychology approach within wellbeing education, proactive interventions in recent years include the notion of developing mindfulness. Emerging from health and therapy fields, mindfulness encompasses a variety of definitions influenced by individuals' perceptions. One particular mindfulness definition describes:

> a natural human capacity, which involves observing, participating and accepting each of life's moments from a state of equilibrium or loving kindness. It can be practiced through meditation and contemplation but may also be cultivated through paying attention to one's every day activities, such as, eating, gardening, walking, listening and school based activities such as class work.
>
> *(Albrecht, Albrecht & Cohen 2012, p. 2)*

Mindfulness has been described as the simultaneous engagement of three mindful practices of: intention (determine the purpose), attention (pay attention, be non-judgemental, focus on the present and be receptive to mind-body thoughts, feelings and sensations) and attitude (qualities one brings to the mindfulness activity) (Shapiro, Carlson, Astin & Freedman 2006). Increasingly, educational settings are applying mindfulness initiatives in addressing both learner and educator wellbeing. Consciousness in understanding oneself and others has been suggested to not only address life stress, trauma, tragedy and negative experiences, but proactively enhance academic, engagement, school climate and wellness outcomes (Garrison Institute 2005) and potentially improve classroom management, teacher-student relationships and instructional strategies (Albrecht, Albrecht & Cohen 2012). To effectively incorporate and teach mindfulness practices in educational settings it is recommended that educators need to embody and practice mindfulness in their own lives (Albrecht, Albrecht & Cohen 2012).

Health and physical approaches

There have been diverse approaches that address the health and physical education dimensions of wellbeing in educational contexts. Essential within these approaches has been an increase in initiatives to address the welfare, rights and basic needs of individuals. These initiatives include Breakfast Clubs, shelter, clothing and care, strategies to improve child protection and safety, and networks of support for individuals under the guardianship of the minister. Embedded within this are the physical needs of individuals such as increased awareness of the importance of sleep, physical exercise, play, recreation, connection with space and place, and a sense of belonging. Campaigns focussing on physical fitness, active lifestyles, healthy eating and self-esteem have been implemented within education policies and programmes; however they may have to compete with alternative messages that learners receive from media, society, community, family and peers.

Within this book we aim to promote a proactive approach and attitude toward wellbeing, in contrast to deficit approaches to the health and physical wellbeing of individuals and communities in need. This is because all children and young people need to be well to achieve life's goals, not just the more fortunate. We believe that the whole educational community needs to be actively engaged in this quest by employing constructive language and initiatives that advocate positive wellbeing rather than focusing on deficit notions of adversity such as young people's obesity, suicide rates, depression, anxiety and risk traits. Deficit models which are often social constructions seemingly perpetuate the issue, single out individuals, reinforce stereotypes and invite interventions to reduce the issues rather than prevent them. It is much more productive to proactively educate and advocate healthy eating, nutrition, health care, healthy sleep behaviours, movement, fitness, active recreational options, reproductive health and physical safety in the pursuit of increasing and/or sustaining healthy wellbeing goals. Keeping in mind that wellbeing is different for each individual and can vary across time and contexts, these elements need to be pursued at varying rates and intensity. Prevention and lifelong education reduces the need for intervention and benefits the health and productivity of society for a sustained period.

These initiatives need to have 'genuine partnerships between health and education sectors' (Stewart, Parker & Gillespie 2000, pp. 253–254) and also government participation and commitment as educational settings cannot be solely responsible. Combining resources, programmes and skills through initiatives such as *Australia's Health Promoting Schools* has demonstrated the benefits of whole school approaches to health promotion (Rissel & Rowling 2000). Frameworks which advocate principles for whole school community approaches such as the *National Safe Schools Framework* (Education Services Australia 2013) are central in positive collaborative initiatives. Given the inextricable link between physical, social, emotional and cognitive wellbeing, holistic positive approaches to education can promote overall wellbeing. This includes contemporary mental health initiatives.

Social and Emotional Learning (SEL)

In addition to the physical dimensions of wellbeing, educational initiatives can influence the mental wellbeing of children and young people. Mentally healthy individuals and communities enjoy numerous wellbeing benefits in terms of identity, self-esteem, confidence, connections with others, sense of belonging and academic achievement. Social and emotional learning (SEL) is a well-researched field which aims to equip individuals with the social and emotional skills, knowledge and disposition to operate and contribute productively to the educational setting and broader societal context. In adopting SEL approaches, one needs to be careful in ensuring that the approach is not underpinned by a deficit model whereby individuals are stereotyped as needing intervention in order to operate and contribute productively to the educational setting and broader societal context. SEL programmes may include a focus on the ability to work with others, coping, emotional regulation, problem solving, anti-bullying, conflict resolution, resilience and values/character education. Such initiatives contribute to students' improved school performance (academic), problem solving and planning, high level reasoning and pro-social behaviours (Devaney, O'Brien, Resnik, Keister & Weissberg 2006; Greenberg, Weissberg, O'Brien, Zins, Fredericks, Resnik & Elias 2003; Zins, Bloodworth, Weissberg & Walberg 2004). Additionally, improvements can be evidenced in students' social emotional skills, positive attitudes about self, others and their educational setting, fewer conduct problems or emotional distress (Durlak et al. 2011). Initiatives that have been adapted and advanced across the world include the *KidsMatter R-7* and *MindMatters Years 8-12* programmes in Australia. SEL initiatives are designed to build 'whole educational community' approaches to advancing mentally healthy attitudes and behaviours and counteracting traditional negative stereotypes of mental health. Being able to discuss positive behaviours, resources and support networks creates a healthy environment which is supportive and responsive to the context. Michael Bernard refers to:

> a new 'mental health roadmap' that enables us to achieve two things. One is to understand and through education weaken those attitudes and ways of thinking that negatively impact mental health. The other is to strengthen, through education, those attitudes that support positive thinking, feeling and behaving to promote the wellbeing of young people.
>
> *(Bernard 2008)*

This philosophy is also transferable to the field of bullying and cyberbullying, whereby educating individuals and groups empowers bystanders to model positive behaviours and attitudes and intervene in bullying situations rather than passively observing. Such education can possibly contribute to a more widespread influence on both bullies and victims with the potential to reduce the persistent nature of bullying. This is particularly important given that bystanders form the predominant population, being present in 85 to 88 per cent of traditional bullying situations, but intervening only 11 to 25 per cent of the time (Atlas & Pepler 1998; Craig & Pepler 1997). Positive behaviours and attitudes can also play a role in educating the hybrid-bystander (Price, Green, Spears, Scrimgeour, Barnes, Geer & Johnson 2014), one who traverses between bullying face-to-face, then reverts to being an online bystander who subsequently watches the consequences of their actions as they unfold in social media. SEL approaches also highlight the importance of wellbeing education in promoting values, respect and responsibility, where people take responsibility for their own behaviours. Addressing such issues sometimes needs a holistic educational commitment and approach rather than individual initiatives.

Relational, community and school ecology approaches

Learner wellbeing must be considered within the context of the entire educational community (Fraillon 2004, p. 17). Zaff, Smith, Rogers, Leavitt, Halle and Bornstein (2003) argue that supportive social environments promote the wellbeing of learners by assisting them to develop a positive sense of identity, agency, self-worth and connectedness within their community. School ecology refers to 'a culturally established social field, which is recognised by individual perceptions and which reflect behavioural norms and regularities' (Thorkildsen, Reese & Corsino 2002, p. 26) and encompasses the procedures and policies that schools implement in order to develop their community. Developing a strong healthy school ecology is emerging as a beneficial strategy to support students' wellbeing. As Noble and colleagues argue, 'Values are the basis of any school culture, and they articulate the essence of the school's philosophy, its goals and how it goes about achieving them' (2008). School ecologies should be developed to encompass the core values and belief systems of the school as advocated by a committed school leadership team. School leaders need to model, through their values, policies, procedures, curriculum, learning environment and community partnerships, how wellbeing is central to learning. For example, in a Finnish study, praise given to teachers by the leadership was seen as an important factor in enhancing good social relationships in the workplace, and this contributed to the wellbeing of the whole school community (Konu, Viitanen & Lintonen 2010, p. 55).

Students spend over a third of their waking hours at school, during which time they embark on a personal journey constructing their identity and establishing lifelong values and habits. A strongly supportive school ecology provides an encouraging setting for students on this journey and promotes school connectedness. It is well evidenced that school connectedness is linked to increased learner engagement and participation, higher levels of academic achievement, higher school completion rates, increased pro-social behaviours, reduced health-risk behaviour, and improved teacher-student and peer relationships (Noble et al. 2008).

Educational initiatives conducted in collaboration with the community play a role in not only promoting individual and community wellbeing, but also enhance personal wellbeing through increasing opportunities to contribute to the wellbeing of other individuals and/or groups. Citizenship and community projects encourage participants to look at the perspectives of others and proactively contribute to the planning, action and evaluation of such initiatives. This challenges individuals to move from sometimes being consumerist and egocentric to taking a pro-social approach to societal issues and needs. At the same time educational community initiatives can promote a sense of gratitude for what one already has and enhances altruistic attitudes and behaviours. Such initiatives also encourage engagement with community issues which can include connection with the local environment or broader global environmental issues and projects. In support of Connell (2007) and White and Wyn (2013) advocate that wellbeing initiatives need to 'take greater account of people's connectedness to place, with land and landscapes, as well as with people in local and global spaces' (White & Wyn 2013, p. 3). Community projects build relationships and partnerships within the educational site with families, support agencies, services and community groups. Such projects can entail specific educational initiatives or contribute to the broader societal goals of the community, and hold inherent educational and wellbeing outcomes for those who participate. This promotes the development of citizens who are committed to and responsible for the sustainability of their community and environment.

Measuring wellbeing

Given the range of wellbeing initiatives being advanced within education, how do we know how well learners are? And how does this impact in relation to academic achievement? 'Student wellbeing is positively related to academic performance' and 'just as there are formulas and practices used to teach the skills of literacy and numeracy, there are formulas and practices that can be used to teach the skills for wellbeing' (Waters 2011, p. 77). As described aptly:

> The challenge for educators is to promote happiness, health and wellbeing, however it may be defined, in practical educational settings. At a time when there are so many different pressures on the timetable and schools are dominated by targets and tests, approaches which bring 'softer' benefits are liable to lose out. Curriculum and policy-makers tend to avoid terms which are difficult to identify and which cannot easily be graded or put into a neat progression in favour of those that are easier to measure.
>
> *(Scoffham & Barnes 2011)*

As traditional curriculum areas increasingly become subjected to standardised measurement for evidence-based and quantifiable data that assess interventions, measure outcomes and identify priorities to spend funding, so too is wellbeing being placed under such pressures. The questions are being asked across sectors including health and education, how well are our young people? How healthy are they? Are they improving in their wellbeing? As described by Wyn (2009) 'the imperative to measure wellbeing, to create metrics that can 'capture' levels of individual wellbeing, to have 'hard' evidence of the outcomes of interventions intended to improve wellbeing and to target the health dollar is especially powerful for governments and organisations today' (p.115). This has significant implications for education especially in light of global or local wellbeing indices created and currently under construction.

Wellbeing measures span a diverse range of separate measures on individual or behavioural outcomes, or a combination of these measures. More recently there has been a shift to include more holistic wellbeing measures which include not only individual, but social and community notions of wellbeing. White and Wyn (2013) support this holistic notion, describing how the majority of research about health takes a medicalised, 'disease/impairment' approach and argue for more relational and social process assessments of wellbeing (p. 209). For example, global organisations such as WHO, UNICEF and the OECD, have issued wellbeing and health reports that rank countries on a scale. Developed countries such as Australia can compare their rankings in relation to other developed countries and assess their levels of improvement and decline. These reports include measures of physical activity, obesity, healthy eating and diet. While large-scale data is important to inform policy and resource investment, interpreting such data requires caution and needs to factor in variables such as the context and timing, and the unique population and community characteristics. The *International Classification of Functioning, Disability and Health Children and Youth (ICF-CY)* (WHO 2007) is a framework aimed at assisting professionals, services and governments around the world to consider in a more holistic way the health of children from birth to 18 years of age. This framework addresses: the interactions between body structures and functions, activities and participation, and personal and environmental factors. In addition to global measures, individual countries can select particular measures to address areas of wellbeing based on their contextual needs, political agendas and priorities. For example, the *Millennium Cohort Study* includes scales designed to measure happiness, worry and parent perceptions of a child's happiness/unhappiness. Happiness has also been measured across areas of school work, appearance, family, friends, the schools they attend and life as a whole (Public Health England 2013). Psychological factors measured include life satisfaction, quality of life, optimism, hope, gratitude and resilience.

In Australia research into the measurement and reporting of wellbeing has risen in priority. The Australian Institute of Health and Welfare (AIHW) provides annual reports on scales encompassing mental health, obesity, communicable diseases, inequality, illicit and licit drug use as well as overall reports on the wellbeing of young people aged 12–24 years. In addition, the Australian Research Alliance for Children and Youth (ARACY) has produced an annual *Report card: The wellbeing of young Australians* which compares Australia with other OECD countries and which categorises Australia's ranking in the top, middle or bottom third across key research areas: being loved and safe; having material basics; learning (reading, maths and science); participation; and supportive systems and environment (ARACY 2013). This report card was based on *The Nest: A national plan for child and youth wellbeing* which consulted with young people and families about 'What was important for children and young people to have a good life?' (ARACY 2014).

Health Behaviour in School-Aged Children (HBSC) is a global survey of health and wellbeing for older children and adolescents, and contributes to initiatives including the design of a survey of Australian children's wellbeing as part of the *Australian Child Wellbeing Project* (ACWP) (Lietz, O'Grady, Tobin, McEntee & Redmond 2014, p. i). ACWP has integrated a range of stakeholder perceptions to support this design since its formation, to specifically address the Australian context. Consultation with children, youth, families, community members, educators, policy makers and service providers, is important and has been increasing in wellbeing measures. In addition, longitudinal studies contribute to our understanding, and accessing the voice of those at the centre is essential. For example, the *Longitudinal Surveys of Australian Youth* explore life satisfaction for youth aged 16–25 years and implications for transitions such as school to work (Nguyen 2011).

We propose that, whilst it is important to identify and intervene in any areas of risk which may be identified through wellbeing measurement, we need to place further emphasis on measuring the positive attributes of wellbeing. This includes mapping the contributing factors, supports, resources, capacities, access, opportunities and capital that together promote individual and community wellbeing. Such an approach would inform the allocation of resources on a preventative rather than reactionary and interventionist basis. Additionally, changing the language associated with measures and indicators can shift the emphasis to positive wellbeing discourses. For example, rather than focussing on measuring the numbers of obese children, wouldn't we rather report on the number of children with a healthy weight? It is essential that educators know the wellbeing of every individual within their care; likewise educators need an understanding of their own wellbeing. How this is achieved needs to be based on a diversity of tools and approaches which deliver far more context and insight than purely quantifiable data. Measuring wellbeing also needs to take into account changes according to time, context, experience, emotions, values, resources and relationships.

Studies to measure teacher wellbeing have also been adopted and trialled across the world. Konu, Viitanen and Lintonen (2010, p. 44) identify two large frameworks for schools, the *Health Promoting School (HPS)* (Parsons, Stears & Thomas 1996; WHO 2003) and the *Coordinated School Health Program (CSHP)* (Allensworth & Kolbe 1987; Marx & Wooley 1998), are examples of wellbeing evaluations which include school personnel in their models. In addition Konu, Viitanen and Lintonen (2010) describe how Savolainen (2001) investigated teachers' perceptions of work conditions, atmosphere, interaction and wellbeing in her study *School as a worksite* whilst Saaranen, Tossavainen, Turunen et al. (2007) studied school as a working community in Finland. They argued that the community and its functionality (e.g. work management and organisation, leadership, social support, information) are essential factors in school personnel's occupational wellbeing (cited in Konu, Viitanen & Lintonen 2010, p. 46). In Finland, Konu, Viitanen and Lintonen (2010) developed a questionnaire for a *School Wellbeing Profile* based on previous studies that promoted school health on international school surveys. The questionnaires for the School Wellbeing Profile were developed for school personnel and for pupils at three levels: elementary (grades 4–6, aged 10–12 years), lower secondary (grades 7–9, aged 13–15 years) and upper secondary (grades 10-12, aged 16–18 years). The questions were essentially the same for school personnel and pupils although the wording was made age-appropriate (p. 46).

Importance of promoting learner and teacher wellbeing in education

Given the significant interrelationship between all aspects of an individual's wellbeing, including academic engagement, performance, quality of life and ultimate contribution to society, wellbeing needs to be the overarching philosophy underpinning education, not just a throw away concept that is addressed intermittently and in reactive response to areas of social and political concern. Addressing wellbeing education across the lifespan provides a proactive and necessary curriculum to enhance the opportunities and capacities of young people. Beginning wellbeing education in the early years 'is critical for children's wellbeing and development in the present (being); and it also has important implications for their future (becoming)' (Hunter Institute of Mental Health 2014, p. i). This needs to be a lifelong endeavour. The education sector is a key stakeholder in promoting learner and educator wellbeing, regardless of the diversity of wellbeing definitions and educational approaches. Learner and educator wellbeing needs to be done in collaboration with whole community services and agencies. Learners, educators, communities and educational institutions hold responsibility in this regard and, as Scoffham and Barnes (2011) describe: 'The challenge for today is to facilitate an education which is both secure and rigorous, and based upon a pedagogy which promotes the present and future happiness of the child in the context of positive social and environmental change' (p. 547).

Our wellbeing definition

So to revisit our definition of wellbeing, we propose that wellbeing is diverse and fluid respecting individual, family and community beliefs, values, experiences, culture, opportunities and contexts across time and change. It encompasses intertwined individual, collective and environmental elements which continually interact across the lifespan. Wellbeing is something we all aim for, underpinned by positive notions, yet is unique to each of us and provides us with a sense of who we are which needs to be respected. Our role with wellbeing education is to provide the opportunity, access, choices, resources and capacities for individuals and communities to aspire to their unique sense of wellbeing, whilst contributing to a sense of community wellbeing.

Conclusion

The aim of this chapter has been to critically analyse the educational discourse pertaining to the definition of wellbeing whilst providing an overarching view of current wellbeing educational initiatives including the roles and responsibilities of learners, teachers and the broader education sector. *Nurturing wellbeing development in education: 'From little things, big things grow'* aims to show how educational settings can nurture wellbeing in education. In particular, the book aims to provide proactive wellbeing education initiatives which enhance learner and teacher wellbeing, in contrast to perpetuating deficit responses to wellbeing issues. In doing so, each chapter's initial vignette will challenge readers across themes of whole school approaches to wellbeing, wellbeing within disability education, alternative education, social media and positive uses of technology to support social and emotional wellbeing, rural education and teacher wellbeing. The book aims to provide individual and collective issues and strategies to promote wellbeing. In particular, we advocate a holistic view to reinforce that everyone has roles and responsibilities for ensuring the wellbeing of children, young people and educators. Education is the most logical place to promote and develop this notion for improved societal outcomes.

Wellbeing follow-up activities

1. What is your definition of wellbeing?
2. What are the factors which influence your wellbeing definition?
3. How do you determine the wellbeing of others (i.e. family members, friends, students, staff etc.)?
4. How do you promote your own sense of wellbeing?
5. What is your role in supporting the wellbeing of others?
6. What is the role of education in promoting wellbeing of its school/site community members?
7. How equitable is wellbeing in relation to core curriculum within your current context?
8. How is wellbeing represented in your settings policy, practice and curriculum? How effectively is this applied?

References

Albrecht, NJ, Albrecht, PM & Cohen, M (2012) Mindfully teaching in the classroom: A literature review. *Australian Journal of Teacher Education*, 37(12), Article 1.

Allensworth, D & Kolbe, L (1987) The comprehensive school health program: Exploring an expanded concept. *Journal of School Health*, 57, pp. 409–412.

Anspaugh, D, Hamrick, M & Rosato, F (2009) *Wellness: Concepts and applications*. McGraw-Hill Higher Education, New York, NY.

ARACY (2013) *Report card: The wellbeing of young Australians*. Australian Research Alliance for Children and Youth, Sydney, NSW.

ARACY (2014) *The Nest action agenda: Improving the wellbeing of Australia's children and youth while growing our GDP by over 7%*. Australian Research Alliance for Children and Youth, Canberra, ACT.

Atlas, RS & Pepler, DJ (1998) Observations of bullying in the classroom. *The Journal of Educational Research*, 92(2), pp. 86–99.

Bernard, M (2004) *The you can do it! Early childhood education program: A social-emotional learning curriculum (4–6 year olds)*. Australian Scholarships Group, Oakleigh, VIC.

Bernard, M (2008) The psychology of children's mental health: It's time to educate all young people that 'things are neither good nor bad but thinking makes it so'. *Education Connect*, 13, pp. 3–5.

Connell, R (2007) *Southern theory: The global dynamics of knowledge in social science*. Allen & Unwin, Sydney, NSW.

Craig, W & Pepler, DJ (1997) Observations of bullying and victimization in the schoolyard. *Canadian Journal of School Psychology*, 13, pp. 41–60.

Csikszentmihalyi, M (1991) *Flow: The psychology of optimal experience*. Harper & Row, New York, NY.

DECS (2007) *DECS Learner Wellbeing Framework for birth to year 12*. Department of Education and Children's Services, Adelaide, SA.

Devaney, E, O'Brien, MU, Resnik, H, Keister, S & Weissberg, RP (2006) *Sustainable schoolwide social and emotional learning (SEL): Implementation guide and toolkit*. CASEL, University of Illinois at Chicago, Chicago, IL.

DfES (2003) *Every child matters*. Department for Education and Skills, Nottingham, UK.

Diener, E (1984) Subjective well-being. *Psychological Bulletin*, 95, pp. 542–575.

Dodge, R (2012) The challenge of defining wellbeing. *International Journal of Wellbeing*, 2(3), pp. 222–235.

Dunn, H. L. (1959). High-Level Wellness for Man and Society. *American Journal of Public Health and the Nations Health*, 49(6), 786–792.

Durlak, JA, Weissberg, RP, Dymnicki, AB, Taylor, RD & Schellinger, KB (2011) The impact of enhancing students' social and emotional learning: A meta-analysis of school-based universal interventions. *Child Development*, 82(1), pp. 405–432.

Education Services Australia (2013) *National Safe Schools Framework (updated 2013)*. Standing Council on School Education and Early Childhood, Carlton South, VIC.

Eid, M & Larsen, RJ (2008) *The science of subjective well-being*. Guilford Press, New York, NY.

Ereaut, G & Whiting, R (2008) *What do we mean by 'wellbeing'? And why might it matter?* Department for Children, Schools and Families, London.

Fordyce, M (1988) A review of research on the happiness measures: A sixty second index of happiness and mental health. *Social Indicators Research*, 20(4), pp. 355–381.

Foresight Mental Capital and Wellbeing Project (2008) *Final Project report – Executive summary*. The Government Office for Science, London.

Forgeard, MJ, Jayawickreme, E, Kern, ML & Seligman, ME (2011) Doing the right thing: Measuring wellbeing for public policy. *International Journal of Wellbeing*, 1(1), pp. 79–106.

Fraillon, J (2004) *Measuring student well-being in the context of Australian schooling*. Paper prepared for the Ministerial Council on Education, Employment, Training and Youth Affairs, Carlton South, VIC.

Garrison Institute (2005) *Contemplation and education – A survey of programs using contemplative techniques in K-12 educational settings: A mapping report*. Garrison Institute, Garrison, NY.

Gillham, J, Jaycox, L, Reivich, K, Seligman, M & Silver, T (1990) The Penn Resiliency Program (unpublished manual). University of Pennsylvania, Philadelphia, PA.

Greenberg, MT, Weissberg, RP, O'Brien, MU, Zins, JE, Fredericks, L, Resnik, H & Elias, MJ (2003) Enhancing school-based prevention and youth development through coordinated social, emotional, and academic learning. *American Psychologist*, 58(6–7), pp. 466–474.

Hunter Institute of Mental Health (2014) *Connections: A resource for early childhood educators about children's wellbeing.* Australian Government Department of Education, Canberra, ACT.

Kelly, P & Carmody, K (1991) From little things, big things grow. Performed by Paul Kelly and the Messengers, *Comedy*, Mushroom Records, Melbourne, VIC.

Konu, A, Viitanen, E & Lintonen, T (2010) Teachers' wellbeing and perceptions of leadership practices. *International Journal of Workplace Health Management*, 3(1), pp. 44–57.

Larson, R, Diener, E & Emmons, R (1985) An evaluation of subjective well-being measures. *Social Indicators Research*, 17, pp. 1–18.

Lietz, P, O'Grady, E, Tobin, M, McEntee, A & Redmond, G (2014) *Towards the ACWP questionnaire. The Australian Child Wellbeing Project: Final phase two report.* Flinders University, University of NSW and the Australian Council for Educational Research, Adelaide, SA.

Marx, E & Wooley, S (eds) (1998) *Health is academic: A guide to coordinated school health programs.* Teachers College Press, New York, NY.

Maslow, A (1943) A theory of human motivation. *Psychological Review*, 50(4), pp. 370–396.

Masten, AS, Best, KM & Garmezy, N (1990) Resilience and development: Contributions from the study of children who overcome adversity. *Development and Psychopathology*, 2(4), pp. 425–444.

McCallum, F & Price, D (2010) Well teachers, well students. *Journal of Student Wellbeing*, 4(1), pp. 19–34.

McCallum, F & Price, D (2012) Keeping teacher wellbeing on the agenda. *Professional Educator*, 11(2), pp. 4–7.

MCEETYA (2008) *Melbourne Declaration on Educational Goals for Young Australians (December 2008).* Ministerial Council on Education, Emploment, Training and Youth Affairs, Melbourne, VIC.

McGrath, H & Noble, T (2012) *Bounce back! A classroom resilience program: Teacher's handbook.* Pearson Longman, Sydney, NSW.

Michalos, AC (2008) Education, happiness and wellbeing. *Social Indicators Research*, 87(3), pp. 347–366.

National Curriculum Board (May 2009) *The shape of the Australian curriculum.* Commonwealth of Australia, Barton, ACT.

Nguyen, N (2011) *Trends in young people's wellbeing and the effects of the school-to-work transition. Longitudinal Surveys of Australian Youth Briefing Paper 27.* NCVER, Adelaide, SA.

Noble, T, McGrath, H, Wyatt, T, Carbines, R & Robb, L (2008) *Scoping study into aproaches to student well-being: Literature review. Report to the Department of Education, Employment and Workplace Relations.* Australian Catholic University & Erebus International, Sydney, NSW.

Nussbaum, M (2003) Capabilities as fundamental entitlements: Sen and social justice. *Feminist Economics*, 9(2–3), pp. 33–59.

OECD (2009) *Doing better for children.* Organisation for Economic Co-operation and Development, Paris.

Parsons, C, Stears, D & Thomas, C (1996) The health-promoting school in Europe: Conceptualizing and evaluating the change. *Health Education Journal*, 55, pp. 311–321.

Pollard, EL & Lee, PD (2003) Child well-being: A systematic review of the literature. *Social Indicators Research*, 61(1), pp. 59–78.

Price, D, Green, D, Spears, B, Scrimgeour, M, Barnes, A, Geer, R & Johnson, B (2014) A qualitative exploration of cyber-bystanders and moral engagement. *Australian Journal of Guidance and Counselling*, 24(1), pp. 1–17.

Price, D & McCallum, F (2015) Ecological influences on teachers' well-being and 'fitness'. *Asia-Pacific Journal of Teacher Education*, 43(3), pp. 195–209.

Price, D & McCallum, F (2014) Teacher wellbeing: Initial teacher education capability approach. Paper presented at the British Educational Research Association Conference, London, 23–25 September 2014.

Price, D (2015) Pedagogies for inclusion of students with disabilities in a national curriculum: a human capabilities approach. *Journal of Educational Enquiry* 14(2). Special edition: Social Justice and Pedagogies.

Public Health England (2013) *How healthy behaviour supports children's well-being.* Health & Wellbeing Directorate, Public Health England, London.

Reivich, K & Shatté, A (2002) *The resilience factor: 7 keys to finding your inner strengths and overcoming life's hurdles.* Broadway Books, New York, NY.

Rissel, C & Rowling, L (2000) Intersectoral collaboration for the development of a national framework for health promoting schools in Australia. *Journal of School Health*, 70(6), pp. 248–250.

Ryff, C (1989) Happiness is everything, or is it? Explorations on the meaning of psychological well-being. *Journal of Personality and Social Psychology*, 57(6), pp. 1069–1081.

Saaranen, T, Tossavainen, K, Turunen, H, Kiviniemi, V & Vertio, H (2007) Occupational wellbeing of school staff members: A structural equation model. *Health Education Research*, 22(2), pp. 248–260.

Savolainen, A (2001) *Koulu työpaikkana (School as a worksite)*. Tampere University Press, Tampere, Finland.

Scoffham, S & Barnes, J (2011) Happiness matters: Towards a pedagogy of happiness and well-being. *Curriculum Journal*, 22(4), pp. 535–548.

Seligman, M & Csikszentmihalyi, M (2000) Positive psychology: An introduction. *American Psychologist*, 55, pp. 5–14.

Seligman, ME (1998) *Learned optimism*. Simon and Schuster, New York, NY.

Seligman, ME (2012) *Flourish: A visionary new understanding of happiness and well-being*. Free Press, New York, NY.

Seligman, ME, Ernst, RM, Gillham, J, Reivich, K & Linkins, M (2009) Positive education: Positive psychology and classroom interventions. *Oxford Review of Education*, 35(3), pp. 293–311.

Sen, A (1985) *Commodities and capabilities*. North-Holland, Amsterdam.

Shapiro, SL, Carlson, LE, Astin, JA & Freedman, B (2006) Mechanisms of mindfulness. *Journal of Clinical Psychology*, 62(3), pp. 373–386.

Snyder, C (1995) Conceptualising, measuring and nurturing hope. *Journal of Counseling & Development*, 73, pp. 355–360.

Stewart, D, Parker, E & Gillespie, A (2000) An audit of health promoting schools policy documentation. *Journal of School Health*, 70(6), pp. 253–254.

Thorkildsen, T, Reese, D & Corsino, A (2002) School ecologies and attitudes about exclusionary behaviour among adolescents and young adults. *Merrill-Palmer Quarterly*, 48(1), pp. 25–51.

Tregenza, V (2008) Looking back to the future: The current relevance of Maria Montessori's ideas about the spiritual wellbeing of young children. *Journal of Student Wellbeing*, 2(2), pp. 1–15.

United Nations (1989) *United Nations Convention on the Rights of the Child*. United Nations, New York, NY.

Van Petegem, K, Aelterman, A, Rosseel, Y & Creemers, B (2007) Student perception as moderator for student wellbeing. *Social Indicators Research*, 83(3), pp. 447–463.

Waters, L (2011) A review of school-based positive psychology interventions. *The Australian Educational and Developmental Psychologist*, 28(2), pp. 75–90.

White, RD & Wyn, J (2013) *Youth and society*. 3rd edn, Oxford University Press, South Melbourne, VIC.

WHO (1947) *WHO definition of health (preamble to the Constitution of the World Health Organization as adopted by the International Health Conference, New York, 19–22 June, 1946)*. World Health Organization, New York, NY.

WHO (1986) *Ottawa Charter for Health Promotion*. World Health Organization, Ottawa, 21 November 1986.

WHO (2003) *Creating an environment for emotional and social well-being: An important responsibility of a health promoting and child friendly school*. World Health Organization, Geneva.

WHO (2007) *The international classification of functioning, disability and health children and youth (ICF-CY)*. World Health Organization, Geneva.

Witmer, J & Sweeney, T (1992) A holistic model for wellness and prevention over the life span. *Journal of Counseling & Development*, 71(2), pp. 140–148.

Wong, PT (2011) Positive psychology 2.0: Towards a balanced interactive model of the good life. *Canadian Psychology*, 52(2), pp. 69–81.

Wrench, A, Hammond, C, McCallum, F & Price, D (2013) Inspire to aspire: Raising aspirational outcomes through a student well-being curricular focus. *International Journal of Inclusive Education*, 17(9), pp. 932–947.

Wyn, J (2007) Learning to 'become somebody well': Challenges for educational policy. *Australian Educational Researcher*, 34(3), pp. 35–52.

Wyn, J (2009) *Youth health and welfare: The cultural politics of education and wellbeing.* Oxford University Press, South Melbourne, VIC.

Yager, Z (2009) Developing wellbeing in first year pre-service teachers: A trial of a personal approach to professional education. *Journal of Student Wellbeing,* 3(1), pp. 52–72.

Zaff, J, Smith, D, Rogers, M, Leavitt, C, Halle, T & Bornstein, M (2003) Holistic well-being and the developing child. In M Bornstein, L Davidson, C Keyes & K Moore (eds), *Well-being: Positive development across the life course.* Lawrence Erlbaum Associates, Mahwah, NJ, pp. 23–32.

Zins, JE, Bloodworth, MR, Weissberg, RP & Walberg, HJ (2004) The scientific base linking social and emotional learning to school success. In JE Zins, RP Weissberg, MC Wang & HJ Walberg (eds), *Building academic success on social and emotional learning: What does the research say?* Teachers College Press, New York, NY, pp. 2–22.

2

WELLBEING FOR ALL

Faye McCallum and Deborah Price

> *I have lots of friends that make me happy*
> *I have teachers that help me when I need help*
> *There are lots of things I can do that I like*
> *There is always time to have fun and talk with friends*
> *There are always new things to do and people to meet*
>
> (9-year-old student)

Introduction

As the previous chapter has substantiated, wellbeing is not a new concept in education, health and other sectors. What is unclear is an agreed definition of wellbeing, and how we achieve and sustain quality wellbeing for all. However, what is clear is that wellbeing is needed so that people can aspire to succeed and to live long, happy and productive lives. This chapter will take a holistic approach to wellbeing in order to highlight that raising our children and young people to be cognitively, socially, physically, emotionally and spiritually well is a community responsibility. This holistic concept (which we call *positive school ecology*) will be discussed from an ecological viewpoint situated in a school site that used an overarching framework that aimed for all its students to be well. The brief vignette above, written by a young primary school participant in one of our research projects, points out that life satisfaction and happiness is achievable if we feel we belong and work together as a community heading towards the same life goals, whatever they may be.

We know that wellbeing contributes to the hope, friendliness and happiness of many within the educational setting and in the community. Schools and educational institutions have emerged as important sites for the implementation of strategies designed to improve health and that counter anti-social behaviour and under-achievement. When the wellbeing concept is applied to schools or other educational sites, it refers to the cultivation of positive emotions and the engagement of character strengths in order to enhance student and staff

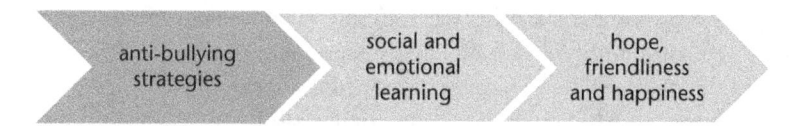

FIGURE 2.1   Historical initiatives that address the whole child

wellbeing, resilience, belonging, and the overall holistic benefits of being happy and having a sense of hope. We suggest that the holistic concept is one of *positive school ecology* and would argue that this is a third wave in a series of historical initiatives (Figure 2.1) that address the whole child, evolving from anti-bullying strategies, to an emphasis on social and emotional learning to the current focus on hope, friendliness and happiness.

School programmes that address bullying, conflict and other forms of adversity have been implemented across the world with some success, and predominately in upper primary and secondary settings. Like bullying, cyberbullying programmes have also received much attention in schools with the aim of equipping children and young people to be more resilient and to keep themselves safe from emotional and psychological harm. Likewise, social and emotional learning (SEL) programmes have also been successful in acknowledging the importance of developing the social and emotional capacities of children and young people and thus potentially improving behaviour and achievement (Durlak, Weissberg, Dymnicki, Taylor & Schellinger 2011). Freeman, Wertheim and Trinder (2014) identify several factors that facilitate the effectiveness of SEL programmes when implemented across the whole school. These factors include: having a whole school vision; maximising pre-programme engagement; linking the new programme with existing ones in the school; having leadership and staff support; ensuring the programme matches the specific context; and monitoring and feedback processes to sustain motivation (p. 853).

In this chapter, we introduce the concept of *positive school ecology*. The term *school ecology* is described by Thorkildsen, Reese and Corsino (2002) as 'the sociocultural norms that are prevalent within a given educational institution'. They elaborate further:

> School ecologies are culturally established social fields that are regulated by individuals' perceptions. Individuals' perceptions of school ecologies are comprised of observations that are constrained by their feelings and evaluations of behaviour.
> *(Thorkildsen, Reese & Corsino 2002, p. 26)*

The *positive* school ecology concept takes a proactive rather than a reactive approach to wellbeing, integrating a whole school community commitment in promoting individual, social, relational, behavioural, environmental and political wellbeing components. A positive school ecology highlights the need for individuals to have tools, which can include student voice, positive student perceptions, positive thinking, resilience and coping, flexible thinking, developing and sustaining a sense of community, and being friendly and respectful to others despite life's challenges.

Positive school ecology promotes an environment that helps to minimise adverse emotions, therefore supporting student learning and wellbeing. Wellbeing is a holistic state that encompasses the social, emotional, physical, spiritual and cognitive dimensions of the individual (McCallum & Price 2010). When people are asked about their wellbeing they generally refer to quality of life, quality of relationships, achievements and individual values. Simultaneously a community and individual phenomenon (Wyn 2009, p. 108), wellbeing contributes to the successful development of individuals across the life course, so that they are better able to realise their full potential, to experience satisfying personal relationships and to enjoy a rich life.

Supportive social environments contribute significantly to the happiness and wellbeing of children, assisting them to develop a positive sense of identity, agency, worth and connectedness within their community (Zaff, Smith, Rogers, Leavitt, Halle & Bornstein 2003). In educational settings, student wellbeing must be considered within the context of the entire school community (Fraillon 2004, p. 17). As a multidimensional construct, wellbeing cannot be measured via a single indicator, but through a composite analysis of the contributory factors.

Much can be learned by understanding the attitudes and behaviour of the 'most happy' students. Numerous reports and research around the world have focussed on negative influences that impact on children's growth and development, particularly children from low-socio economic backgrounds or countries. Few have studied the positive influences that ensure our children and young people are successful and happy. A sense of happiness at school can be derived from various factors including the level to which we feel we belong and how friendly the school is. In a study conducted by McCallum and Price in 2009 at one elite school which we will call 'GreenLeaf Primary', the most significant factors for predicting childhood happiness were found to be optimistic thinking and having quality friendships, a finding also supported by the work of O'Rourke and Cooper (2010). Our research also identified the importance of developing strong and healthy staff-student relationships whereby staff knew their students, and taught and related to them using individualised interactions, thus assisting in the prevention of social isolation. What happens beyond the classroom or school may be beyond the influence of staff, however they can still create the opportunity for developing an atmosphere where students feel included and perceive that they have friends. Additionally, the most committed school principals/leaders are those that identify a connection between wellbeing principles and their own school culture and vision, which incorporates a strong and happy learning environment where children and young people flourish and aspire.

Positive social ecology

Central to this book and the theme of 'wellbeing for all' is what we term *positive social ecology*. Drawn from the work of Bronfenbrenner (1992) and explained extensively in Price and McCallum (2014) where the concept of social ecology was applied to teachers' wellbeing, here we take the concept further to describe how an ecological perspective can influence everyone's sense of wellbeing and belonging to a community.

We suggest there are four domains of Intrapersonal, Environmental, Behavioural and Political influence factors in the Natural, Information, and Social and Cultural environments of a community, as clarified in Table 2.1. The first domain, *Intrapersonal*, includes factors like the demographics of the specific community, biological and psychological factors, and the inter-relationships of the people that live in that community. The second domain, *Environmental*, includes the actual or perceived views or experiences that may impact on the immediate environment. These are often in relation to crime, safety, physical attractiveness, comfort, convenience, and accessibility of the area in which one lives. The third domain, *Behavioural*, relates to active living and includes activities, services or access to certain tools or

TABLE 2.1 Characteristics of the social ecology concept

	Natural	*Information*	*Social and Cultural Environments*
Intrapersonal	Demographic data of the specific people who make up the community.	Biological factors of the people that live there including family situation, cultural groups, age etc.	Psychological factors of the people that live and how they interact.
Environmental	Actual or perceived views or experiences that may impact on the immediate environment.	Statistics related to issues that impact on the environment, e.g. crime rates and prevalence. And media alerts that build community connections.	Programmes and activities that promote community safety, attractiveness, comfort, convenience, and accessibility of the area in which we live.
Behavioural	Active living in the community.	Information, promotion and advertisement of opportunities to interact positively together including special events and celebrations.	Includes activities, services or access to certain tools or structures that enable people living and working in a community to be positively engaged and physically, intellectually and emotionally active.
Political	Relevant localised policies and practices that enhance the natural environment.	Communication of past, present and future policies that affect people living in the community.	Developments to infrastructure or operations that enhance community socialisation.

structures that enable people living and working in a community to be positively engaged and physically, intellectually and emotionally active. Factors included here are related to recreation, for example: entertainment; parks; trails; programmes; private facilities; community groups and activities; and availability of sports. This domain is multifaceted and can be different for households, educational settings or the neighbourhood.

To put the model into practice, we could consider the social ecology of a single household within a community. Within this household we would look at: entertainment facilities and equipment; gardens; space to play and belong; stairs; electronic entertainment; labour-saving devices; access to good babysitters and carers; cleanliness and hygiene; employment of parents/carers; siblings (number, age, gender, health); and social capital.

In a school, factors that influence the social ecology include: the neighbourhood; walkability; facilities; academic achievement outcomes; Physical Education programmes; health programmes and professional services; breakfast programmes; social programmes; special academic programmes, e.g. music or language; parking; transit access; child safety; accessibility; student profile and population; stairs and physical access; signage; community climate; and school norms. And in a neighbourhood, the important factors include: healthcare access and facilities; counselling; sports; parks; recreation space for walking and riding bikes; aesthetics; child safety; shopping availability and access; parking; congestion; and social support and activities.

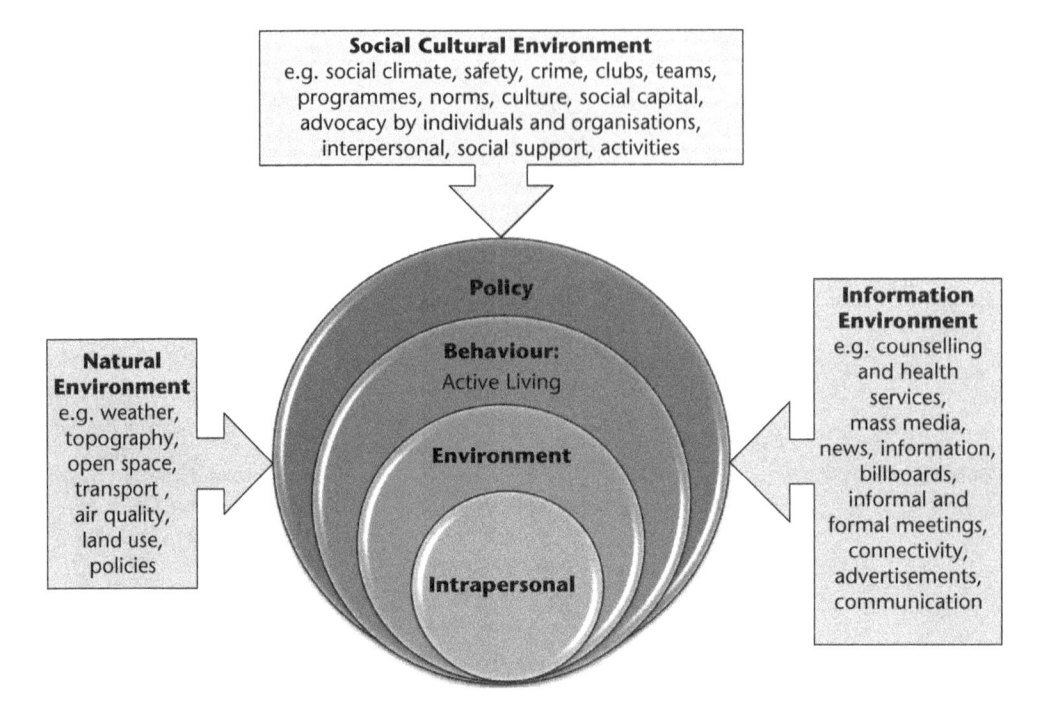

FIGURE 2.2 Positive social ecology concept

The final domain is the political environment which ultimately impacts on all activities in a community both within the educational setting and the broader community. These include local, national and global educational policies; development regulations (fire, building traffic etc.); zoning codes; transport investments; community management; regulations; incentives; community belonging; budgets and investment; safe routes; advocacy for communities, individuals and groups; media regulations; healthcare policies and practices; business practices; subsidised equipment and facilities; home prices; housing–job balance; public investments; park policies; and infrastructure investment.

The degree to which each of these aspects are valued and implemented influence the overall social ecology and the positive connectedness to the community. Three significant environments—Natural, Information, and Social and Cultural—will benefit from the quality of the experiences within each domain and how these interconnect with one another. Examples are provided in Figure 2.2. At the centre of a *positive social ecology* is a commitment to learners' wellbeing, in particular their fundamental rights for fulfilling and productive lives.

The rights of the child

Central to all communities must be a focus on children and young people. All children have the right to an education that supports their wellbeing and development. The *United Nations Declaration of the Rights of the Child* states that 'the child, by reason of his physical and mental immaturity, needs special safeguards and care, including appropriate legal protection, before as well as after birth' (United Nations General Assembly 1959, p. 164). The *United Nations on the*

Rights of the Child Convention expanded upon this notion to include not only the promotion of the rights of children, but also emphasised their wellbeing and development (United Nations General Assembly 1989). Within Australia, *The Human Rights and Equal Opportunity Commission* plays an official role in protecting and promoting the rights of children and young people (AHRC 2010, p. 2). In an official description of this role, the promotion of wellbeing is not specifically mentioned, however, it does refer to the right to an education (AHRC 2010, p. 3). The *National Framework for Protecting Australia's Children* has a strong focus on protecting children from abuse and neglect. One measure for identifying this is through wellbeing indicators (COAG 2009, p. 11). The focus on wellbeing is increasingly being noticed when promoting children's rights.

The *South Australian Children's Protection Act 1993* aims to provide for the care and protection of children and to do so in a manner that maximises a child's opportunity to grow up in a safe and stable environment and to reach his or her full potential. The most recent version of the Act (Version 1.7.2014) explicitly mentions the wellbeing of children. One of the four Objects of the Act is listed as:

> [promoting] caring attitudes and responses towards children among all sections of the community so that the need for appropriate nurture, care and protection (including protection of the child's cultural identity) is understood, risks to a child's wellbeing are quickly identified, and any necessary support, protection or care is promptly provided ...
>
> *(Attorney-General's Department 2014)*

At local, national and international levels, child rights are protected and promoted. Given the large amount of time students spend at school and given that wellbeing is linked to child rights, a *positive social ecology* is well-placed to promote wellbeing for all.

Wellbeing in educational policies?

Based on section 10(2) of the *Children Act 2004* (DCSF 2010, p. 3), the *Every Child Matters* policy (ECM) (2003) published in the United Kingdom recognised wellbeing as achieving five positive outcomes: be healthy; stay safe; enjoy and achieve; make a positive contribution; and achieve economic wellbeing. In the United States of America, the *No Child Left Behind Act 2001* (NCLB) supports standards-based education reform based on the premise that setting high standards and establishing measurable goals can improve individual outcomes in education. The main goal of the Act is to close the achievement gap that separates disadvantaged children and their peers. However, no distinction is made between achievement and wellbeing. NCLB focuses on standardised testing and undesirable motivational methods which have gained much criticism and suggests that student achievement was placed ahead of student wellbeing (Noddings 2005, p. 8). Although critics and policymakers believe the NCLB legislation has major flaws and modifications will be made, it appears the policy will be in effect for the long-term (see http://en.wikipedia.org/wiki/No_Child_Left_Behind_Act).

In Australia, the *National Safe Schools Framework* (Student Learning and Support Services Taskforce 2003) placed emphasis on creating a safe and supportive school environment by addressing issues of bullying, violence, harassment, and child abuse and neglect. It failed to address the concept of wellbeing. However, in the 2014 revision, the *National Safe Schools*

Framework provides Australian schools with a vision and a set of guiding principles that assists school communities to develop positive and practical student safety and wellbeing policies as well as practical tools and resources that will help build a positive school culture. Endorsed by all Australian Ministers of Education in December 2010, the vision statement declares that: 'All Australian schools are safe, supportive and respectful teaching and learning communities that promote student wellbeing' (Department of Education 2010, para. 6).

In South Australia, the former Department of Education and Children's Services (DECS), in its *Statement of Directions 2005–2010*, identified as one of its goals the improvement of learner engagement and wellbeing (DECS 2005). As discussed in Chapter 1, DECS developed a *Learner Wellbeing Framework*, targeting all children and young people in South Australian educational sites and schools from birth to Year 12 (DECS, 2007). Noting that few learner wellbeing frameworks exist, Kickbusch and colleagues (2011) claim that the DECS framework is a good example that can be applied internationally.

Such a framework promotes wellbeing for all learners, signalling wellbeing and learner engagement as key directions for educators. It acknowledges the interconnection between wellbeing and learning and states that wellbeing is more than the absence of problems. It recognises the influences of change on today's learners and the complexity of their lives.

The framework supports educators to build and improve effective wellbeing policies and practices and is consistent with the *Declaration of the Rights of the Child* (United Nations General Assembly 1959) and the *Adelaide Recommendations on Healthy Public Policy* (WHO 1988). Five dimensions of wellbeing are identified in the DECS framework: emotional, social, cognitive, physical and spiritual, and these dimensions need to be considered in the context of four domains within the site or school:

- learning environment;
- curriculum and pedagogy;
- partnerships; and
- policies and procedures.

With an embedded wellbeing education philosophy supported by partnerships with family, community and other agencies, and made explicit in the policies and practices of the site, what students learn via curriculum content and skill development will be practised in the learning environment. Integrating these domains through a whole school approach promotes *positive school ecology* and advocates educational responsibility for the wellbeing of all learners. As educational policies help to shape schools, the importance of wellbeing within them is paramount to the development of school ecologies.

Positive school ecology

The previously mentioned concept of social ecology can be applied to the promotion of wellbeing at specific sites or school settings. In order to foster wellbeing, schools should aim to create an inclusive and supportive environment. One way of managing this is through the development of a school ecology that reflects the wellbeing policy of the school. School ecology is defined as a culturally established social field, which is recognised by individual perceptions and which reflect behavioural norms and regularities (Thorkildsen, Reese & Corsino 2002, p. 26).

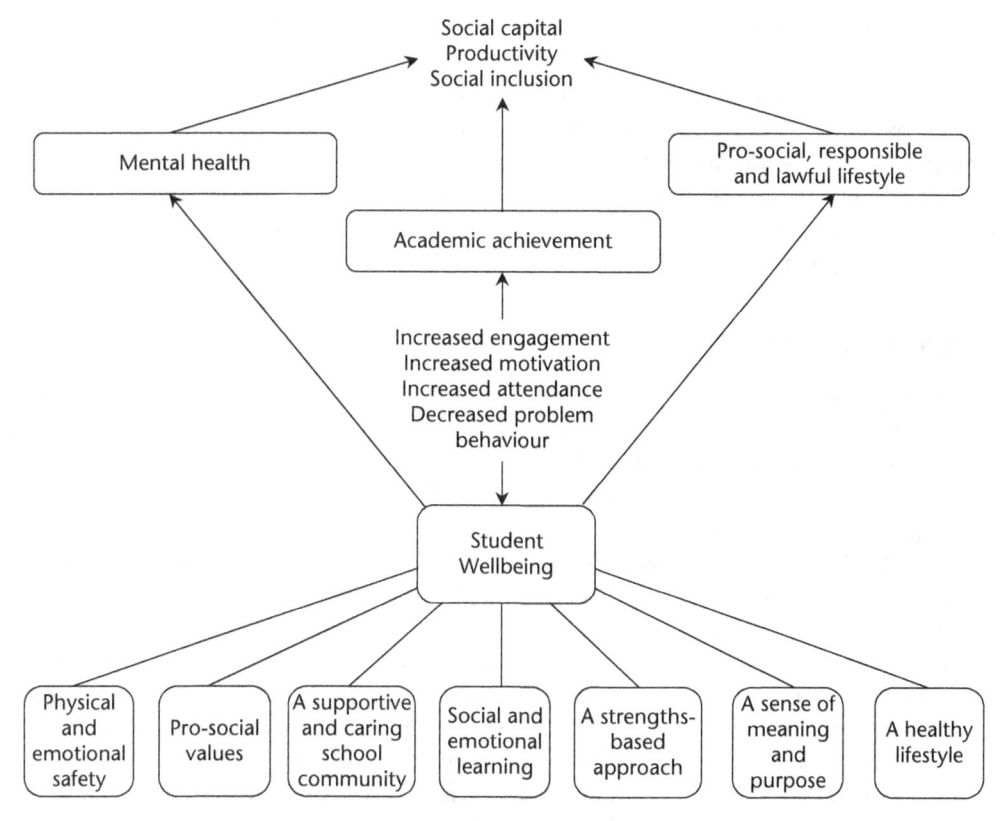

FIGURE 2.3 Seven pathways to student wellbeing (Noble, McGrath, Wyatt, Carbines & Robb 2008, p. 92)

Caring school communities play a vital role in the establishment of a *positive school ecology*. There is a strong focus on social relationships, as members become active participants in developing an identity by being active participants in the community (Wenger 1998, p. 4). Effective schools are communities of practice and by promoting and supporting relationships with students; their wellbeing is at the core of school business. In Australia, the Department of Education, Employment and Workplace Relations (Noble, McGrath, Wyatt, Carbines & Robb 2008, p. 92) produced a framework that describes seven pathways to student wellbeing (Figure 2.3). This framework is useful here in determining the school's contribution to school ecology, and shows the link with wellbeing which is at the core. Each pathway contributes to student wellbeing *and a positive school ecology* develops from these.

The school ecologies that reflect behavioural norms and regularities (Thorkildsen, Reese & Corsino 2002, p. 26) establish in children good health and positive social behaviours (AIHW 2007, p. viii). Cahill and Freeman (2007, p. 95) state that more than two decades of research on student engagement, motivation, school connectedness and mental health has demonstrated that supportive classroom environments are a critical factor in enhancing student engagement, academic learning and wellbeing. Students in supportive classrooms feel that they belong, are cared for and valued by the teacher and other students; these positive feelings that contribute towards wellbeing (Cahill & Freeman 2007, p. 95). Yet despite this, in many schools there is still an over-emphasis on achievement and results rather than learning and relationships (Dinham 2014; Harris 2008, p. 369; Hattie 2009). Our understanding of the connections between wellbeing and learning are only getting stronger.

As Figure 2.3 shows, a school that has a positive sense of wellbeing, developed through programmes and initiatives established in the pathways, realises outcomes associated with a greater sense of achievement. Furthermore, achievement, positive mental health and pro-social, responsible and lawful student behaviours are ultimately investments in increased productivity, social capital and inclusion. Thus, individual traits contribute to a much more effective and positive community for all.

Adverse effects on wellbeing

Not to be ignored are adverse factors that continually challenge our wellbeing. For example, within the educational context, Nagel (2005, p. 70) identifies a growing body of research that indicates that stress, fear, anxiety and other emotional responses to environmental stimuli experienced by school students can directly impact on their neurological capacities to learn. And globally, children and young people continue to experience adversity. Thus, Garvis and Pendergast (2014) claim that, in order to maximise learning, there is a global imperative to improve the health and wellbeing of children (p. 18).

In the educational context, numerous ecological buffers can mitigate the potentially negative effects of risk factors. Such buffers include a positive, rewarding school environment and a sense of connectedness to the school. These buffers are achievable in all schools, regardless of academic scores, socio-economic status, location and clientele. Evidence of such achievement is demonstrated by Reid and McCallum (2014) and Wrench, Hammond, McCallum and Price (2013) in studies undertaken with secondary school students living in the northern urban fringe of Adelaide in South Australia; a region that is characterised by socio-economic challenge (Prosser, Lucas & Reid 2010). These studies demonstrated that students from low socio-economic backgrounds have aspirations for their future which are influenced by their schooling experiences and the positive trust relationships that they develop with teachers within their school community. Further to this, connections between place and learning were highlighted as critical factors in achieving more equitable schooling outcomes. These studies explored the identification of factors within a 'community' that shape young people's aspirations and the ways in which they can be supported in navigating toward their aspirations. Wrench et al. (2013) used a curriculum redesign process with middle year teachers which applied a wellbeing framework to empower students in self-awareness and agency. Their study argues that pedagogy and curriculum have a direct influence on student engagement (p. 932). In an earlier study undertaken in the same geographic area Prosser, McCallum, Milroy, Comber and Nixon (2008) argued for middle school students to be taken seriously by others so they can achieve high grades to aspire to go to university and seek employment and careers. The stereotypes often placed on students in low socio-economic areas can have a deleterious effect on their ambition, satisfaction and attendance at school, and academic achievement.

Elements to a positive school ecology: Hope, happiness and belonging

One approach to a positive school ecology, promotes three key elements: hope, happiness and belonging as depicted in Figure 2.4. Hope, as a variable of happiness and wellbeing, is itself

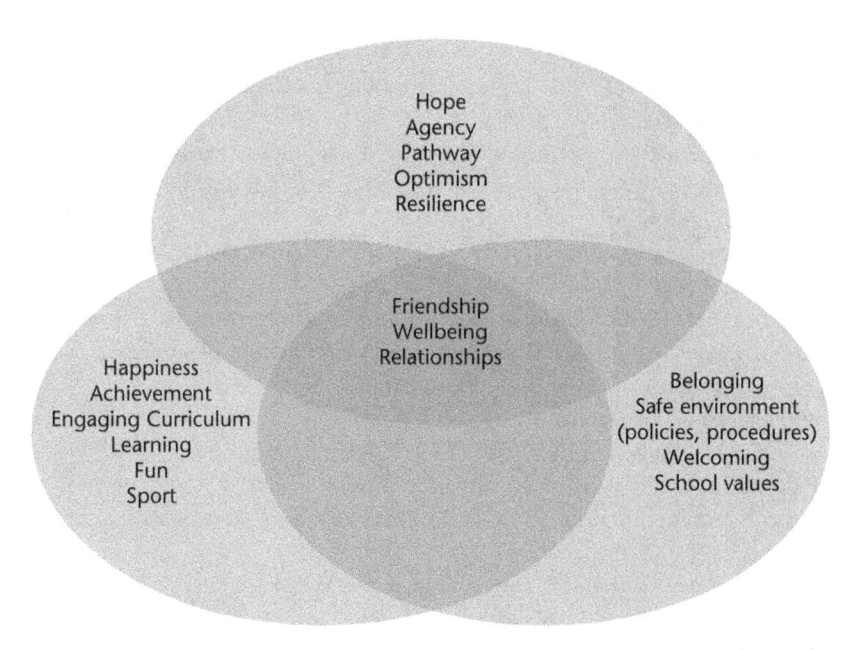

Hope
Agency
Pathway
Optimism
Resilience

Friendship
Wellbeing
Relationships

Happiness
Achievement
Engaging Curriculum
Learning
Fun
Sport

Belonging
Safe environment
(policies, procedures)
Welcoming
School values

FIGURE 2.4 Positive school ecology

comprised of two dimensions: the mental willpower to move towards one's goal (agency) and the perceived ability to generate routes to reach that goal (pathway). Snyder (1995) states that 'persons with a higher sense of hope and agency, and pathways for situations in general, approach a given goal with a positive emotional state, a sense of challenge, and a focus on success rather than failure' (p. 355). Such attitudes are vital for success in school and beyond. The subjective state of wellbeing encompasses two key dimensions: happiness (*I feel good about my life*) and satisfaction (*I think that the various aspects of my life are satisfactory*) (Triandis 2000, p. 15). These elements allow relationships to develop which results in a sense of belonging where children and young people feel safe, welcomed and valued at school.

A positive school ecology model (Figure 2.4) was applied to McCallum and Price's (2009) study of GreenLeaf Primary referred to earlier in this chapter. This 12-month project at one Australian primary school involved 277 child participants (Reception to Year 7) who completed an online survey in school term two which collected both quantitative and qualitative data. The Year 7 students (n=66) also completed an art activity in term three where they brainstormed ideas and feelings about their wellbeing at school and then represented these in drawings which were used as the basis for questions in focus groups. In addition, the researchers collected a range of documents, policies and artefacts (e.g. student diaries, school vision statement, staff handbook, anti-bullying and student behaviour policies, wellbeing policy, school code of conduct, student leadership document, uniform policy, excursions and camps policy, and sports code of behaviour policy) which they analysed for wellbeing themes and foci. Of significance in this study was the overall positive sense of belonging and connectedness that students identified.

These children felt they belonged at school (81 per cent *most* or *all of the time*) and 85 per cent felt they could 'be themselves' at school. So what did contribute to such a high level of belonging at this school? The contributing factors were identified as:

- feeling safe (89 per cent);
- having friends that were close and cared; and being treated fairly by others most of the time (66 per cent);
- a set of core values were identified both by the students themselves and through the document analysis. These core values were respect, trust, kindness, understanding, acceptance, care and inclusion;
- daily rituals: for example, my friends greet me every morning and say 'seeya' at the end of the day;
- teachers treated students fairly (reported by 82 per cent of students);
- the school welcomed new students (reported by 85 per cent of students);
- school environment was friendly and familiar;
- the curriculum was rigorous;
- school structure worked as there were lots of meaningful groups;
- extra-curricular activities were available for all; and
- there was an accepted school ethos, tradition, celebrations, and uniform.

One year seven student portrayed her feelings about wellbeing at school (Figure 2.5) and articulated in the focus group how balanced she felt because of the positive school ecology she experienced at this school. The vignette at the beginning of this chapter also displays another student's perspective of wellbeing at this particular school. It was evident that many of the students were flourishing and they exhibited strong socio-emotional development

FIGURE 2.5 Artwork displaying a balanced view of wellbeing in a positive school ecology which values academic thinking and learning, and art and creativity

through a healthy sense of self-esteem, confidence and connectedness with their school community. Such children are resilient in the face of adversity and have a positive orientation towards the future (futures perspective or hope). Positive school ecology is an important proactive response against health challenges, anti-social behaviour and under-achievement.

Tools of positive school ecology

As previously stated, the concept of positive school ecology takes a proactive rather than a reactive approach to wellbeing. To achieve a positive school ecology, it is essential to apply specific tools in order to promote proactive wellbeing initiatives. Such tools include actively promoting: student voice, student perceptions, positive thinking, resilience and coping, flexible thinking, developing and sustaining a sense of community, and friendliness.

Student voice is an imperative factor in shaping school ecology. In the United Kingdom, the Cambridge Review (Alexander & Armstrong 2010, p. 56) identified that student voice was noticeably missing from the findings of many research studies, despite the fact it is an important perspective. Students' own perception of their quality of life is one of the most important indicators of their level of wellbeing (Suldo & Huebner 2004). Given that students are most in tune with their own wellbeing, authentic accessing of their voice is central. Of particular importance is that this voice is actively integrated to inform policy, curriculum, practice, learning environments and community partnerships. This values all learners' unique wellbeing needs and builds the sense of connectedness and a united approach to a positive school ecology.

Student perceptions of wellbeing have not been explored in much depth in the literature (Wyn 2009, p. 90), however, in 2007, the New South Wales Commission for Children and Young People (NSW CCYP) conducted a research project on student wellbeing. The project found that children understood the complexities of wellbeing and their responses indicated they understood the differences between categorical and relational wellbeing (NSW CCYP 2007, p. 1). The study revealed that children's perceptions of wellbeing focused around three main themes—having agency, security, and a positive sense of self (NSW CCYP 2007, p. 1). A similar study conducted in 2005, and reinvestigated in 2009, found that students recognised the role that schools played in the development of their wellbeing (NSW CCYP 2010, p. 1). Children were expressive about the 'promoters and inhibitors of well-being at school', or more explicitly what made them feel good and what made them feel bad (NSW CCYP 2010, p. 1). A 1998 New Zealand study focussing on students' perceptions of health and wellbeing had similar findings (Burrows & Wright 2004, p. 197). White and Wyn (2008, p. 231) report that students' understanding of wellbeing has a social emphasis and can revolve around feeling good with friends. Schools need to promote and raise issues about wellbeing by involving their students and building proactive initiatives based on first-hand student voice and perceptions of wellbeing.

Positive thinking is a mental and emotional attitude that focuses on the bright side of life and expects positive results. A positive person anticipates happiness, health and success, and believes he or she can overcome obstacles and difficulties. Thus, positive thinking is integral to one's wellbeing and to that of a positive school ecology. In earlier studies cited in this chapter (namely Prosser et al. 2008; Reid & McCallum 2014; Wrench et al. 2013) positive thinking was a strategy introduced with children and young people to raise their aspirations for schooling and life. Teachers as participants in these studies used strategies to enhance positive thinking in the curriculum and through their pedagogy to engage children in schooling and to help establish goals of high achievement. In the 2013 study by Wrench and colleagues, parents/carers were also involved; they completed surveys about their hopes for their children's future. And the parents of the children at GreenLeaf Primary were active members of the school community, displaying futures oriented positive thinking through extra-curricular activities, in-school academic pursuits, and interactions with staff and other avenues that could influence policy.

Resilience and coping are terms that have been well researched and referred to in many disciplines and sectors. Reference to initiatives, interventions and programmes appear in policy, curriculum and resource applications globally. Resilience or coping are relevant to all children, young people and adults regardless of context and is often described as 'the capacity to cope with change and challenge and bounce back during difficult times' (Kids Helpline 2014). For resilience to be fostered in a positive school ecology, there need to be trusting relationships between students and their teachers and other adults, programmes that can build students' confidence and provide hope, and an emotionally safe learning environment. Although all children can experience moments where their resilience is compromised, schools and parents/carers must work together as a school community to ensure children know they have strategies in place to 'bounce back'.

Flexible thinking plays a key role in children's learning, at school and beyond. Children need to learn and know they can change direction, look at things differently or even 'unlearn' old ways of doing things. Flexible thinking is a cognitive function but is also supported by a safe learning environment—including classrooms that allow children to make mistakes, try new ways of doing things, and ask questions that enable them to understand how and why. This proactive stance is central to a positive school ecology, encouraging children to be happy, to have hope and to belong.

Developing and sustaining a sense of community is integral to a positive school ecology. The children at GreenLeaf Primary displayed a strong sense of belonging to the school community. They felt that they were an important part of the school fabric, describing how they felt they belonged at school and could be themselves. Feeling safe at school is a significant factor in one's sense of belonging with 89 per cent of the students in the study indicating they did feel safe. Knowing that you have close and caring friends around contributes to this sense of safety as this student commented:

> *Because I feel happy around other students and have friends that care for me and make me feel happy.*
>
> *(Student aged 9)*

And also:

> *All the children are relatively nice to me and I feel comfortable here. It has a nice atmosphere and Because i [sic] have lots of friends and we all try and stick together.*
>
> *(Student aged 10)*

Being friendly is a theme critical to children's sense of belonging at school. At GreenLeaf Primary, the theme of 'friends' was dominant which indicated that friends contribute to the development and maintenance of a *positive school ecology*. Responses to the question *What makes*

FIGURE 2.6   Wordle representing student responses to an online survey question: What makes me happy at school? (from McCallum & Price 2009)

me happy at school? generated a very strong feeling towards friends as depicted in the Wordle analysis of responses to the question (Figure 2.6). Students reported that they felt happiest at school when they were with friends, making new friends, having friends to cheer them up or working with friends. This research indicates that the following factors are important in generating a positive school ecology: friends; holistic curriculum choices; school structures and processes that enable positive social and intellectual interactions; student voice; learning from the most resilient and happy children; and the importance of teacher/child relationships. The whole school approach to student wellbeing at GreenLeaf Primary demonstrates that a holistic state of wellbeing exists. This state may take on different characteristics and emphases for individuals and communities across time and contexts. Of particular importance is the notion that a whole school community commitment to developing and maintaining a positive school ecology influences the level of student engagement, achievement, hope and happiness.

This section has described a whole school wellbeing approach where happiness, hope and a sense of belonging to the school community contributed to student wellbeing through the development of a positive school ecology. Applying explicit tools to enhance wellbeing for all and to promote a positive school ecology is important across the diversity of educational settings and in response to the life events and experiences. Much can be learned by understanding the attitudes and behaviour of the 'most happy' students including optimistic thinking and quality friendships. Hope, happiness and belonging, as antecedents to a sense of wellbeing, contribute substantially to one's success and satisfaction at school and beyond. Therefore, in applying a whole school wellbeing approach within Greenleaf Primary, a new model of wellbeing developed which was driven by student voice and which responded to their particular needs. It involved a specific cohort, at a particular time and in a specific context. This model (Figure 2.7) can be adapted within any educational setting to respond to the needs of any group of children and young people and in any particular context.

Let us now reflect on this new model of wellbeing, positive school ecology, referred to in Table 2.1. This table presented four domains (intrapersonal, environmental, behavioural and political) and argued that for wellbeing to exist, certain factors needed to be present in the Natural, Information, and Social and Cultural Environments of a community. Community examples were provided. A positive school ecology model suggests that hope, happiness and belonging are the central themes needed for optimum wellbeing and these are influenced by

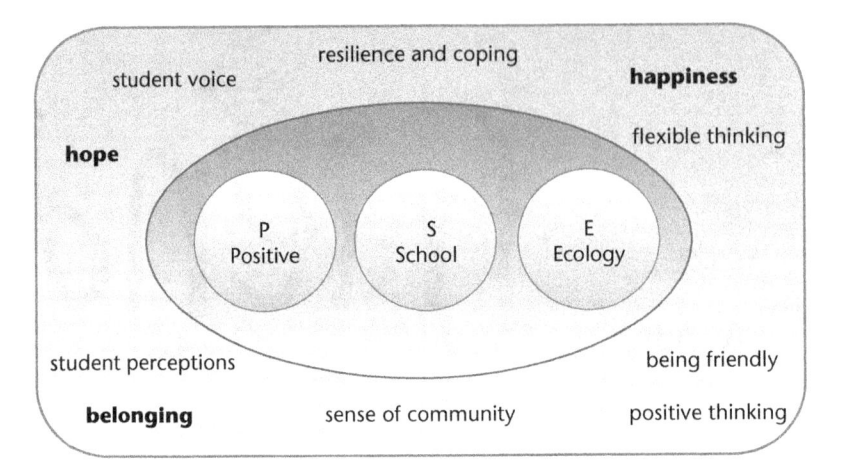

FIGURE 2.7 A new model of wellbeing

seven critical factors that make a well community: student voice, resilience and coping, flexible thinking, student perceptions, sense of community, positive thinking and being friendly. A community and individual phenomenon (Wyn 2009, p. 108), wellbeing contributes to the successful development of individuals across the life course, so that they are better able to realise their full potential, to experience satisfying personal relationships and to enjoy a rich quality of life (Bornstein, Davidson, Keyes & Moore 2003).

So, in advancing the notion of 'wellbeing for all', we note that the concept of 'wellbeing' has developed into an official educational discourse in recent years. The constructs of wellbeing are complex and wellbeing is often used as an 'umbrella' term to encapsulate the ideal state in different dimensions such as the emotional, cognitive, social, physical and spiritual. Healthy development and a positive sense of wellbeing is a right of every child and young person and education providers are increasingly focusing on developing frameworks and policies to promote wellbeing in schools. Student perceptions of wellbeing are integral to this process. Creating a strong, supportive and inclusive school ecology—one that advocates communities of practice—helps to create a strong sense of wellbeing within the school community. This is particularly important for school students who are experiencing rapid technological development and change.

Conclusion

In conclusion, this chapter sought to argue for a wellbeing concept for all. We are reminded of research by Kickbusch, Gordon, Kropf and O'Toole (2011) who take up the theme of rapid change and challenge for our children and young people, warning how this has become a policy priority in Europe and elsewhere. This is highly relevant to all communities around the globe given the assertion that the wellbeing of children and young people is key to sustainable development and well communities; it is about our present and our future. But such a priority is sometimes driven by views in some contexts that we do not treat our children well enough. One reason for this is that children themselves are not offered the opportunity to have their voices heard and have weak or no political representation. Another is that we are not creative and daring enough in effecting change. We need to radically shift our mindsets (Kickbusch et al. 2011).

Wellbeing is *for all*; therefore the wider community and educational sites have a responsibility in advancing positive school ecologies.

> When a child is happy and secure, he takes chances and explores. This makes him feel good, which in turn generates more exploration and more mastery. He becomes a veritable mastery machine.
>
> *(Seligman 1995)*

Wellbeing follow-up activities

1. How might your community develop a positive school/educational site ecology? Refer to Figure 2.2 to unpack the features in your local community in each of the domains. Summarise how 'well' your Natural, Information, and Social and Cultural Environments are at present. Identify what could be initiated within these areas to enrich wellbeing for all.
2. Guiding principles for developing safe, supportive and respectful school communities exist around the globe. For example, in Australia there is the 2014 *National Safe Schools Framework's* vision which has the following principle for schools to consider: acknowledge that being safe and supported at school is essential for student wellbeing and effective learning. How safe and supportive is your educational community for enabling student wellbeing and effective learning? What strategies are in place to achieve wellbeing and effective learning? How effective are these strategies and how do you know?
3. Consider the seven pathways to wellbeing (Figure 2.3). Draw a chart to represent these pathways and include the policies, strategies, practices and programmes at your educational site that contribute to an over-arching positive school ecology.
4. Educational sites with a positive school ecology (PSE) take a proactive rather than a reactive approach to wellbeing. Various tools enable children and young people to work with the school community to achieve a PSE. How would you value and measure these tools at your school: student voice, student perceptions, positive thinking, resilience and coping, flexible thinking, developing and sustaining a sense of community, and being friendly? What other tools might be important within your context?

References

AHRC (2010) *How does the Australian Human Rights Commission promote the rights of children and young people?* Australian Human Rights Commission, Sydney, NSW. Viewed 12 April 2010, available from http://www.hreoc.gov.au/human_rights/children/hreoc_promote_rights_of_children.html.

AIHW (2007) *Young Australians: Their health and wellbeing 2007.* Australian Institute of Health and Welfare, Canberra, ACT.

Alexander, RJ & Armstrong, M (2010) *Children, their world, their education: Final report and recommendations of the Cambridge Primary Review.* Routledge, London.

Attorney-General's Department (2014) *South Australia Children's Protection Act 1993 (Version 1.7.2014).* Government of South Australia, Adelaide, SA.

Bornstein, MH, Davidson, L, Keyes, CL & Moore, KA (2003) *Well-being: Positive development across the life course.* Lawrence Erlbaum Associates, Mahwah, NJ.

Bronfenbrenner, U (1992) Ecological systems theory. In R Vasta (ed), *Six theories of child development: Revised formulations and current issues.* Jessica Kingsley, London, pp. 187–249.

Burrows, L & Wright, J (2004) The good life: New Zealand children's perspectives on health and self. *Sport, Education and Society*, 9(2), pp. 193–205.

Cahill, H & Freeman, E (2007) Creating school environments that promote social emotional wellbeing. In M Keefe & S Carrington (eds), *Schools and diversity*, 2nd edn. Pearson Education Australia, Frenchs Forest, NSW, pp. 90–107.

COAG (2009) *Protecting children is everyone's business: National framework for protecting Australia's children 2009–2020*. Council of Australian Governments, Commonwealth of Australia, Canberra, ACT.

DCSF (2010) *Children's trust: Statutory guidance on cooperation arrangements, including the Children's Trust Board and the Children and Young People's Plan*. Department for Children, Schools and Families, UK.

DECS (2005) *DECS statement of directions 2005–2010*. Department of Education and Children's Services, Adelaide, SA.

DECS (2007) *DECS Learner Wellbeing Framework for birth to year 12*. Department of Education and Children's Services, Adelaide, SA.

Department of Education (2010) *The National Safe Schools Framework*. Australian Government. Viewed 11 November, 2014, available from https://www.education.gov.au/national-safe-schools-framework-0

Dinham, S (2014) Current developments in Australian education: A tsunami approaches. *Professional Educator*, 13(3), pp. 7–8.

Durlak, JA, Weissberg, RP, Dymnicki, AB, Taylor, RD & Schellinger, KB (2011) The impact of enhancing students' social and emotional learning: A meta-analysis of school-based universal interventions. *Child Development*, 82(1), pp. 405–432.

Fraillon, J (2004) *Measuring student well-being in the context of Australian schooling*. Paper prepared for the Ministerial Council on Education, Employment, Training and Youth Affairs, Carlton South, VIC.

Freeman, E, Wertheim, EH & Trinder, M (2014) Teacher perspectives on factors facilitating implementation of whole school approaches for resolving conflict. *British Educational Research Journal*, 40(5), pp. 847–868.

Garvis, S & Pendergast, D (2014) *Health and wellbeing in childhood*. Cambridge University Press, Port Melbourne, VIC.

Harris, B (2008) Befriending the two-headed monster: Personal, social and emotional development in schools in challenging times. *British Journal of Guidance & Counselling*, 36(4), pp. 367–383.

Hattie, J (2009) *Visible learning: A synthesis of over 800 meta-analyses relating to achievement*. Routledge, London.

Kickbusch, I, Gordon, J, Kropf, D & O'Toole, L (2011) *Learning for well-being: A policy priority for children and youth in Europe. A process for change*. Report based on a verbal presentation given to the *Quality of Childhood Group* at the European Parliament, September 2011. Viewed 11 November 2014, available from http://www.ecswe.net/downloads/publications/QOC-V3/Chapter-6.pdf

Kids Helpline (2014) *Being resilient*. Available from http://www.kidshelp.com.au/teens/get-info/hot-topics/being-resilient.php

McCallum, F & Price, D (2009) *The friendliest school in the world. Report to Independent Schools*. University of South Australia, Adealide, SA.

McCallum, F & Price, D (2010) Well teachers, well students. *Journal of Student Wellbeing*, 4(1), pp. 19–34.

Nagel, M (2005) Understanding the adolescent brain. In D Pendergast & N Bahr (eds), *Teaching middle years: Rethinking curriculum, pedagogy and assessment*. Allen & Unwin, Crows Nest, NSW, pp. 65–76.

Noble, T, McGrath, H, Wyatt, T, Carbines, R & Robb, L (2008) *Scoping study into aproaches to student well-being: Literature review. Report to the Department of Education, Employment and Workplace Relations*. Australian Catholic University & Erebus International, Sydney, NSW.

Noddings, N (2005) What does it mean to educate the whole child? *Educational Leadership*, 63(1), pp. 8–13.

NSW CCYP (2007) *Ask the children: Overview of children's understandings of well-being*. NSW Commission for Children and Young People, Sydney, NSW.

NSW CCYP (2010) *Children's perceptions of their well-being at school*. NSW Commission for Children and Young People, Sydney, NSW.

O'Rourke, J & Cooper, M (2010) Lucky to be happy: A study of happiness in Australian primary students. *Australian Journal of Educational & Developmental Psychology*, 10, pp. 94–107.

Price, D., & McCallum, F. (2014) Teacher wellbeing: Initial teacher education capability approach. Paper presented at the British Educational Research Association Conference, London, 23–25 September 2014.

Price, D & McCallum, F (2015) Ecological influences on teachers' well-being and 'fitness'. *Asia-Pacific Journal of Teacher Education*, 43(3), pp. 195–209.

Prosser, B, Lucas, B & Reid, A (eds) (2010) *Connecting lives and learning: Renewing pedagogy in the middle years*. Wakefield Press, Kent Town, SA.

Prosser, B, McCallum, F, Milroy, P, Comber, B & Nixon, H (2008) 'I am smart and I am not joking': Aiming high in the middle years of schooling. *Australian Educational Researcher*, 35(2), pp. 15–35.

Reid, A & McCallum, F (2014) 'Becoming your best': Student perspectives on community in the pursuit of aspirations. *The Australian Educational Researcher*, 41(2), pp. 195–207.

Seligman, ME (1995) *The optimistic child*. Random House, Sydney, NSW.

Snyder, CR (1995) Conceptualizing, measuring, and nurturing hope. *Journal of Counseling & Development*, 73(3), pp. 355–360.

Student Learning and Support Services Taskforce (2003) *National Safe Schools Framework*. Ministerial Council on Education, Employment, Training and Youth Affairs, Carlton South, VIC.

Suldo, SM & Huebner, ES (2004) Does life satisfaction moderate the effects of stressful life events on psychopathological behavior during adolescence? *School Psychology Quarterly*, 19(2), pp. 93–105.

Thorkildsen, T, Reese, D & Corsino, A (2002) School ecologies and attitudes about exclusionary behaviour among adolescents and young adults. *Merrill-Palmer Quarterly*, 48(1), pp. 25–51.

Triandis, HC (2000) Cultural syndromes and subjective well-being. In E Diener & E Suh (eds), *Culture and subjective well-being*. MIT Press, Cambridge, MA, pp. 13–36.

United Nations General Assembly (1959) *Declaration of the rights of the child*. United Nations, General Assembly Resolution 1386(XIV).

United Nations General Assembly (1989) *Convention on the rights of the child*. United Nations, New York, NY.

Wenger, E (1998) *Communities of practice: Learning, meaning, and identity*. Cambridge University Press, Cambridge.

White, RD & Wyn, J (2008) *Youth and society*. 2nd edn, Oxford University Press, Melbourne, VIC.

WHO (1988) Adelaide Recommendations on Healthy Public Policy. Adopted at the Second International Conference on Health Promotion, Adelaide, South Australia, 5–9 April 1988. http://www.who.int/healthpromotion/conferences/previous/adelaide/en/

Wrench, A, Hammond, C, McCallum, F & Price, D (2013) Inspire to aspire: Raising aspirational outcomes through a student well-being curricular focus. *International Journal of Inclusive Education*, 17(9), pp. 932–947.

Wyn, J (2009) *Youth health and welfare: The cultural politics of education and wellbeing*. Oxford University Press, South Melbourne, VIC.

Zaff, J, Smith, D, Rogers, M, Leavitt, C, Halle, T & Bornstein, M (2003) Holistic well-being and the developing child. In M Bornstein, L Davidson, C Keyes & K Moore (eds), *Well-being: Positive development across the life course*. Lawrence Erlbaum Associates, Mahwah, NJ, pp. 23–32.

3

WELLBEING IN DISABILITY EDUCATION

Deborah Price

What is important to me?

So many things that I want to tell you.

I know exactly what is important to me.

I follow my friends, school support officer (SSO) and class teacher as they take photos around the school using a digital camera. They ask me, 'Amy, is the sensory room important to you?' I tap my hand enthusiastically on my wheelchair tray signalling it is so important to me. My inner voice pleads for them to take a photo of it. They do so immediately in response to my communication. I love the sensory room lights, the quiet and calm atmosphere, the feeling of flying in the swinging chair; it is such a change from the busy classroom. We pass by my favourite teacher in the corridor, I tap my hand vigorously on the tray and my friend is quick to connect with my communication, asking 'Do you want me to take a photo of Ms Smith? Is she important to you?' Excitedly I respond by tapping my hand. We move through the entire school repeating this process, where I select photos of objects, people, space and places. I feel so happy to be able to choose and share what is important to me with others.

[A day passes]

Sitting in my classroom, my school support officer places a whole selection of printed digital photographs on the table in front of me. These included photos that I had chosen the day before and others taken by my classmates. He pointed one by one to each photo asking 'is this important to you?' Once again I tap my hand on the tray as photos of my friends, favourite places, activities and objects are identified. In contrast, I move my hand from side to side when I don't think the photo is important. This is fun. But suddenly I stop, my eyes fixed to a photo. Tears begin to well and trickle down my face. Oh, this photo is so important to me, look at that smiling face, I miss her so much; whilst we weren't what I would call best friends, we would sit in the same class together every day, go swimming, listen to music, laugh at our crazy teacher. Stacey was part of our small community. I lift my gaze from the photo to notice the shock on my SSO's face at my reaction. Yes ... didn't you know that when Stacey left the school I was devastated? I wanted to tell you but didn't know how; I couldn't find a way to communicate my feelings. That is why I haven't been concentrating on my work as well as I normally would, I just don't seem to be able to focus. Thank goodness these photos have let me share my sadness, I feel so relieved that you know.

Stacey was so important to me and I miss her ... I wonder how she is?

(Amy, student, aged 10)

Introduction

As evidenced by Amy's vignette, empowering students with disability to have a valued voice (whether verbal or non-verbal) advances opportunities for them to communicate their perceptions of place, space, community and wellbeing. As you engage in this chapter, you are challenged to question how well you know the wellbeing of *all* learners in your care. This chapter aims to contribute to social inclusion and wellbeing initiatives for students with disability to address issues pertaining to access, transition, and higher level achievement in schooling (South Australian Social Inclusion Board July 2010). As we are well aware, society shapes individual experiences and choices and, in the case of students with disability, this can be complicated by life inequities (Wilkinson & Pickett 2010).

When referring to students with disability within this chapter, this is inclusive of students officially meeting diagnostic criteria as specified by the *Diagnostic and statistical manual of mental disorders* (American Psychiatric Association 2013), as well as students unofficially identified with disabilities and/or learning difficulties. However, extreme caution needs to be exercised as such labelling can place additional pressures and reinforce stereotypical attitudes which influence the wellbeing of these students. On the other hand, explicit wellbeing education initiatives are essential for students with disabilities in order to support their particular needs. However these require proactive approaches rather than reacting to medical discourse and categorisation. Educational personnel and carers need to expand opportunities for how an individual's life is spoken and thought about. This can be achieved through provision of experiences to break down barriers which have been created by limiting societal structures and educational arrangements (Barnes 1999; Finkelstein 1980; Oliver 1992; Oliver 1996; Reddington 2014).

As discussed in earlier chapters, all children and young people have a right to wellbeing, including individual emotional, social, physical, cognitive and spiritual dimensions, as well as relational and community dimensions. Wellbeing is inclusive of everyone and their contexts; it offers opportunity to flourish, belong, be resilient, experience happiness and contentment, which ultimately provides quality of life. And just as educational curriculum and pedagogies require differentiation, the wellbeing of students with disabilities may need support through appropriate accommodations, adjustment and negotiation. Such an holistic educational approach which integrates wellbeing and learning advances human rights initiatives, fundamental rights and equal opportunity as advocated in the United Nations Educational, Scientific and Cultural Organization *Salamanca Statement* (UNESCO 1994), *The Individuals with Disabilities Education Improvement Act of 2004* (IDEIA) and Australian legislation, including the *Disability Discrimination Act of 1992* and the *Disability Standards for Education* (Australian Government 2005).

It has been well documented that inclusive education provides social, emotional, economic and educational benefits for marginalised groups; in particular students with disabilities (Peetsma, Vergeer, Roeleveld & Karsten 2001; Price, in review; Ruijs, Van der Veen & Peetsma 2010; UNESCO 1994). However, efforts advancing inclusion and wellbeing continue to be interrupted by issues of fair treatment, stigmatisation and exclusion which particularly impacts on students who need atypical arrangements and care (Price, forthcoming 2015). In a recent Australian Human Rights Commission National Disability Forum review (2014), 'respondents identified that the rights issues facing persons with disabilities are interconnected. In particular, barriers encountered in relation to access to services, education and employment were interlinked with negative attitudes, stereotypes and discrimination' (p. 7). In addition, 'income security, freedom from discrimination and violence and social connection are the three most critical areas for anyone's health and wellbeing. They are particularly hard to realise for people with disabilities in a world that excludes' (p. 7). Unfortunately 'violence, abuse and neglect is too commonly experienced by persons with disabilities, especially persons with an intellectual disability' (Australian Human Rights Commission 2014, p. 7). Furthermore, the wellbeing of students with disabilities is further compounded by global concerns regarding mental health difficulties (Armstrong, Price & Crowley, 2015). Armstrong and Hallett (2012) report on national and international research which identifies a significant overlap between children and young people identified in an educational context as having Social, Emotional or Behavioural Difficulty (SEBD) but who might otherwise be categorised as suffering from clinically significant mental health disorders such as generalised anxiety or conduct disorder. It is of particular concern that children and young people categorised beneath the banner of special or inclusive education have co-occurring mental health problems (Armstrong 2013; Armstrong, Price & Crowley, 2015; Macleod 2010; Mowat 2009).

When addressing the wellbeing of students with disabilities, caution is needed to avoid assessing or attributing their wellbeing entirely in the context of disability. This, in my opinion, undermines an individual's fundamental rights to wellbeing, and may provide excuses for not making the necessary adjustments and accommodations that the individual rightfully deserves. For example, in reference to distinct populations such as children with intellectual disability, co-occurring mental health problems are frequently overlooked because of diagnostic overshadowing whereby professionals, carers and/or family incorrectly attribute a child's behaviours to their disability whereas, in fact, these behaviours are the expression of chronic mental health difficulties (Armstrong, Price & Crowley, 2015; Coughlan 2011). This is just one example which reflects the immense body of international data reporting on the negative experiences of individuals within the field of disability. Whilst such findings are highly important in challenging educators, policy makers and caregivers to achieve positive wellbeing outcomes for students with disabilities, in this chapter I deliberately avoid continual bombardment with statistics, which only reinforce 'at risk' categorisations of students with disabilities. Instead, to advocate for a truly inclusive philosophy, I intentionally focus on the capabilities of students with disabilities—that is, what they *can do* and *be* (Nussbaum 2003; Price, in review; Sen 1985) by sharing their first-hand perspectives in relation to their own wellbeing and educational experience. In order to authentically include students with disabilities in the wellbeing educational agenda, we need to learn from their perspectives, desires and what is important to them. Within this chapter, I challenge you think about how often you seek out the perspectives of students with disabilities in relation to wellbeing, before jumping straight to stereotypical assumptions of what you deem as appropriate for their wellbeing. In particular, for students such as Amy in the vignette, who presents as non-verbal and is extremely eager to share her thoughts and feelings, what accommodations and how much effort is typically invested in seeking out her perspective? And even when you as an individual are extremely responsive to the wellbeing needs of students with disabilities, how responsive is the broader educational curriculum, the policies, pedagogy and the wider community attitudes and structures?

Drawing on an ethnographical place-based case study of a secondary special educational setting in South Australia, this chapter provides insights into what students with disability perceive as important in terms of the educational places and spaces they occupy and the implications for their wellbeing. Empowering students with disability as visual ethnographers advances opportunities to authentically communicate their perceptions of place, space, community and wellbeing. All students in the case study setting participated by communicating, through digital imagery, their response to the question, 'What is important to me?' According to the *United Nations Convention on the Rights of the Child* (United Nations General Assembly 1989) all children have a right to have their opinion heard regarding issues that affect their lives (Hallett & Prout 2003; John 1996; Lewis & Lindsay 1999; Qvortrup, Bardy, Sgritta & Wintersberger 1994).

Within this case study, student's wellbeing was evidenced through positive emotions regarding place and space, including a strong sense of belonging and community, happiness, pride, care and respect. A desire to attend school was underpinned by relationships with key people including teachers, leadership, school support officers and friends. This supports the notion that individual wellbeing dimensions are influenced by relations and connectedness. Additionally, images that acknowledged students' sense of self were recorded, including images of individual achievements, extrinsic rewards, work products and public displays. The students engaged in a curriculum that integrated workplace and work experience programmes along with physically safe and relaxing spaces. Predominantly, this chapter focuses on enabling community wellbeing initiatives and considers the perceptions of students with disabilities in relation to school ecology and sense of place. Ultimately, the relationship between social space and physical space (Bourdieu 1999) plays a role in enhancing the happiness and wellbeing for students with disabilities. As you progress through this chapter, challenge yourself by critiquing how effectively your community promotes wellbeing inclusive of all individuals.

For the purpose of this chapter, the terms *students with disabilities* and *special educational site* are used in the context of the case study. However the implications for learner wellbeing reach far wider having relevance for children and young people with special educational needs who may not be officially diagnosed with a disability and/or attend a mainstream educational setting. Inclusive education is the focus here but we know that regardless of diagnosis or setting, all learners are entitled to opportunities that support their wellbeing.

The inclusion debate: Which educational setting bests supports the wellbeing needs of a child or young person with disabilities?

The inclusion debate has been extensive over a long period and the aim of this chapter is not to delve into the complexity, rather to acknowledge how inclusion issues influence the wellbeing of students with disability. While contemporary global educational discourse and policy is permeated with calls for 'inclusive education' and 'education for all', it has been argued that these parallel yet interrelated agendas need to be brought closer together in order to improve teaching and learning for all children (Miles & Singal 2010). Changes in educational policy have promoted initiatives designed to keep students with disabilities in mainstream educational settings instead of referring them to special schools (de Boer, Pijl & Minnaert 2011). The key motive is to foster social interaction between students with disabilities and mainstream students. As a result, many countries have largely abandoned the special school system (Meijer, Soriano & Watkins 2006) whilst others, such as the United Kingdom, continue such practices. Within the Australian context, a national agenda that promotes equitable access and participation in education and training is reflected in the *Disability Standards for Education* (Australian Government 2005) and a national inclusive curriculum introduced by the Australian Curriculum, Assessment and Reporting Authority (ACARA 2011). These initiatives are primarily dictated by adult stakeholders making decisions based on perceived benefits to the child/student. Furthermore, knowledge about disability has largely come from people without disabilities (Boxall & Ralph 2009). What is often overlooked in such debates and initiatives is an overarching and explicit focus of the wellbeing the children and young people at the centre. Essentially, wellbeing is often an afterthought.

Some educators and stakeholders consider segregated special schooling to be dehumanising (Kenworthy & Whittaker 2000), unregulated, poor quality and a 'watered down form of schooling' (Miles & Singal 2010, p. 6). Others argue that the special treatment of difference further perpetuates disadvantage. This argument presents a dilemma: if differences aren't recognised there is a likelihood that they will not be addressed (Minow 1991). Efforts aimed to empower people with learning difficulties have been described as possibly endangering to individuals as it reinforces the victim status (Goodley 2007). Ainscow, Booth and Dyson (2006) describe how initiatives focused solely on disability tend to undermine and detract from broader efforts to promote system and organisational change which was largely the original intention of inclusive education. Such tensions potentially create reactive wellbeing initiatives, rather than broader proactive measures.

Wilkinson and Pickett (2010) interrogate how individual's experiences and choices are shaped by the society they live in, particularly in relation to deprivation and inequality. Students with special needs and disabilities try to cope with the many difficulties that inequality inflicts on their lives, including the social stigma of attending a special education school. These complexities compound enrolment decisions for students with disabilities in either mainstream or special education settings, which are influenced not only by caregivers, but the broader educational system and stakeholder perspective. Thereby limited attention is given to integrating the voices of students with disabilities to identify their desires and feelings about schooling settings. Consequently, student sense of belonging, wellbeing and achievement within the educational place that is selected for them may be jeopardised.

Sense of place and space from the students' perspective

Educational place and space—that is, the physical and social setting, whether a special educational or mainstream site—is of great significance to the wellbeing of a student with disability. Exploring sense of place, space and community of students with disabilities in special education schools is a neglected area of research. In particular, adult perceptions may be challenged or reinforced by listening to the authentic voices of students with disabilities as they explore how they perceive their sense of place and community within the site they inhabit. Gibson (2006) argues that a culture of silence exists and serves as a barrier to eliciting voice in the special education field; space needs to be provided where voices can be heard. Capturing what students love about their place and space and what makes them proud should be the driving rationale for student enrolment, participation and subsequent achievement. In mainstream schooling, efforts to promote the student voice are compounded for students with disabilities because orthodox understandings of *voice* often ignore diverse forms of expression and exclude those who articulate differently (Goodley 2007). Deficit views marginalise students with disabilities as *othered* and in need of empowerment (Clough & Barton 1998) this implies that they are considered to be entities with limited agency or capacity to articulate their perceptions of their connection to educational space and place. This failure to generate knowledge from children who are viewed as being less capable of participating in informed and rational ways has been challenged by researchers such as Epstein, Stevens, McKeever and Baruchel (2008). The present case study promotes the need for socially just pedagogies which emphasise productivity and liberate subject and identity with students *becoming* rather than *being* in order to open up spaces and places of resistance and to promote social justice (Deleuze & Guattari 1987/2004). Inviting the bodies and minds of students with disabilities to share perceptions, desires and connections to space and place, promotes opportunities for reconfiguring the classroom, the learning environment, the school, the space and pedagogy (Goodley 2007), whilst engaging students with disabilities in discourses around disability and decision-making processes (Boxall & Ralph 2009).

The case study in this chapter provided a place-based critical inquiry for students with disabilities to reimage, re-inscribe and re-inhabit their sense of place through images and stories about their special education site community (Gannon 2009). The meaning of place is viewed in relation to the identities and experiences of the people sharing the location; specifically, place is viewed 'as a lived entity that results from a dialogical transaction between a community and its material environment at a particular moment in cultural historical time and which hence shapes and is shaped by the identity of the people' (van Eijck & Roth 2010, p. 869). McInerney, Smyth and Down (2011) express the need for informed critical reading of the physical, social and cultural aspects of place whilst not just focusing on what is wrong with the place. Specifically, the case study integrated enabling pedagogy inviting multiple voices and representations from students with disabilities through exploration, critique and multi-media generation (Gannon 2009). Such methods promoted the exploration of more complex themes in relation to these students' wellbeing which, Aldridge (2007) suggests, would not have emerged using non-visual methods. These students' perceptions of place in relation to their identity, attachment, and dependence was analysed with the aim of identifying the level of wellbeing interconnectedness between the dimensions of self, physical place and sociality of individuals and culture (Antonsich 2010; Kemp 2006). As such, this work challenges stereotypical and normative educational pedagogies which tend to marginalise and exclude the voices of students with disabilities. It potentially provides opportunities for students to counter or resist public narratives including deficit perceptions held by the media and public cultures in relation to the special education setting and their sense of 'place' within this setting. Such initiatives are central to enhancing the individual and collective wellbeing of these students.

Case study: What is important to me?

Building on enabling pedagogies (Somerville 2006) and place-based critical inquiry (Beach & Thein 2006), this case study adapted the methodology from an Australian Research Council Discovery grant pilot project *Rewriting 'the road to nowhere'* which addressed negative public images of a disadvantaged school setting (Gannon 2009). Within this study, students within the domains of Arts and English invited multiple voices and representations to 'aestheticize the environment and to idealize a view of the environment [as] an object for personal representation and reflection' (Cormack, Green & Reid 2003, p. 10). Gannon's research was adapted to the context of students with disabilities in order to ascertain their perceptions of place and space within a special education school. Amongst other objectives, the research aimed to:

1. Identify what students love about the place and community they live
2. Describe the spaces students occupy in their everyday lives
3. Speculate on elements that make them proud of the place they inhabit
4. Generate critical and creative responses to the relations between the structures of social spaces and those of physical space (Bourdieu 1999).

(Gannon 2009, p. 614)

Driving this study was the 'vibe' that one experienced upon entering this particular school setting. Regardless of who you were, a student, parent/carer, staff member, visitor, a sense of warmth, welcome, belonging and respect permeated the atmosphere. Similar to the notion of a homely feeling that a house provides within the Australian iconic movie *The Castle* (Sitch 1997), the school environment presented 'not a house, but a home' feeling. As stated by a character in the movie: 'it's the vibe of the thing, your honour'. So what was it about this unique vibe that contributed to the whole school community sense of wellbeing? Encouraging students to capture this vibe was central.

Thirty-seven students from a secondary special educational school in metropolitan Adelaide, South Australia participated in this study ranging across years 8–12 (13 to 19 years of age). These students were identified across a diverse range of disabilities. These included autism spectrum disorder (70 per cent), down syndrome, intellectual and physical disabilities, language and communication disabilities, and incorporating severe and/or multiple disabilities. The school's philosophy aims to provide quality teaching and care to enable students to achieve their full potential and experience quality of life. They are committed to the South Australian Department for Education and Child Development (DECD) priorities for all students. Integrity, optimism, respect and responsibility are the values that underpin this school's commitment to developing the most appropriate teaching and learning methodologies for their community. As such, students become lifelong learners. In addition, they aim for the development of self-respect and respect for others through intellectual, physical and social challenges.

Students in this school are assigned to one of five home groups, primarily based on developmental needs rather than chronological age. To support the wellbeing of students and maintain classroom routines, the researcher worked alongside class teachers in their home groups to provide an initial discussion about the operation, care and ethical use of digital cameras. Students were each provided with a digital camera over two days in order to take photos of *whatever they see as important for them*. Following this, each student discussed with the researcher what was important about each photo and these responses were categorised across conceptual themes comprising of: significant places; curriculum, learning; policies and procedures; relationships/significant people; future aspirations; transition to work/society; sense of self, self-esteem, wellbeing, identity; safety, Child Protection Curriculum, community connections; and home and family.

As can be seen in Amy's vignette at the outset of this chapter, adaptations were made to be inclusive of all students. To ascertain the most significant influences on wellbeing, students were asked to choose from their portfolio of photos the 20 photos that were the most important to them and explain the reason for their choice. To celebrate what was important to these students they produced their own photo story (favourite digital images and music). For students with severe and multiple disabilities, a class photo story was produced. Such a process outlines how all students' wellbeing and perceptions can be captured and communicated through creative approaches, including the expansive opportunities digital technologies provide. As Taylor (2005) suggests, arts education provides the potential for self-empowerment through visual representations of lived experience. Such initiatives attempt to break down the culture of silence by providing a space where voices can be heard (Gibson 2006). This was evidenced by the students being empowered with the independence and responsibility of using digital cameras.

What students love about the place and community they live in

The social and emotional wellbeing benefits of this process was highly evident in the enthusiasm, exuberant body language and facial expressions of the students when provided with an individual camera and having total ownership of making decisions about what was important to them. The smiles, animated gestures, eager discussions and questions dominated the students' initial use of the cameras and when they were provided with the task of taking photos of *what is important to me,* they quickly responded by racing off to take photos with exclamations of *I know exactly what is important to me!* Overall, a total of 2,181 digital photos were taken, averaging 59 images per student and ranging from 13 photos to 147. To fully analyse the most important dimensions of place and community for these students, the 20 favourite photos selected by each student or class were categorised across the five home classes (refer to Table 3.1).

Class 1 consisted of five lower functioning students aged 14–17 years, mainly presenting as non-verbal, with multiple and complex disabilities. Overall these students took a total of 145 photos, at an average of 29 photos per student. In identifying their most important photos these students selected images of themselves with a total of 17 images of individuals. These students are the centre of this classroom, and they displayed pride and enthusiasm in having their photos taken and choosing to take photos of themselves. When related to wellbeing, the feelings experienced during the process included a sense of belonging within the classroom, and provision of artistic spaces as a way of sharing their identity and self-concept (Hall 2010). The second most prominent image category for these students centred on their swimming programme (see Figure 3.1), which was a weekly routine promoting community access, coordination and muscular conditioning, while also broadening movement opportunities whilst engaging in socialisation with friends and community members.

The images depicted the swimming centre as an enabling physical place to which the students communicated their attachment, dependence, identity and sense of place (Antonsich 2010). Kemp (2006) describes the interconnectedness of communication, physical place, sociality of individuals and culture, whereby, 'the self and place are inseparable as one helps define the other'

TABLE 3.1 Students' top 20 selected photographs

	Class 1	Class 2	Class 3	Class 4	Class 5	All Classes
Number of students:	5	3	8	8	13	37
Total photos taken:	145	165	308	748	815	2181
20 most important themes:						
Photo of self	*17*	7	17	*26*	26	**93**
Friends	3	11	*29*	21	28	**92**
Cafe	0	2	1	2	*62*	**67**
Teachers	5	6	13	7	17	**48**
Art/work products	1	4	17	18	5	**45**
SSO	10	3	8	7	5	**33**
Outside/garden	0	7	6	6	8	**29**
Swimming	11	0	9	4	1	**25**
Excursions	6	1	0	4	9	**20**
Bikes	0	3	0	9	5	**17**
Signage	0	*13*	2	1	1	**17**
Bus	3	0	1	6	3	**13**
Sensory Room	0	0	7	1	0	**8**
Library	0	1	0	2	5	**8**

Note: Entries in *italics* indicate the most important theme for each class

(p. 126). In moving beyond purely independent notions of space and place, the students in Class 1 selected ten photos of the school support officers (SSOs) who provided one-to-one support to students, as their third most important category. Particularly for these students experiencing severe and multiple disabilities, the importance of their place within their special education setting was emphasised in relation to the identities and experiences of people sharing the location

FIGURE 3.1 Swimming programme

(van Eijck & Roth 2010). Given the specialised care provided by significant people, such as SSOs, for personal care, hygiene, feeding, communication, mobility, sensory stimulation and learning, students' emotional attachment and trust is central to meeting their wellbeing needs. Connection with staff and peers is integral to a student's level of spiritual wellbeing and sense of belonging within the classroom environment. As Baskin, Wampold, Quintana and Enright (2010) discuss, a sense of belonging is a potentially important buffer against the negative effects of low peer acceptance and high levels of loneliness.

Class 2, was comprised of three students aged 14–17 years with verbal skills and lower literacy abilities (five to six year reading age assessment). These students took a total of 165 photos averaging 55 per student, and images of signs were considered to be of most importance to them. As can be evidenced in Figures 3.2 to 3.5, signs communicating safety, rules, procedures and directions were significant.

These explicit, clear signs were explained by the students to be highly important for their safety in case of emergencies and to prevent accidents. Safety was a key element of their own wellbeing and they continually reinforced the need for everyone to follow the rules and procedures of the school. Following a close second, friends were ranked as important to students in Class 2, with 11 images chosen. When discussing the images, students made numerous affirmative comments including:

> *I like having friends … not being left alone*
> *Having friends with the same interest … like listening to music*
> *Hanging out with friends*
> *Having friends you can trust … cause you can tell them your secrets.*

FIGURE 3.2 Exit sign

FIGURE 3.3 Safety instructions

FIGURE 3.4 Fire extinguisher instructions

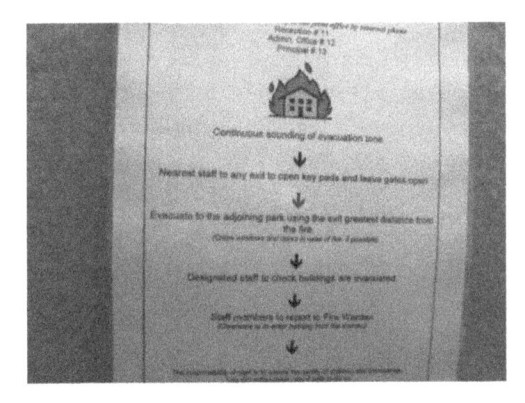

FIGURE 3.5 Fire evacuation procedure

These students described their friends as being *interesting, kind, understanding* and *helpful*. Such relationships were deemed by the students to be central to their sense of belonging, motivation to come to school, happiness and overall wellbeing.

Within Class 3, eight students aged 14–19 years were working at a Year 3 level and presented with mild intellectual disabilities and/or had been diagnosed on the Autism Spectrum. These students took a total of 308 photos, at an average of 38 photos per student. For these students, friendships dominated their choice of the top 20 important photos, with 29 images selected across the class.

In particular, in addition to the characteristics described by Class 2, these students described the importance of *friends who are happy* and *friends in the home group*. This reinforces the significance of developing a collective identity whereby multiple histories and voices contribute to creating a place and engage in dialogue to dwell together (Lim 2010). Demir and Özdemir (2010) identify the correlation between friendship and happiness; however they go beyond this to pose how individuals need their basic needs satisfied in which friendship experiences provide such a context.

Within a mainstream setting, Hamm and Faircloth (2005) describe how friendships serve as a secure base and buffer that help adolescents to cope with the psychological challenges of the social ecology of high school. Through these relationships, adolescents develop a stronger sense of belonging to their schools. As Majors (2013) suggests, being accepted and having friends is essential to mental health and wellbeing, and is a significant factor in terms of life quality and enjoyment. Young children need to learn the complex social and emotional management skills and that enable them to gain acceptance from peers and sustain mutually satisfying interactions leading to, in some cases, life-long friendships. The rewards of friendship are immense, but the consequences of not being accepted by peers and failing to develop friendships are also significant in terms of long-term mental health and wellbeing.

Of interest for this cohort of students in Class 3, their second most important element of the educational setting was pride in art and work products. As illustrated in Figures 3.6 to 3.9, public displays were important for students in order to feel a sense of accomplishment. They loved engaging with visitors and pointing out their creative products. Working collaboratively on projects created a collective bond and sense of joint ownership of the final products.

Teachers were also an important image for Class 3 students, with 13 images selected. Student comments included:

> *Always organised for me around the school*
> *There when I need it*
> *They are friends*
> *Have the same interests such as soccer*
> *Happy teachers, trusting*
> *Safe*

FIGURE 3.6 Mural of a public store

FIGURE 3.7 School gate painting

FIGURE 3.8 Mosaic tile mural

FIGURE 3.9 Hot air balloon

The importance of teacher/student relationship has been well documented and for these students' notions of *inclusion, respect* and *safety* underpinned their discussion of the teachers who were significant to them.

Students in Class 4 were enrolled in a Year 8/9 Asperger's Programme (prior to DSM-V release, now ASD). Eight students aged 14–16 years (six male, two female) took a total of 748 photos with an average of 93 photos per student, indicating that they were extremely engaged in this activity. Of note, the students primarily selected photos of themselves as the most important (a total of 26 selected). They were active in taking 'selfies' or asking others to take photos of them across a range of settings and poses. As they reviewed their photo collections, the students reinforced the personal significance of the images of themselves, with comments such as *I like myself, I like taking photos of myself and seeing the special places in the school, this is me.* Some photos incorporated personal items alongside the student, prompting comments such as: *This is me and my name; This is me on my bike; This is me at my desk.* A focus on identity and self-concept permeated the discussions and images. Given the inter-relationship between self-concept, achievement and wellbeing (Wei & Marder 2011), it is imperative to acknowledge these individuals and their capacities. In ranking the importance of photos, images of friends closely followed photos of self, with a total of 21 images selected. Art and work products ranked third in importance with 18 images selected. This aligns with Class 3 priorities.

There were 13 students in Class 5. Aged 16–19 years, and presenting with mild intellectual disabilities and/or high functioning ASD, these students were known as the seniors of the school. They took a total of 815 photos, averaging 62 photos per student. As part of their community engagement programme, these students were responsible for planning, shopping, catering, hospitality, cooking, budgeting for a community café located in their school site; they selected photos of the café as their most important photos, with a total of 62 selected. The individual and collective pride that these students felt in providing a service to the community and interacting with clients, was evidenced through these images. Education needs to be receptive to change and provide participation rights to *all* children (Quennerstedt 2011) inclusive of students with disabilities. These students were vocal in their self-advocacy, identifying their capabilities and their contribution to the broader community. As Test and colleagues (2005) state, self-advocacy is linked to self-determination, leading to better opportunities and outcomes. Such notions challenge notions of citizenship whereby some individuals with disabilities are unfortunately seen as not having the competence to participate (Vorhaus 2005). Whilst individual education plans (IEPs) are seen as important to support individuals in achieving goals, Adams, Beadle-Brown and Mansell (2006) describe how those with higher quality plans spend more time engaged in meaningful activity with increasing community presence and participation, which promotes lifestyle satisfaction and quality of life (p. 75). Students in Class 5 provided images (see Figures 3.10 and 3.11) and rich descriptions of their experiences in the café:

> *I find cooking fun, every Tuesday we have to set up tables and then yeah people come round and sit at them. That's a picture of the roster, who's working … like who does what part, what part of the kitchen, so like the person.*
>
> *We take it in turns to work together to get the job done. That's a close up of the table so it's all nice and neat and set up. I like the tulips they make me feel happy seeing them on the table.*

Overall, the most important photos for this cohort of students were people-centred, that is, their own photo (n=93), friends (n=92), teachers (n= 48) and SSOs (n=33). With four of the top six categories focused on people, the significance of personal identity and relationships with others provided the foundation of wellbeing within this educational setting. Students were extremely clear about how they view themselves, evidenced by comments such as:

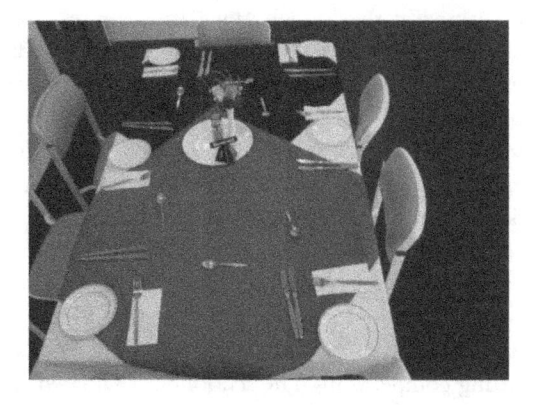

FIGURE 3.10   Café table

FIGURE 3.11 Café kitchen

I like myself, my name, my personal items
I like taking pictures of myself
I don't like anything about myself
Reading makes me feel nice and calm and I feel like I am in the story when I am reading.

Such insights provide valuable information for educators and carers about what is important for the authentic inclusion of students with disabilities, rather than imposing judgements, negative attitudes and expectations (Balandin & Duchan 2007). In advancing and sustaining wellbeing of students with disabilities, an in-depth understanding is needed of how their everyday movements within the place and space of educational settings are intricately intertwined.

The spaces students occupy in their everyday lives

In understanding the relations between the structures of social space and physical space (Bourdieu 1999) students provided examples which connected the physical school setting and wider community with the social interactions and connections with individuals. As Gannon (2009) describes, 'physical and social spaces are entwined in their (students) lived experience of place' (p. 620). For example, the significance of work experience and community access programmes, such as working at the local hospital (see Figure 3.12) and connecting with nature at the Botanical Gardens at lunch times (see Figures 3.13 and 3.14), provided a sense of purpose, contribution to society, self-respect and confidence in work skills and communication, whilst offering space to relax, interact with nature and time out from work demands. These elements are central to the wellbeing of students with disabilities, through providing safe and scaffolded learning opportunities which enhance academic achievement and post-school transition work opportunities. Fundamental to these elements is how they contribute in supporting a mentally healthy approach to learning, work and play.

The school bus (Figure 3.15) was very important to the students. Their photos and the accompanying discussion emphasised its integral role as the means of connecting with the community, including visits to the local library, swimming, excursions, work experience, charity events and sporting competitions. The school bus facilitated access to the community and was therefore an important connection between education and wellbeing.

FIGURE 3.12 Hospital work experience: filing patient records

FIGURE 3.13 Botanical Gardens

FIGURE 3.14 Botanical Gardens

In describing the images taken on outings, such as to the Adelaide Oval, South Australia (Figures 3.16 and 3.17), students' exuberance was captured with exclamations such as:

> *Going out – see people … ah it's good, it's good to see people*
> *It's fun you get fresh air*
> *I like meeting new people 'cause when you meet new people you can get to know them.*

FIGURE 3.15 School bus

FIGURE 3.16 Adelaide Oval, South Australia

FIGURE 3.17 Adelaide Oval scoreboard

One student who excelled in statistics and numbers loved studying the cricket scoreboard (Figure 3.17), which provided an opportunity for complex mathematical learning.

Additionally, the bike education programme for the students provided another highly important opportunity to move freely amongst the local community, whilst learning about safety and healthy lifestyle activities. Bicycles were provided for all students to access and they were evidently proud of having their own bike with comments including: *this is my bike; Bikes – make me feel happy* (Figure 3.18).

Within the educational setting, significant rooms were identified by students as places and spaces that were highly important to them. For example, the sensory room (Figures 3.19 and 3.20)

FIGURE 3.18 Bicycles

FIGURE 3.19 Sensory room swinging bed

FIGURE 3.20 Sensory room toys

provided an emotional escape from the school routine, whilst meeting the sensory stimulation preferences of individual students. As one student commented, *I like to go in there and sleep in the darkness or relax in the hammock here … I actually go there if I'm feeling stressed or relaxed, I need to relax … yeah, very calming.*

Other students identified the school's auditorium (hall) as a place of refuge. One student described the auditorium as a place for *quiet time – be quiet, not talking to your friends – don't like it when it's loud.* Such revelations highlight the interconnections between social spaces and physical place. For some students with disabilities this is even more important given heightened

FIGURE 3.21 School garden

senses. Designing spaces and places which reduce stimulation for some students, whilst heighten senses for others requiring intense stimulation, is important in accommodating and differentiating learning and life experiences. Acknowledging that all individuals have preferences for how and when they move through spaces and places, and incorporating this into educational plans, is key to enhancing educational inclusion and wellbeing. Sometimes these elements are overtaken by a focus on curriculum content rather than providing a physical and spatial environment conducive to learning and concentration. Such an environment includes an increased focus on outdoor classrooms and on the importance of nature and the environment in both learning and wellbeing. For these students, outside spaces made them feel 'happy'. One student commented: *I like to sit in the sun*. Comments relating to gardens included: *We have been planting a lot of gardens*; and *the garden makes me feel relaxed* (Figure 3.21).

A vital element of one's wellbeing is being able to feel safe. These students were acutely aware of the people and places which made them feel safe. Due to the ethical considerations of this research, images of individuals are not able to be displayed. However student comments included:

> *Friends make me feel safe and happy*
> *Teachers make the yard safe*
> *I go and talk to teacher*
> *Leadership makes me feel safe*
> *Rules make it safe*

Many students were quick to take images of their favourite places. A bench (Figure 3.22) was seen as a source of fun, social interaction, communication with friends whilst eating recess and lunch; a place the student looked forward to every schooling break. Favourite places such as this bench were referred to as important as they were places to go to for breakfast, learning, research, artwork, reading, music, science, quiet, friends and help.

Students' acute sense of what was important to them is aptly depicted by the image in Figure 3.23. When questioned about the choice of taking a photo of a power point on an exterior school wall, the student replied: *It's my space, I listen to music, we hang out … um … you can just sit and relax, go there every recess and lunch.*

This space was the meeting place for all his friends, where they sang, danced, laughed and bantered about the popular songs. It also offered this student a sense of identity as the leader

FIGURE 3.22   An important place

FIGURE 3.23   Power point on exterior wall

of a music group, organising the music equipment and inviting people into the group. This example showcases how important it is to share young people's insights and interpretations, as what another person could have deemed to be an unimportant photo was highly significant for the student.

Additionally, for students with disabilities, music (Figure 3.24) provides opportunities to reflect and share emotions. It is a source of collective interest and freedom to move and/or express oneself, and a form of communication.

FIGURE 3.24   Music source: iPod

Central to how spaces and places promoted the wellbeing of students with disabilities was their sense of pride in navigating these spaces and places.

Elements that make students proud of the place they inhabit

Students' level of wellbeing was linked to how proud they felt about themselves and their efforts at school. The significant number of photos of themselves signifies that they are proud of who they are, what they do and their capabilities. This pride was expressed in individual possessions, in seeing their own name displayed in the educational setting and in achievements such as the *trophy that I won as a team* (Figure 3.25).

Being proud of achievements and both individual and collective products dominated many images and discussions, including photos of posters, projects and food cooked in the café. For many students there was a strong motivation to strive for individual recognition by attaining a school leadership position. This was both for their own identity and self-worth, but also to gain staff, school leadership and family/carer recognition, whilst receiving aspired privileges (i.e. extra time for favourite activities, access to specialised rooms/equipment, rewards cabinet) based on their interests. Gaining school 'leadership passes' included permanent passes, diamond, gold and silver. As one student described: *Having a permanent pass which gives special access to the computer room.*

Acknowledging student achievement and effort was important as well. For example, a student was recognised by the whole school upon graduation and was given a crown at assembly (see Figure 3.26). He commented:

> *Ah my crown, I love my crown, it makes me feel happy, it was given to me on graduation day …*
> *always been making me a perfect time'.*
>   When asked *How do you feel when you have your crown on?* he replied: *Like a king! …*
> *without it – a little bit not appreciated*

Such dialogue provides insight into how this student feels and clearly shows a strong sense of wellbeing through the gesture of receiving a crown to publicly acknowledge his status. Of interest was this student's insight into his own emotional wellbeing at not feeling appreciated when not wearing his crown. For this student his desire for peer, staff and parent/caregiver

FIGURE 3.25 Soccer team trophy

FIGURE 3.26 Student crown

recognition and appreciation was central to his wellbeing. Such visual images provided opportunities to share these experiences and emotions as well as open up opportunities for students with disabilities to showcase their immense creativity.

Creative and critical responses

The students chose their top 20 most important digital images and designed a photo story with music to showcase their wellbeing message to others including their peers, staff, parents/carers and wider community. Providing students with freedom to demonstrate and apply their decision making, information and communication technology (ICT) knowledge, music appreciation, literacy skills, creativity and imagination motivated students and empowered them. The following sequences of figures are screenshots of one student's photo story, which was based around a *Star Wars* theme. The initial image was a rolling screen using the opening narrative from movie *The Empire Strikes Back* accompanied by the corresponding *Star Wars* music. Whilst for ethical purposes images with peers, staff, community members have been removed, the remaining images and captions demonstrate a highly creative imagination, a cheeky sense of humour, pride in own work products and an acute ability to sequence an engaging message within the *Star Wars* theme (Figure 3.27). Above all, the most important themes for this student are highly visible.

An enabling pedagogy which incorporated digital images, ICT, music and captions provided the opportunity for this student to express his interests and humour. It is particularly important that this pedagogy provided rich opportunities for those students who have difficulty in expressing themselves or who are not confident to express in more traditional forms of writing and speaking. By transferring the power to the student, we gain a more informed

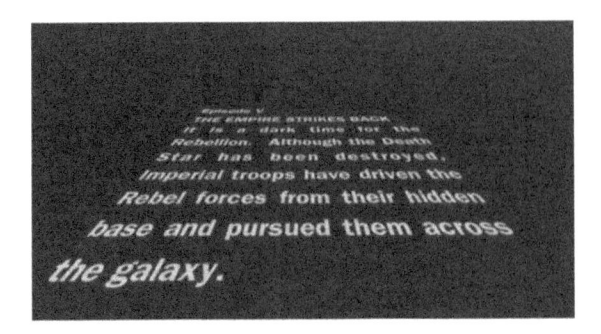

FIGURE 3.27A Star Wars photo story excerpt

FIGURE 3.27B Reading in the library is important

FIGURE 3.27C Visual attractiveness of the student run café is important

FIGURE 3.27D Producing delicious food to serve to café patrons is important

FIGURE 3.27E Displaying learning and work products is important

FIGURE 3.27F Space to express humour is important

FIGURE 3.27G Creative space linking with Star Wars theme is important

FIGURE 3.27H Creative space linking with Star Wars theme and surveillance

FIGURE 3.271 Bike education and creativity in expression is important

insight into their wellbeing, skills and understandings. For this student, wellbeing is at its peak when he is immersed in the literary world, where he traverses between fictional narratives such as *Star Wars* and his everyday life. Using his photos, he takes on from the movie a strong character that moves and interacts confidently and powerfully. Peers and staff are also represented as fictional characters and their roles within the school are creatively integrated into the photo story; for example, a school leader is named as the Enforcer. These images and characterisations skilfully project the student's experience of respectful relationships with members of the school community. Having the freedom to traverse these fictional and everyday realms provides this student with spaces and places to share his wellbeing perspectives as well as his highly acute literary competence. Enabling pedagogies are vital in order to open up opportunities for the expression of young people's voices and representations.

Integration of enabling pedagogy inviting multiple voices and representations

The enabling pedagogy of providing students with a camera, gave freedom, creativity and the opportunity for individual response. Inclusion, belonging, place and artistic spaces were employed as a way of developing identity and stronger self-concepts (Hall 2010) for students with disabilities. When students were given the camera, heightened engagement and enthusiasm was observed. This was complemented by increased communication, with students asking people to pose for photos and engaging in animated discussions focussed on what they were taking photos of and why. Such opportunities promoted socialisation between peers as well as experimenting with language, literacy and communication skills. Students were overheard debating what they thought others should take photos of based on their opinions of what they thought was important to others; these opinions and suggestions were sometimes acted upon and other times students assertively claimed *no that is not important to me*. In advancing the identity and wellbeing of students with disability, such self-belief, confidence and assertiveness is essential in advancing their own self-advocacy and independence.

For Amy, the student in the vignette at the beginning of this chapter, who presents as non-verbal with severe and multiple disabilities, the use of photos gave her the opportunity to communicate. During their daily routines, Amy's class teacher and peers would point to places and spaces asking her what she would like to take photos of and whether it was important to her. She would tap her tray to acknowledge *yes* or move her hand from side to side to signal *no*. The insight provided by this enabling pedagogy within the vignette highlights the intense emotional feelings Amy was experiencing at the loss of her friend who had recently left the school. The cumulative impact of experiencing emotional distress permeated Amy's outward expressions of happiness, her desire to interact with peers, staff and parents and her capacity to concentrate and invest effort in everyday learning tasks. For the SSO, the enabling pedagogies of visual images opened the door to understanding why Amy's behaviour and application to learning had changed. As a consequence, appropriate support for her wellbeing was able to be put into place. In the busy and often fast-paced educational environment, making time and increasing opportunities to communicate are essential in order to fully understand each student's wellbeing and the support needed to maximise this.

Through engaging students as visual ethnographers (Figure 3.28), images become a communication tool and a way of transferring power to the students (White, Bushin, Carpena-Méndez & Ní Laoire 2010). Carroll-Lind, Chapman, Gregory and Maxwell (2006) describe how accessing authentic information about students can be problematic. Adults often represent student's views and experiences on behalf of them; children's own views may be perceived as lacking validity or honesty, and ethical issues often prevent access to children's own opinions. As Boxall and Ralph (2009) suggest, techniques such as visual ethnography challenge the monopoly on knowledge claimed by researchers and educators, and address the complexities of ethical research for fully informed participation when participants may have communication difficulties. Banks (2001) identifies the value of photos in reducing awkwardness where students feel self-conscious, as the attention is turned to the images where direct eye contact is not required. Addressing these issues for truly inclusive wellbeing education is essential for students with disabilities.

For full understanding of their wellbeing, we are all responsible for opening accessibility and opportunities for students with disabilities to share and communicate their perspectives.

FIGURE 3.28 Students with disabilities as visual ethnographers

This chapter has aimed to share a proactive example designed to address tensions between meeting academic research criteria and ensuring the needs and views of people with disabilities are genuinely met and represented (Aldridge 2007). This includes addressing the gatekeepers who, for every good intention of care, safety and protection, can sometimes inadvertently perpetuate stereotypes and barriers which are aversive to true inclusion and access. For example in this case study, gatekeeper questions, behaviours and comments included:

- What if they don't take the photos I think they should?
- What if they take inappropriate photos?
- What if they break the camera?
- What if they take a whole lot of photos of the same thing?
- Telling students what photos they should be taking

In response to such gatekeeping, we restate that enabling pedagogical initiatives aim to explore what is important to the student, not the gatekeeper. Unnecessary assumptions of inappropriate or careless use of a camera reflect a stereotypical bias by the gatekeeper. I suggest the need to challenge the power relationships between students with disabilities and those charged with educational responsibility. Students with disabilities need to be involved in education in a way that acknowledges their rights and makes space for their voices, acknowledging that children are competent and have valid opinions (Einarsdóttir 2007). It is the educator's responsibility to be creative in accessing this voice and opinion. This requires stepping outside traditional methodologies, in order to invite multiple voices and representations which better inform our understanding of young people's wellbeing. Whilst a duty of care for students with disabilities is paramount, applying a 'capabilities' rather than a 'gatekeeper' approach is essential in building their self-esteem, confidence and overall wellbeing. In advocating for a proactive capabilities approach suggested by Sen (1985) and Nussbaum (2003), the focus is on what students *can do* and *be*. Students with disabilities have a right to wellbeing which includes Nussbaum's (2003) central human capability entitlements of: life; bodily health; bodily integrity; senses, imagination and thought; emotions; practical reasoning; affiliation; other species; play; and control over one's emotions. Price (2015) describes the need for educators to be proactive for the inclusion of students with disabilities in curriculum through advocating positive attitudes and self-efficacy; student progression and achievement; and equity, flexibility, access and choice. These elements aptly apply to wellbeing education for students with disabilities.

Conclusion

As expressed so vividly in Amy's vignette at the outset of this chapter:

> *Thank goodness these photos have let me share my sadness, I feel so relieved that you know.*
> *(Amy, 10 years old)*

This chapter has aimed to show how, for students with disabilities, photo voice authorises people to re-author and re-imag(in)e themselves in order to address the deficit perceptions of media and public cultures (Gannon 2009). As such, visual ethnography provides students with opportunities to express their level of wellbeing, their identity and what is important to them. How students view their sense of space and place is central to their overall wellbeing.

In relation to the wellbeing of the students discussed in this chapter, key factors include:

- These students love the people who occupy their place.
- These students take significant pride in themselves, their belongings, work products and space.
- An enabling pedagogy as visual ethnographers engaged students, opened opportunities for communication and encouraged critical and creative responses.
- Space and place interconnections provided opportunities for learning, interactions, safety and happiness.

Given the right of all young people to wellbeing, the definition provided in Chapter 1 is inclusive of the diverse needs of students with disabilities and reminds us that we need to be mindful of the fluid and unique characteristics of wellbeing:

> Wellbeing is diverse and fluid respecting individual, family and community beliefs, values, experiences, culture, opportunities and contexts across time and change. It encompasses intertwined individual, collective and environmental elements which continually interact across the lifespan. Wellbeing is something we all aim for, underpinned by positive notions, yet is unique to each of us and provides us with a sense of who we are which needs to be respected. Our role with wellbeing education is to provide the opportunity, access, choices, resources and capacities for individuals and communities to aspire to their unique sense of wellbeing, whilst contributing to a sense of community wellbeing.
>
> *(from Chapter 1)*

Ultimately, in advancing an inclusive wellbeing educational agenda 'a strong commitment by curriculum developers and educators to the good of others should be a shared conception from the outset, which promotes what students with disabilities can do and be, provide opportunity, dignity and respect' (Price in review 2015, p. 11). We must also guard against succumbing to stereotypical judgements of individuals' wellbeing, particularly students with disabilities. As Huppert and So (2009) emphasise, some people in very favourable objective circumstances do not necessarily flourish, whilst others who live in relatively harsh circumstances have high levels of wellbeing. For learners, being diagnosed with a disability does not automatically imply reduced wellbeing or rights to wellbeing. If we aim to remove societal categorisations and divisions of 'us and them' (Hamber 2004) and focus inclusively on 'us', then this will be a significant step in supporting wellbeing for all.

Wellbeing follow-up activities

1. In relation to your setting, engage as a visual ethnographer taking photos of *what is important to you* and then adopt Gannon's (2009) approach to critique:

   - Identify what you love about the place and community in which you live.
   - Describe the spaces you occupy in your everyday life.
   - Speculate on elements that make you proud of the place you inhabit.
   - Generate critical and creative responses to the relations between the structures of social spaces and those of physical space (following Bourdieu 1999).

2. Analyse your responses to the above questions in relation to the students with disabilities' perceptions. How are they similar and/or different? The key here is to critique:

    •   How might your individual perceptions possibly influence decisions and actions made in relation to the education and wellbeing of students with disabilities? How can you ensure students with disabilities genuinely have their voice?
    •   Are there foundational elements of what is important to both you and students with disabilities? If so, what might these be? If not, then why?

3. Empower children and young people in your care as visual ethnographers by inviting them to take digital images and create multimedia presentations (such as photo stories) around the theme 'What is important to me?'
4. Critique how your setting/environment promotes wellbeing for all? In particular, analyse whether policies, practices, curriculum and pedagogy promote 'us and them' wellbeing divisions or an inclusive 'us' wellbeing philosophy as suggested by Hamber (2004).
5. Critique the role of the gatekeeper in relation to the wellbeing of students with disabilities.
6. Analyse your role (as an educator, caregiver, stakeholder) and consider how you can further apply a capabilities approach (Nussbaum 2003; Sen 1985) to the wellbeing of students with disabilities; that is, a focus on what they can do and be.

References

ACARA (2011) *Shape of the Australian curriculum*. Australian Curriculum, Assessment and Reporting Authority. Available from http://www.acara.edu.au/home_page.html.

Adams, L, Beadle-Brown, J & Mansell, J (2006) Implementation and effect of individual programme planning. *British Journal of Learning Disabilities*, 34, pp. 69–76.

Ainscow, M, Booth, T & Dyson, A (2006) Inclusion and the standards agenda: Negotiating policy pressures in England. *International Journal of Inclusive Education*, 10(4–5), pp. 295–308.

Aldridge, J (2007) Picture this: The use of participatory photographic research methods with people with learning disabilities. *Disability & Society*, 22(1), pp. 1–17.

American Psychiatric Association (2013) *Diagnostic and statistical manual of mental disorders*. 5th edn, APA, Washington, DC.

Antonsich, M (2010) Searching for belonging – An analytical framework. *Geography Compass*, 4(6), pp. 644–659.

Armstrong, D (2013) Educator perceptions of children who present with social, emotional and behavioural difficulties: A literature review with implications for recent educational policy in England and internationally. *International Journal of Inclusive Education*, 18(7), pp. 731–745.

Armstrong, D & Hallett, F (2012) Private knowledge, public face: Conceptions of children with SEBD by teachers in the UK – A case study. *Educational & Child Psychology*, 29(4), pp. 77–87.

Armstrong, D, Price, DA & Crowley, T (2015) Thinking it through: a study of how pre-service teachers respond to children who present with possible mental health difficulties. *Emotional and Behavioural Difficulties*. Onlilne 18 March 2015. DOI: 10.1080/13632752.2015.1019248

Australian Government (2005) *Disability standards for education*. Australian Government, Department of Education and Training. Available from http://education.gov.au/disability-standards-education.

Australian Human Rights Commission (2014) *National Disability Forum 2014: Summary of survey results*. Australian Human Rights Commission, Sydney, NSW.

Balandin, S & Duchan, J (2007) Communication: Access to inclusion (editorial). *Journal of Intellectual and Developmental Disability*, 32(4), pp. 230–232.

Banks, M (2001) *Visual methods in social research*. SAGE, London.

Barnes, C (1999) A working social model? Disability and work in the 21st century. Paper presented at the *Disability Studies Conference and Seminar*, Edinburgh, 9 December 1999.

Baskin, TW, Wampold, BE, Quintana, SM & Enright, RD (2010) Belongingness as a protective factor against loneliness and potential depression in a multicultural middle school. *The Counseling Psychologist*, 38(5), pp. 626–651.

Beach, R & Thein, A (2006) Challenging standardisation through place-based critical inquiry. In B Doecke, M Howie & W Sawyer (eds), *Only connect: English teaching, schooling and community*. Wakefield Press and The Australian Association for the Teaching of English, Kent Town, SA, pp. 263–280.

Bourdieu, P (1999) Site effects. In P Bourdieu, A Accardo, G Balazs, S Beaud, F Bonvin, E Bourdieu, P Bourgois, S Broccolichi, P Champagne & R Christin (eds), *The weight of the world: Social suffering in contemporary society*. Stanford University Press, Palo Alto, CA, pp. 123–129.

Boxall, K & Ralph, S (2009) Research ethics and the use of visual images in research with people with intellectual disability. *Journal of Intellectual and Developmental Disability*, 34(1), pp. 45–54.

Carroll-Lind, J, Chapman, JW, Gregory, J & Maxwell, G (2006) The key to the gatekeepers: Passive consent and other ethical issues surrounding the rights of children to speak on issues that concern them. *Child Abuse & Neglect*, 30(9), pp. 979–989.

Clough, P & Barton, L (eds) (1998) *Articulating with difficulty: Research voices in inclusive education*. SAGE, London.

Cormack, P, Green, B & Reid, J-A (2003) River literacies: Discursive constructions of place and environment in children's writing about the Murray-Darling Basin. Paper presented at the Senses of Place Conference, University of Tasmania, Hobart, 5–8 April 2003.

Coughlan, BJ (2011) Critical issues in the emotional wellbeing of students with special educational needs in the 21st century. *Reach*, 24(2), pp. 57–75.

de Boer, A, Pijl, SJ & Minnaert, A (2011) Regular primary schoolteachers' attitudes towards inclusive education: A review of the literature. *International Journal of Inclusive Education*, 15(3), pp. 331–353.

Deleuze, G & Guattari, F (1987/2004) *A thousand plateaus: Capitalism and schizophrenia*. Continuum, London.

Demir, M & Özdemir, M (2010) Friendship, need satisfaction and happiness. *Journal of Happiness Studies*, 11(2), pp. 243–259.

Einarsdóttir, J (2007) Research with children: Methodological and ethical challenges. *European Early Childhood Education Research Journal*, 15(2), pp. 197–211.

Epstein, I, Stevens, B, McKeever, P & Baruchel, S (2008) Photo elicitation interview (PEI): Using photos to elicit children's perspectives. *International Journal of Qualitative Methods*, 5(3), pp. 1–11.

Finkelstein, V (1980) *Attitudes and disabled people: Issues for discussion*. World Rehabilitation Fund, New York.

Gannon, S (2009) Rewriting 'the road to nowhere': Place pedagogies in Western Sydney. *Urban Education*, 44(5), pp. 608–624.

Gibson, S (2006) Beyond a 'culture of silence': Inclusive education and the liberation of 'voice'. *Disability & Society*, 21(4), pp. 315–329.

Goodley, D (2007) Towards socially just pedagogies: Deleuzoguattarian critical disability studies. *International Journal of Inclusive Education*, 11(3), pp. 317–334.

Hall, E (2010) Spaces of social inclusion and belonging for people with intellectual disabilities. *Journal of Intellectual Disability Research*, 54(Supp.1), pp. 48–57.

Hallett, C & Prout, A (eds) (2003) *Hearing the voices of children: Social policy for a new century*. Taylor & Francis, Basingstoke.

Hamber, B (2004) The impact of trauma: A psychosocial approach. Paper presented at the Shared Practice–Victims Work in Action Conference, Limavady, Northern Ireland, 7–8 April 2004.

Hamm, JV & Faircloth, BS (2005) The role of friendship in adolescents' sense of school belonging. *New Directions for Child and Adolescent Development*, 2005(107), pp. 61–78.

Huppert, FA & So, T (2009) *What percentage of people in Europe are flourishing and what characterises them?*, paper presented at the meeting Measuring subjective well-being: An opportunity for NSOs?, Florence, 23–24 July 2009.

John, M (1996) Voicing: Research and practice with the silenced. In M John (ed), *Children in charge: The child's right to a fair hearing*. Jessica Kingsley, London, pp. 3-24.

Kemp, A (2006) Engaging the environment. *Curriculum and Teaching Dialogue*, 8(1/2), pp. 125–142.

Kenworthy, J & Whittaker, J (2000) Anything to declare? The struggle for inclusive education and children's rights. *Disability & Society*, 15(2), pp. 219–231.

Lewis, A & Lindsay, G (1999) *Researching children's perspectives*. Open University Press, Philadelphia, PA.

Lim, M (2010) Historical consideration of place: Inviting multiple histories and narratives in place-based education. *Cultural Studies of Science Education*, 5(4), pp. 899–909.

Macleod, G (2010) Identifying obstacles to a multidisciplinary understanding of 'disruptive' behaviour. *Emotional and Behavioural Difficulties*, 15(2), pp. 95–109.

Majors, K (2013) Friendships: The power of positive alliance. In S Roffey (ed), *Positive relationships: Evidence based practice across the world*. Springer, Dordrecht, pp. 127–143.

McInerney, P, Smyth, J & Down, B (2011) 'Coming to a place near you?' The politics and possibilities of a critical pedagogy of place-based education. *Asia-Pacific Journal of Teacher Education*, 39(1), pp. 3–16.

Meijer, C, Soriano, V & Watkins, A (eds) (2006) *Special needs education in Europe: Provision in post-primary education*. European Agency for Development in Special Needs Education, Middelfart.

Miles, S & Singal, N (2010) The Education for All and inclusive education debate: Conflict, contradiction or opportunity? *International Journal of Inclusive Education*, 14(1), pp. 1–15.

Minow, M (1991) *Making all the difference: Inclusion, exclusion, and American law*. Cornell University Press, Ithaca, NY.

Mowat, J (2009) The inclusion of pupils perceived as having SEBD in mainstream schools: A focus upon learning. *Support for Learning*, 24(4), pp. 159–169.

Nussbaum, M (2003) Capabilities as fundamental entitlements: Sen and social justice. *Feminist Economics*, 9(2–3), pp. 33–59.

Oliver, M (1992) Changing the social relations of research production? *Disability, Handicap & Society*, 7(2), pp. 101–114.

Oliver, M (1996) *Understanding disability: From theory to practice*. MacMillan, Basingstoke.

Peetsma, T, Vergeer, M, Roeleveld, J & Karsten, S (2001) Inclusion in education: comparing pupils' development in special and regular education. *Educational Review*, 53(2), pp. 125–135.

Price, DA (in review 2015) Australian curriculum: Applying a central human capabilities approach to cross curriculum priorities for students with disabilities. *Australasian Journal of Special Education*.

Price, DA (2015) Pedagogies for inclusion of students with disabilities in a national curriculum: a human capabilities approach. *Journal of Educational Enquiry*. 14(2). Special edition: Social Justice and Pedagogies.

Quennerstedt, A. (2011). The construction of children's rights in education – a research synthesis, *The International Journal of Children's Rights*, 19(4), pp. 661 – 678.

Qvortrup, J, Bardy, M, Sgritta, G & Wintersberger, H (eds) (1994) *Childhood matters: Social theory, practice and politics*. Avebury, Aldershot.

Reddington, S (2014) Thinking through multiplicities: Movement, affect and the schooling experiences of young men with autism spectrum disorder. Doctoral thesis, School of Education, University of South Australia, Adelaide, SA.

Ruijs, NM, Van der Veen, I & Peetsma, TT (2010) Inclusive education and students without special educational needs. *Educational Research*, 52(4), pp. 351–390.

Sen, A (1985) *Commodities and capabilities*. North-Holland, Amsterdam.

Sitch, R (dir.) (1997) *The Castle*. Village Roadshow.

Somerville, M (2006) An enabling place pedagogy for new teachers. Paper presented at the Annual AARE Conference: Engaging Pedagogies, Adelaide, 8–9 November 2006.

South Australian Social Inclusion Board (July 2010) *Activating citizenship: A social inclusion approach for disability in South Australia (discussion paper)*. South Australian Social Inclusion Board, Adelaide, SA.

Taylor, M (2005) Self-identity and the arts education of disabled young people. *Disability & Society*, 20(7), pp. 763–778.

Test, DW, Fowler, CH, Wood, WM, Brewer, DM & Eddy, S (2005) A conceptual framework of self-advocacy for students with disabilities. *Remedial and Special Education*, 26(1), pp. 43–54.

UNESCO (1994) *The Salamanca statement and framework for action on special needs education: Adopted by the World Conference on Special Needs Education; Access and Quality. Salamanca, Spain, 7–10 June 1994.* UNESCO, Salamanca, Spain.

United Nations General Assembly (1989) *Convention on the rights of the child.* United Nations, New York, NY.

van Eijck, M & Roth, W-M (2010) Towards a chronotopic theory of 'place' in place-based education. *Cultural Studies of Science Education*, 5(4), pp. 869–898.

Vorhaus, J (2005) Citizenship, competence and profound disability. *Journal of Philosophy of Education*, 39(3), pp. 461–475.

Wei, X & Marder, C (2011) Self-concept development of students with disabilities: Disability category, gender, and racial differences from early elementary to high school. *Remedial and Special Education*, 33(4), pp. 247–257.

White, A, Bushin, N, Carpena-Méndez, F & Ní Laoire, C (2010) Using visual methodologies to explore contemporary Irish childhoods. *Qualitative research*, 10(2), pp. 143–158.

Wilkinson, R & Pickett, K (2010) *The spirit level: Why equality is better for everyone.* Penguin, London.

4

WELLBEING IN ALTERNATIVE EDUCATION

Marnie Best

Lucca, an 11-year-old student in an alternative educational setting, exclaimed:

The teachers at my real [mainstream] school, they didn't like me. They reckon I caused too much trouble so they sent me here [alternative educational setting] to get rid of me. But I don't care, they're just stupid. Their school is shit anyway …

Lucca continued …

My old school was real strict and stuff. That school hates me. If they send me back, I'll probably do something that'll get me excluded again like hit someone or stuff like that. They can't make me go back there. I hate that school and the teachers there.

Needless to say, Lucca wasn't too fond of his mainstream school. He was open and candid about his experiences and made it clear that mainstream school was a place that he did not want to be. Lucca wasn't restrained with his language; he told it as it was. He had opinions, but few of them conveyed a positive impression of education.

Lucca had an extensive history of negative interactions with peers and teachers at the mainstream school, where his latest round of violence resulted in an eight week exclusion from a year six mainstream class. Although aged 11, he had experienced countless detentions and an earlier suspension. He had been in an upper primary class at an alternative education setting for one week when he conveyed his perceptions of the experience. Through meeting the goals of his exclusion, it was anticipated he would return to the mainstream school. Or so the teachers planned.

Introduction

Alternative education, as the name suggests, is an alternative approach to mainstream schooling. Often, the students who attend an alternative educational setting are those who are marginalised through, and by, mainstream school experiences. The reasons students are involved with alternative educational settings are diverse, but learners with social, emotional, educational or behavioural needs are overrepresented in non-mainstream educational contexts (Mills & McGregor

2010; te Riele 2007). Recent trends indicate that enrolments in alternative educational settings are steadily growing and, whilst this may be due to varying definitions of alternative education, schools and teachers are experiencing greater student diversity than existing educational structures have been able to effectively support (Hughes & Adera 2006). This chapter builds on previous ones, arguing that learner wellbeing is paramount to meaningful learning and educational engagement. Therefore, it is reasoned that learner wellbeing and alternative education are inextricably linked: wellbeing is influenced through educational and social environments and interactions in which learners are immersed.

Alternative education can be considered an intervention to support students who have needs which cannot be appropriately accommodated within mainstream educational settings (DCSF 2008; Mills & McGregor 2010; te Riele 2007). This chapter explores the benefits, challenges and implications of supporting the social, emotional, educational and behavioural wellbeing of students marginalising from educational opportunities, with a particular focus on alternative educational opportunities. The vignette opening this chapter reflects the perspective of Lucca, an 11-year-old male student attending an alternative educational setting, emphasising that wellbeing is influenced through our environments and shapes who we are as people and as members of communities.

As earlier chapters have highlighted, all young people have a right to education, irrespective of whether it is mainstream or alternative. Further to this, they have a right to environments which promote their sense of wellbeing. For this reason, there is a growing necessity for school systems to provide alternative educational opportunities which support the wellbeing of students who are on the periphery of mainstream education (Mills & McGregor 2010; Smyth, McInerney & Fish 2013). Whilst this chapter focusses on alternative educational settings and the role they play in supporting students on the periphery of education, modifications to support students' wellbeing can be possible, and in fact achievable, in all educational settings: mainstream and alternative. This chapter draws on the definition of wellbeing provided in Chapter 1 to explore how alternative education can support the academic, social, behavioural and emotional wellbeing of students who are marginalised through, and by, mainstream school settings.

Shifting understandings of 'students at risk' and 'educational marginalisation'

As educators, we often relate school to academic outcomes such as high grades and educational retention, and yet we fail to consider how important non-academic achievements are to learner wellbeing (Best, Price & McCallum 2015). For example, in order for students to attain high grades and remain in school, educators need to foster environments that promote attendance, engagement and a sense of belonging. With this in mind, we need to ask the following questions: What are successful, positive and effective learning experiences? Can we consider student grades and retention irrespective of their wellbeing? And how do we promote success, positivity and effectiveness for students who have had primarily negative experiences of education?

The dilemma presented here surrounds the need to challenge the way in which we think about schools, teachers and students: *Do students fail school or do schools fail students?* The often used term 'at risk', for example, homogenises individuals and infers that a common trait or behaviour exists (te Riele 2006, 2012), failing to consider broader social and contextual influences within educational settings. Through the associated negative stigma and deficit image of individuals, the term 'at risk' has been contested (Smyth, Hattam, Cannon, Edwards, Wilson & Wurst 2004; te Riele 2012; Thomson 2002). As a result, te Riele (2006; 2012) has reasoned for the term *marginalised students*, to shift the definitional focus away from deficits within individuals (and their families), to critically consider the role of educational settings and social interactions in shaping student retention, belonging and wellbeing.

The term marginalised students has been conceptualised to identify youth whose educational outcomes are noticeably low, are at increased risk of not completing secondary school, or who may have experienced school expulsion (te Riele 2006). This shift in terminology is a push away from deficit models—which attribute educational marginalisation to factors *within students* (Faubert 2012; Quinn, Poirier, Faller, Gable & Tonelson 2006; Riordan 2006; te Riele 2006, 2012)—toward the acknowledgement that causal external factors *within educational contexts*, such as school processes, achievement-related experiences, and social interactions, influence learner wellbeing and educational marginalisation (Faubert 2012; Riordan 2006). However, while it is suggested that school and social influences are integral to student wellbeing, family and home environments must likewise be considered as factors which shape a student's sense of self and belonging to school. The nexus which exists between families, home and school are vital contributors to student wellbeing; events at home can shape student dispositions at school, as events at school are similarly taken home by students. If we then reconsider the definition of wellbeing described in Chapter 1, we reinforce the notion that learner wellbeing cannot be considered independently from environmental and social interactions; our understanding of wellbeing must reflect the numerous environments in which students are immersed.

What is alternative education?

Although relatively unknown in wider educational circles, alternative education has an established foundation, both in Australia and internationally. In broad terms, alternative education is designed primarily for students verging on educational disengagement, disconnection, marginalisation or premature withdrawal from the school system, where mainstream school settings cannot, or do not, meet their needs. In essence, alternative education provides different or *alternative* approaches and structures to mainstream school settings (Lagana-Riordan, Aguilar, Franklin, Streeter, Kim, Tripodi & Hopson 2011; McGregor & Mills 2012; Morgan, Brown, Heck, Pendergast & Kanasa 2013). As Figure 4.1 illustrates, students are involved with alternative education for diverse and often complex reasons.

Like wellbeing, there is no widely-adopted definition of alternative education. Varying conceptualisations have resulted in wide-ranging estimates regarding the actual number of students involved with alternative education. Yet, what is known is that the need for alternatives to mainstream schooling is growing. In the United States, where alternative education has grown threefold since mid-1990 (Hughes & Adera 2006), it is estimated that 600,000 students (Gable, Bullock & Evans 2006) are involved across 20,000 sites (Lange & Sletten 2002). United Kingdom data estimates 70,000 students, or 1 per cent of the student population, are involved with alternative education, with approximately the same number in short-term alternative provisions. These figures suggest that approximately 135,000 students per year are involved with some form of alternative education in the UK alone (DCSF 2008). Like Lucca, mentioned in the vignette at the beginning of this chapter, 91 per cent of students involved with alternative education are aged between 11 and 15 years with males representing

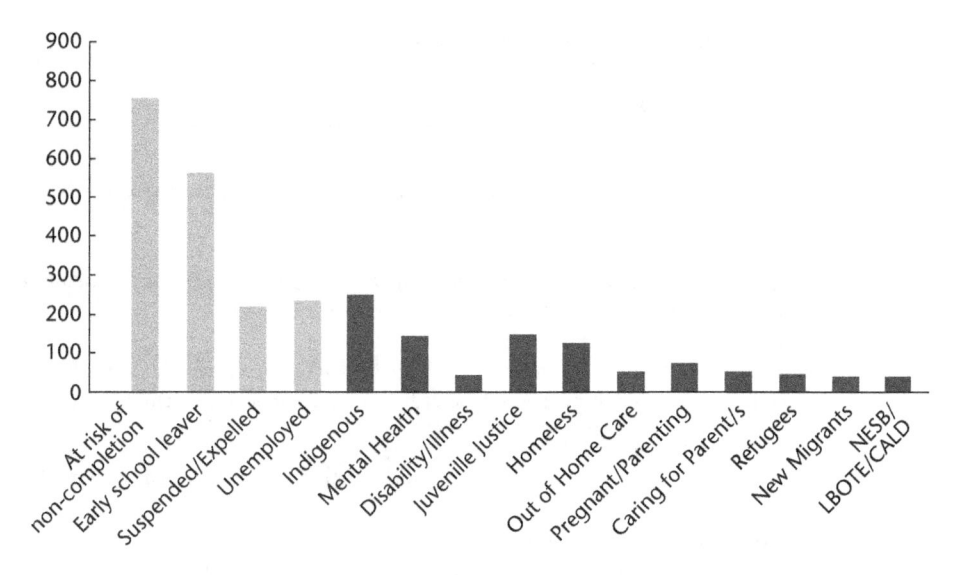

FIGURE 4.1   Alternative education target groups (te Riele 2014)

69 per cent of learners (DCSF 2008). Conservative Australian estimates place 70,000 students across 900 programmes (te Riele 2014), yet this number is likely to be much higher in reality given that many students participate in unreported flexible and alternative learning initiatives. Given the importance of providing alternative educational options and in view of the considerable number of students accessing these options, educational policy and practice, both in Australia and beyond, must be responsive to the changing needs of learners (McGregor & Mills 2012; Social Enterprise Coalition 2010; te Riele 2012).

Types and characteristics of alternative education

Alternative education has been broadly conceptualised by researchers such as Gregg (1999) and Raywid (1994) as unique approaches to education, designed to provide academic options outside of mainstream school contexts. How this broad concept is put into practice differs considerably across sites. However, regardless of the varying conceptualisations of alternative education, considerably more agreement exists regarding the common characteristics of alternative educational settings. These include:

• flexible curriculum linking academic and social skills;
• responsive instructional approaches;
• transitional arrangements which connect alternative and mainstream education;
• access to community-based support; and
• increased staff and resources to serve students with diverse needs (Lehr & Lange 2003; Lehr, Moreau, Lange & Lanners 2004; Powell 2003; Quinn & Rutherford 1998; Raywid 1994; te Riele 2012).

While there are different approaches to alternative education in different countries, many share similar characteristics and models, as highlighted in Table 4.1.

TABLE 4.1 Alternative educational models from US, UK and Australia

Country	Alternative Education Model
United States	*Type I* Optional attendance; emphasis on innovative programmes and practices; centred on *environmental* change *Type II* Predominantly 'last chance' sites; centred on *within-person* change through disciplinary approaches to circumvent exclusion or expulsion *Type III* Remedial or therapeutic in nature, centred on *within-person* change; focus on social or emotional needs that pose academic or behavioural barriers to learning (Raywid 1994)
United Kingdom	*Alternative provision* Students participate in timetabled, educational opportunities away mainstream school *Pupil referral unit* A form of alternative provision for students with academic, behavioural, social or emotional needs that cannot be appropriately accommodated within mainstream school (Taylor 2012)
Australia	*Alternative schools* Focussing on the academic, social, behavioural and emotional needs of students whose return to a mainstream school is improbable *Alternative placements* Characterised as educational contexts designed to support students who have been suspended or excluded, to return to mainstream school (Mills & McGregor 2010) *Alternative programmes* Proactive intervention initiatives designed to strengthen educational connection with mainstream school

Many students who attend an alternative educational setting do so due to school exclusion. Yet, students who are excluded or disengaged from school do not disappear or adjourn their need for academic support during this time (DCSF 2008). Alternative education therefore serves two key purposes: supporting government education (and retention) targets, and providing essential pathways for students to retain connection to educational opportunities (te Riele 2012). What underpins the achievement of these purposes is supporting the wellbeing of these students, and in particular, their personal and social wellbeing.

Why do we need alternative approaches to education?

We all possess a sense of wellbeing, however varied and fluid. Our definition of wellbeing in this book draws attention to the fact that one's sense of self and belonging are influenced through environmental and social interactions. Whilst there is little argument that most students experience relative success throughout their time in school, there remains a population of students who don't appear to fit within existing school structures. Traditionally, research regarding educational retention has focussed on students within the secondary years of school, but how can students successfully traverse the secondary years if they fail to successfully navigate the earlier years? Research is suggesting that students in the middle years of school, incorporating the developmental phases of middle childhood and early adolescence, are exhibiting progressively disengaged, disruptive and violent behaviours (Lagana-Riordan et al. 2011; Mills & McGregor 2010; Sullivan, Johnson, Conway, Owens & Taddeo 2012). As a result, educators need to respond to increasingly diverse student behaviours, which often result in a considerable number of school suspensions and exclusions (DCSF 2008; Lange & Sletten 2002; Lehr & Lange 2003; Riordan 2006).

If we take the South Australian public education system as a case study, 3,842 students (2.28 per cent of students enrolled) accounted for 5,073 suspensions and 261 students (0.16 per cent of students enrolled) represented 263 exclusions in 2013. In both the cases of suspension and exclusion, violence (actual or threatened), were the leading reasons, with 36.1 per cent and 44.5 per cent respectively (DECD, 2013). So, how is this data representative of positive learner wellbeing, and how can educators support students to develop pro-social behaviours to maximise learning?

Delving deeper into the South Australian data, students aged seven to 12 years represented 39.2 per cent of all South Australian suspensions in 2013, with students aged four to six accounting for 4.4 per cent (DECD 2013). The recent South Australian Behaviour at School Study (Sullivan et al. 2012) reported disengaging, disruptive and aggressive behaviours to be more prevalent in primary rather than secondary years of school. Yet these findings are not unique to South Australia, with broader Australian research, such as the *Social and Emotional Well-Being* project (Bernard, Stephanou & Urbach 2007) exploring social and emotional wellbeing across the school years, reporting similar trends. Of concern, they found 35 per cent of students reported low impulse control, 48 per cent experienced difficulty calming from upset or anger and 48 per cent were academically underperforming. With this data emerging from students in the early years of school, and extending across the school years, what can educators take from this information? While research suggests that there is a compelling need for alternative educational options for students in the early years of school, this has not been met in practice, with little evidence of alternative educational offerings within Australia for students under the age of eleven years (te Riele 2014).

It has been argued in this chapter that learners develop within social and contextual environments, yet many alternative educational options focus on within-person change. How can students be 'fixed' when their environments remain constant? A strong case has been put forward to suggest that punitive discipline strategies aimed at 'fixing the student' are counterproductive to addressing problem behaviours or constructing more positive school environments (Skiba & Peterson 2000; Tsai & Cheney 2012). This means that intervention approaches which aim to 'fix' the learner, independent of their social and contextual surrounds, fail to address what may actually be the cause of the perceived 'problem' (Mills & McGregor 2010).

Zero-tolerance or 'get-tough' policies, widely adopted within the United States and some areas of the Australian education system, marginalise students through expulsion for low-scale, first-time misdemeanours (Carroll 2008; Skiba & Peterson 2000). While these policies present 'an example' designed to dissuade other students (Gregory, Skiba & Noguera 2010), they appear to invest less interest in understanding student perspectives and direct more attention toward clearing schools and classrooms of 'problematic' students (Skiba & Peterson 2000). Perhaps one possible solution is to develop greater awareness regarding the need for proactive, early intervention, particularly as we know that students in the early years of school are being suspended and excluded from school (DECD 2013).

What factors influence learner wellbeing and educational marginalisation?

In addition to interactions with parents and family members (OECD 2012; Wang & Eccles 2012; Woolfolk & Margetts 2013), there are a variety of social, contextual and personal influences which impact on learner engagement and wellbeing within (and beyond) educational contexts. These influences may include differences between students' skills/interests and educational activities, perceived irrelevance of academic content, unconstructive relationships with peers or teachers, and rigid, impersonal or authoritarian practices and policies (Fan 2011; Lagana-Riordan et al. 2011). Contextual factors, outside of school, can also contribute to educational marginalisation and its effects such as exclusion and disengagement. Research suggests that factors such as low socio-economic status or minority background, fractured family structure, family mobility, poor previous achievement-related performance or 'deviant' behaviours, may reduce a student's ability to fully engage with educational opportunities (Lyche 2010; McGregor & Mills 2012). As this chapter has strongly argued, these factors are *not* deficits within individuals, but factors which influence student wellbeing and educational engagement. So what responsibility does education play in enhancing learner wellbeing and engagement, or conversely, reinforcing personal and social difficulties?

Learner wellbeing and educational engagement are not only influenced by real-time experiences, but are shaped through previous experiences of success and failure, with low academic achievement or negative reaction to failure in the early years of school related to later perceptions of competence (Wigfield, Eccles, Roeser & Schiefele 2009). When students experience negative events in school, they may be cautious of educational contexts, questioning the relationship between school and subsequent educational outcomes (Best, Price & McCallum 2015; Lange & Sletten 2002; Smyth & McInerney 2012). For example, students who have experienced the disconnecting practice of school suspension or exclusion have been found to invest less effort in undertaking academic tasks and observing school expectations, with consequently reduced educational connection, engagement and motivation (Gregory, Skiba & Noguera 2010; Hemphill, Heerde, Herrenkohl, Toumbourou & Catalano 2012).

The following case study focuses on the educational experience of James, a 12-year-old student involved with alternative education. This case study was part of a larger mixed method study which investigated the influence of alternative education on marginalised middle school students in South Australia (Best 2013). Take time to read through the experiences James shared with the researcher regarding mainstream and alternative education settings and reflect on how mainstream school events have influenced his sense self of identity, wellbeing and belonging.

Case study: James

Why do you think you are here [alternative education setting]?

At my last school I was getting in heaps of fights and so the school kicked me out and now I'm here … Some of the kids at my school would push me and stuff, so I'd push them back and sometimes we'd fight … My teacher and school excluded me after the last fight. Maybe I'll go back … But they suspended me a couple of times before and last term, or the term before, I don't know, they excluded me again. So I don't know if I can go back to that place.

Who do you talk to if you get upset?

There's no one I want to talk to. I don't like to talk to people about my stuff ... I get over it.

What should I know about the teachers here?

The teachers are okay. They're nice and all that ... [I get along better with] these ones. The ones at my other school know that I've been suspended and stuff so they don't really treat me as nice as they treat the good kids ... They yell at me, but they don't yell at other kids that are annoying ... It's not fair ...

As James' story highlights, wellbeing is socially situated and influenced through interacting with others. When we suspend or exclude students as a reprimand, we distance them from pro-social peers, teachers and educational environments (Hemphill, Toumbourou, Herrenkohl, McMorris & Catalano 2006). Negative educational perceptions or experiences are recognised as precursor factors to antisocial behaviour, truancy, suspension, exclusion and attrition (Dryfoos 1996; Eccles 1999; Wigfield, Byrnes & Eccles 2006); thus educators are at the fore of influencing students' educational engagement and wellbeing, both whilst at school and beyond. James clearly voices that his interactions and experiences at school are powerful influences on his wellbeing and perceptions of the educational environment, both reconnecting and disconnecting him with opportunities for engagement with learning.

Alternative education: Reconnection, disconnection and learner wellbeing

Alternative education outcomes have been portrayed in the research as twofold, in the sense that they provide both reconnection and disconnection with mainstream educational opportunities (Mills & McGregor 2010; Quinn et al. 2006; te Riele 2008). Zweig (2003), for example, has contended that whilst alternative education may provide the platform for supporting reconnection to mainstream school, it may also be used to remove 'difficult' students from educational settings. Consequently, alternative education is contentious. Carruthers (1999) has argued that alternative programmes for students with long-term suspensions have little, if any, influence on performance, academic achievement or behaviour when compared to students who were suspended without involvement in alternative education. Other researchers have countered this view, arguing that alternative education provides greater opportunities for positive outcomes than continued suspension or exclusion (Mills & McGregor 2010; Stranger 2002). So how does this translate to learner wellbeing? And where is the 'learner' and their sense of self positioned within this?

In actively challenging a deficit-based approach, Mills and McGregor (2010) have acknowledged a number of positive social and contextual influences within alternative educational settings, and in particular, in relation to teachers. Alternative school educators have been found to generally provide greater flexibility in regards to rules and expectations, challenging the perception of alternative education as a means to 'punish' or 'rehabilitate' students who fail to meet mainstream school expectations. According to Mills and McGregor's (2010) research, the absence of behaviour management discourses is an integral factor. In their research, student participants described alternative education teachers as 'caring' and 'respectful'; compared with mainstream schools, alternative sites were small and felt like a 'community'. Whilst relationships with alternative education staff were identified as central to engagement, it is notable that most students did not object to the rules and expectations of mainstream schools, but rather to the ways in which mainstream teachers enacted these rules and expectations (Mills & McGregor 2010).

Alternative education settings are often associated with small class sizes designed to foster student and teacher relationships and enable specific learner needs to be met. Whilst these factors are also aligned with enhanced learner wellbeing, Faubert (2012) has found that educational connection and engagement are not solely reliant on class size itself. Effective, engaging and responsive pedagogical approaches, including individualised instruction, rigorous and relevant curriculum, regular feedback and assessment, and varied grouping strategies and activities (OECD 2012; Taylor 2012) are stronger influences on student engagement, motivation, outcomes and behaviour (Hughes & Adera 2006). As Figure 4.2 highlights, teachers have the ability to create environments that mitigate student risk and promote wellbeing and engagement.

Whilst alternative education may be characteristically more 'relaxed' than mainstream school to support diverse learner behaviours and engagement (McGregor & Mills 2012), this may present barriers to mainstream school integration. That is, while flexible and lenient approaches provide chances for instructive reminders without reprimand, it is vital that students are supported to develop appropriate strategies that span educational sites, whether alternative or mainstream. Therefore, alternative education approaches that mirror mainstream school do not necessarily accommodate student needs, however interactions and expectations that are too divergent, seemingly do not support mainstream school reintegration (Best 2013).

Genuine alternative education must centre on providing equitable, quality and rigorous academic support to enable opportunities for students to make positive educational and life changes (Flower, McDaniel & Jolivette 2011; Kim & Taylor 2008; McGregor & Mills 2012). Such approaches should be scaffolded through friendly, fair, compassionate, helpful and

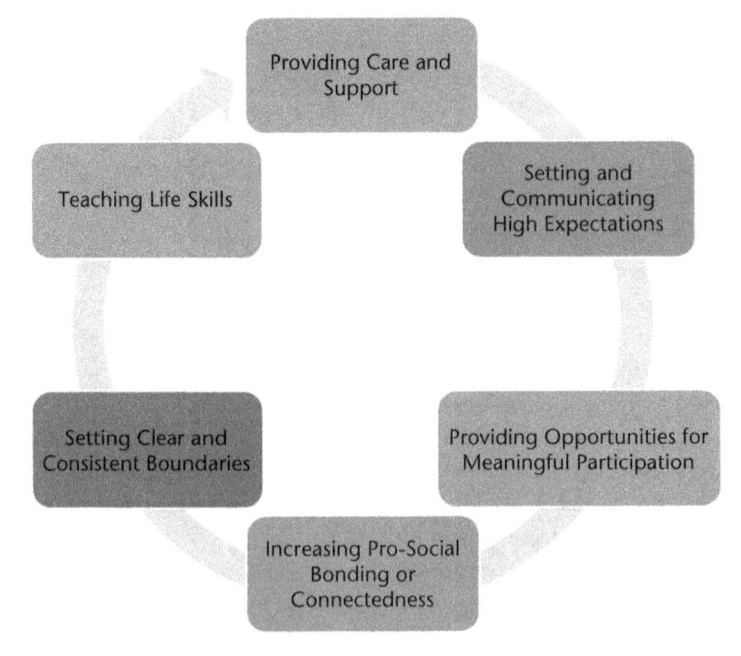

FIGURE 4.2 Mitigating student risk factors through alternative education (Georgia Association for Alternative Education 2006)

respectful interactions between students and teachers (Kim & Taylor 2008; te Riele 2006). As we know and as research confirms, teachers are instrumental to learner wellbeing (Best, Price & McCallum 2015). This is certainly no exception for students who are involved with alternative education (Taylor 2012). In fact, it could be argued that positive teacher relationships are even more crucial for students in alternative education settings. Lagana-Riordan and colleagues' (2011) study, drawing on the views of 33 alternative education students aged 16 to 19 years, illustrates this point clearly. The findings highlighted that students conveyed more positive perceptions of peer and teacher support and understanding, with the students further noting greater flexibility and individualised interactions within alternative education settings. When contrasted with mainstream school experiences, students reported a lack of personal relationships with mainstream peers and teachers.

When we consider how students come to be involved with alternative education, it is not surprising that their social and emotional wellbeing is impacted. That is, students are often the passive recipients of decisions that relate to them, rather than active participants in the decision-making process. As the student voices in this chapter have conveyed, these are the voices of experience. Yet these are not the voices of young people who are necessarily resistant to educational opportunity. Australian research by Mills and McGregor (2010) has revealed that students who rejected or were rejected by mainstream schools often demonstrate increased engagement with alternative education experiences, including the curriculum, teaching practices, teacher-student relationships and the site ethos. So, as asked earlier in the chapter, *Do students fail school or do schools fail students?*

This chapter highlights the need to challenge and reject negative or deficit views of students and alternative education settings. Whilst still evident in educational discourse, terms such as 'at risk', 'dumping grounds', 'problem students' and 'deficits', are counterproductive to learner wellbeing and educational outcomes. In fact, they have no place in educational discourse. Whilst highlighting the right for students to have access to education, this is furthered with the view that students have a right to respectful education. With this in mind, alternative education should be respectfully, rigorously and relevantly designed to support the educational reintegration or connection of some of the most disenfranchised learners and, therefore, such sites must be embraced as positive educational interventions to reconnect learners.

Reconnecting learners through a wellbeing approach

Interacting with positive peers is instrumental during the middle years of school as many students prioritise social activities, peer acceptance and appearance over educational outcomes during these years (Eccles 1999; Wigfield, Byrnes & Eccles 2006). Given that we know that peer group connection is linked to academic performance (Wentzel & Caldwell 1997), it is imperative that we emphasise the connection between the social influence of peers and educational engagement (Battin-Pearson, Newcomb, Abbott, Hill, Catalano & Hawkins 2000). Peers act both as positive and negative role models (Fan 2011) and, through interaction, learners shape their level of engagement, sense of belonging and personal wellbeing (Ladd, Herald-Brown & Kochel 2009). So, in essence, the presence of supportive and academically-oriented peers fosters educational motivation and engagement (Wang & Eccles 2012) which often leads to positive peer relationships and acceptance (Pratt 2006) and improved educational perceptions and participation (Ladd, Herald-Brown & Kochel 2009). Supporting this view, te Riele (2014) has developed a framework of quality flexible learning

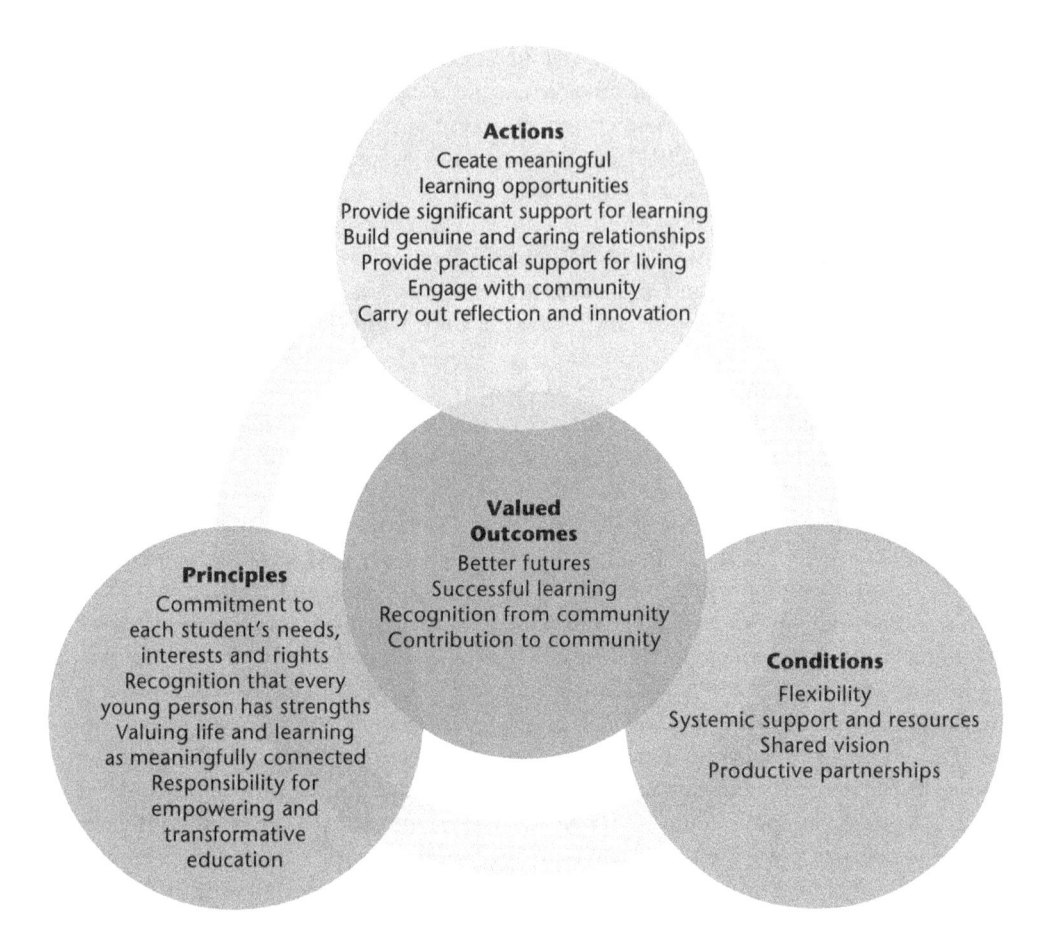

Actions
Create meaningful
learning opportunities
Provide significant support for learning
Build genuine and caring relationships
Provide practical support for living
Engage with community
Carry out reflection and innovation

**Valued
Outcomes**
Better futures
Successful learning
Recognition from community
Contribution to community

Principles
Commitment to
each student's needs,
interests and rights
Recognition that every
young person has strengths
Valuing life and learning
as meaningfully connected
Responsibility for
empowering and
transformative
education

Conditions
Flexibility
Systemic support and resources
Shared vision
Productive partnerships

FIGURE 4.3   Framework of quality flexible learning programmes (after te Riele 2014)

programmes (Figure 4.3) which articulates that valued outcomes, a contributor to learner wellbeing, are a product of three distinct variables: actions, principles and conditions.

Research repeatedly suggests that students in the middle years of school are seeking trusting, caring and supportive relationships with adults beyond their parents (Eccles 1999; Groundwater-Smith, Mitchell & Mockler 2007; Woolfolk & Margetts 2013). In fact, student-teacher relationships are key influences on students' social and academic achievement, motivation and engagement (Lagana-Riordan et al. 2011; Wentzel 2009; Wentzel, Battle, Russell & Looney 2010). Teachers who listen to students, include them, ask questions, check for understanding and provide assistance in positive and productive ways (Newman 2002), and through positive classroom climates (Stipek 2002; Wentzel 2009), convey messages that foster academic engagement (Wang & Eccles 2012) and school retention (Lyche 2010). Below is an extract from Damien, a 13-year-old alternative education student, reflecting on his experiences with education. As you read through it, take note of the comparisons that Damien makes between mainstream school and alternative education teachers and the tensions that arise.

As Jussim et al. (2009) have contended, students perceive little value in active engagement when they feel that autonomy is limited, resulting in decreased motivation, engagement and

---

Case study: Damien

Why do you think you are here [alternative education setting]?
'Cos I've been naughty at my old school … Fighting … Getting suspended and then just get-
ting into trouble. [I had issues with] the teacher and with the students … Sometimes it was
the teacher's fault for blaming me for stuff that I didn't do. One of the students always got
me in to trouble. I felt like bashing him.

Who do you talk to if you get upset?
No one … I forget about it … let it go …

What should I know about the teachers here?
They're all nice … Way better [than mainstream school teachers] … They listen first then they
work it out from there … I think they care … [They help with] my work, my maths, spelling,
reading and writing.

---

commitment to learning tasks. That is, students need to feel a sense of connectedness, not only to their educational community, but to a curriculum which is founded on rigour, relevance and high expectations for student outcomes. Since students have been found to take on perceived expectations conveyed by their teachers (Stipek 2002), teachers who convey high expectations are more likely to have a positive influence on students' academic development (Wentzel 2009). Furthermore, students who perceive teacher support have generally reported increased wellbeing and greater peer belonging (Roeser, Urdan & Stephens 2009; te Riele 2006; Wentzel 2009). Yet these views are not confined to students involved with alternative education, but are equally relevant to students who are involved with mainstream schooling: student wellbeing is informed through interactions and experiences with others.

When students are marginalised from or by education, it is often because they are experiencing equity, inclusion and accessibility complexities relating to curriculum, pedagogy, policy and resourcing. As Chapter 1 highlighted, there has been a growing emphasis on the wellbeing of children and young people, both in Australia and internationally. In the context of learning, wellbeing, through its connection to inclusive and equitable access to education for all young people, has been reflected within international policies such as the *No Child Left Behind Act 2001* in the United States, and *Every Child Matters* (HM Treasury 2003) in the United Kingdom. Within Australia, broad educational reform including the *Melbourne Declaration on Educational Goals for Young Australians* (MCEETYA 2008) and the *Review of Funding for Schooling* (Gonski 2011) have highlighted the need to improve learner wellbeing and, correspondingly, educational outcomes through equity and access initiatives.

However, almost paradoxically, many educational reform agendas that legislate for increased school retention are at odds for students who are educationally marginalised (Best, Price & McCallum 2015). This is reinforced though educational policies which silence young people, excluding their perspectives from decisions regarding what they learn, how they learn and with whom (Smyth & McInerney 2012). When we consider the wellbeing of young people, educational policies that push for educational retention with an emphasis on academic outcomes can further marginalise students who are already questioning the value, practices and relevance of education, potentially forcing them further away from educational opportunities.

Conclusion

> Young people in flexible learning programs want to learn, and want access to the improved life opportunities that such learning enables ... They demonstrate great insight in what they want and need to learn as well as how this is best accomplished.
>
> *(te Riele 2014, pp. 28, 81)*

The focus of this chapter has been on the wellbeing of learners within alternative educational settings. In particular, this chapter has drawn attention to the interactions that students have with both peers and teachers, and the subsequent impact these interactions can have on an individual's wellbeing and educational trajectory. This chapter has highlighted the ways in which we can actively include students and, conversely, the ways in which we actively exclude them.

And yet, as educators, we wonder why students who are excluded from school, or who are 'educationally rejected', often invest little interest in educational opportunities, or hold little expectation of succeeding. When we really consider the experiences that these students have encountered, more often than not as passive recipients, we could actually understand why they may think like this. We know that many students who have been marginalised by, or through, education make conscious decisions regarding educational opportunities. Students clearly possess a capacity to make choices. They make choices with both their minds and their feet.

Wellbeing follow-up activities

1. What is your understanding of alternative education?
2. The question, '*Do students fail school or do schools fail students?*' was asked several times in this chapter. How would you respond to this question?
3. How can alternative educators balance an educative approach to behaviour management, student wellbeing and supporting students for mainstream school integration?
4. What can mainstream educational settings learn from alternative education practices?
5. What type of wellbeing focus may be useful as an early intervention approach for students who are marginalising away from education?

References

Battin-Pearson, S, Newcomb, M, Abbott, R, Hill, K, Catalano, R & Hawkins, J (2000) Predictors of early high school dropout: A test of five theories. *Journal of Educational Psychology*, 92(3), pp. 568–582.

Bernard, M, Stephanou, A & Urbach, D (2007) *The ASG student social and emotional health report*. Australian Scholarships Group, Oakleigh, VIC.

Best, M (2013) Reconnection or disconnection: The influence of alternative education for marginalised students in the middle years of school. Doctoral thesis, University of South Australia, Adelaide, SA.

Best, M, Price, D & McCallum, F (2015) 'Go over there and look at the pictures in the book': An investigation of educational marginalisation, social interactions and achievement motivation in an alternative middle school setting. *International Journal of Inclusive Education*, 19(4), pp. 422–434.

Carroll, M (2008) Educating expelled students after No Child Left Behind: Mending an incentive structure that discourages alternate education and reinstatement. *UCLA Law Review*, 55(6), pp. 1909–1969.

Carruthers, W (1999) *Collected evaluations on the WCPSS alternative school program for students with long-term suspensions. Executive summary. Eye on evaluation*. Wake Country Public Schools System, Rayleigh, NC.

DCSF (2008) *Back on track: A strategy for modernising alternative provision for young people*. Department for Children, Schools and Families, London, UK.

DECD (2013) *Suspension and exclusion*. Department for Education and Child Development, Adelaide, SA.

Dryfoos, J (1996) Adolescents at risk: Shaping programs to fit the need. *The Journal of Negro Education*, 65(1), pp. 5–18.

Eccles, J (1999) The development of children ages 6–14. *The Future of Children*, 9(2), pp. 30–44.

Fan, W (2011) Social influences, school motivation and gender differences: An application of the expectancy-value theory. *Educational Psychology*, 31(2), pp. 157–175.

Faubert, B (2012) *A literature review of school practices to overcome school failure*. OECD, Paris.

Flower, A, McDaniel, SC & Jolivette, K (2011) A literature review of research quality and effective practices in alternative education settings. *Education and Treatment of Children*, 34(4), pp. 489–510.

Gable, R, Bullock, L & Evans, W (2006) Changing perspectives on alternative schooling for children and adolescents with challenging behavior. *Preventing School Failure*, 51(1), pp. 5–9.

Georgia Association for Alternative Education (2006) *Home page*. Available from http://www.georgiaaae. org/.

Gonski, D (2011) *Review of funding of schooling, final report*. Australian Government, Canberra, ACT.

Gregg, S (1999) Creating effective alternatives for disruptive students. *The Clearing House*, 73(2), pp. 107–113.

Gregory, A, Skiba, R & Noguera, P (2010) The achievement gap and the discipline gap: Two sides of the same coin? *Educational Researcher*, 39(1), pp. 59–68.

Groundwater-Smith, S, Mitchell, J & Mockler, N (2007) *Learning in the middle years: More than a transition*. Thomson, Melbourne, VIC.

Hemphill, S, Heerde, J, Herrenkohl, T, Toumbourou, J & Catalano, R (2012) The impact of school suspension on student tobacco use: A longitudinal study in Victoria, Australia, and Washington State, United States. *Health Education & Behavior*, 39(1), pp. 45–56.

Hemphill, S, Toumbourou, J, Herrenkohl, T, McMorris, B & Catalano, R (2006) The effect of school suspensions and arrests on subsequent adolescent antisocial behavior in Australia and the United States. *Journal of Adolescent Health*, 39(5), pp. 736–744.

HM Treasury (2003) *Every Child Matters* Green Paper. HMSO, Norwich.

Hughes, A & Adera, B (2006) Education and day treatment opportunities in schools: Strategies that work. *Preventing School Failure*, 51(1), pp. 26–30.

Jussim, L, Robustelli, S & Cain, T (2009) Teacher expectations and self-fulfilling prophecies. In K Wentzel & A Wigfield (eds), *Handbook of motivation at school*. Routledge, New York, NY, pp. 349–380.

Kim, J-H & Taylor, K (2008) An alternative for whom? Rethinking alternative education to break the cycle of educational inequality. *The Journal of Educational Research*, 101(4), pp. 207–219.

Ladd, G, Herald-Brown, S & Kochel, K (2009) Peers and motivation. In K Wentzel & A Wigfield (eds), *Handbook on motivation at school*. Routledge, New York, NY, pp. 323–348.

Lagana-Riordan, C, Aguilar, JP, Franklin, C, Streeter, CL, Kim, JS, Tripodi, SJ & Hopson, LM (2011) At-risk students' perceptions of traditional schools and a solution-focused public alternative school. *Preventing School Failure*, 55(3), pp. 105–114.

Lange, C & Sletten, S (2002) *Alternative education: A brief history and research synthesis*. National Association of State Directors of Special Education, Alexandria, VA.

Lehr, C & Lange, C (2003) Alternative schools serving students with and without disabilities: What are the current issues and challenges? *Preventing School Failure*, 47(2), Winter, pp. 59–65.

Lehr, C, Moreau, R, Lange, C & Lanners, E (2004) *Alternative schools: Findings from a national survey of the states (Research Report 2)*. University of Minnesota, Institute on Community Integration, Minneapolis, MN.

Lyche, C (2010) *Taking on the Completion Challenge: A literature review on policies to prevent dropout and early school leaving*. OECD Education Working Papers, No. 53, OECD Publishing.

MCEETYA (2008) *Melbourne Declaration on Educational Goals for Young Australians (December 2008)*. Ministerial Council on Education, Emploment, Training and Youth Affairs, Melbourne, VIC.

McGregor, G & Mills, M (2012) Alternative education sites and marginalised young people: 'I wish there were more schools like this one'. *International Journal of Inclusive Education*, 16(8), pp. 843–862.

Mills, M & McGregor, G (2010) *Re-engaging young people in education: Success factors in alternative schools.* Youth Affairs Network of Queensland, Brisbane, QLD.

Morgan, A, Brown, R, Heck, D, Pendergast, D & Kanasa, H (2013) Professional identity pathways of educators in alternative schools: The utility of reflective practice groups for educator induction and professional learning. *Reflective Practice*, 14(2), pp. 258–270.

Newman, R (2002) What do I need to do to succeed … when I don't understand what I'm doing!?: Developmental influences on students' adaptive help seeking. In A Wigfield & J Eccles (eds), *Handbook of achievement motivation*. Academic Press, San Diego, CA, pp. 285–306.

OECD (2012) *Equity and quality in education: Supporting disadvantaged students and schools.* OECD Publishing, Paris.

Powell, DE (2003) Demystifying alternative education: Considering what really works. *Reclaiming Children and Youth*, 12(2), pp. 68–70.

Pratt, H (2006) Adolescence. In N Salkind & L Margolis (eds), *Encyclopedia of human development*. SAGE, Thousand Oaks, CA, pp. 28–35.

Quinn, M & Rutherford, R (1998) Alternative programs for students with social, emotional, or behavioural problems. In L Bullock & R Gable (eds), *CCBD Mini-Library series: Successful interventions for the 21st century*. Council for Children with Behavioural Disorders, Restin, VA.

Quinn, MM, Poirier, JM, Faller, SE, Gable, RA & Tonelson, SW (2006) An examination of school climate in effective alternative programs. *Preventing School Failure: Alternative Education for Children and Youth*, 51(1), pp. 11–17.

Raywid, MA (1994) Alternative schools: The state of the art. *Educational Leadership*, 52(1), pp. 26–31.

Riordan, J (2006) Reducing student 'suspension rates' and engaging students in learning: principal and teacher approaches that work. *Improving Schools*, 9(3), November, pp. 239–250.

Roeser, R, Urdan, T & Stephens, J (2009) School as a context of student motivation and achievement. In K Wentzel & A Wigfield (eds), *Handbook of motivation at school*. Routledge, New York, NY, pp. 381–410.

Skiba, RJ & Peterson, RL (2000) School discipline at a crossroads: From zero tolerance to early response. *Exceptional Children*, 66(3), pp. 335–346.

Smyth, J, Hattam, R, Cannon, J, Edwards, J, Wilson, N & Wurst, S (2004) *Dropping out, drifting off, being excluded: Becoming somebody without school*. Peter Lang Publishing, New York, NY.

Smyth, J & McInerney, P (2012) Sculpting a 'social space' for re-engaging disengaged 'disadvantaged' young people with learning. *Journal of Educational Administration and History*, 44(3), pp. 187–201.

Smyth, J, McInerney, P & Fish, T (2013) Re-engagement to where? Low SES students in alternative-education programmes on the path to low-status destinations? *Research in Post-Compulsory Education*, 18(1–2), pp. 194–207.

Social Enterprise Coalition (2010) *Social enterprise and alternative education*. Croydon Enterprise, London.

Stipek, D (2002) Good instruction is motivating. In A Wigfield & J Eccles (eds), *Handbook of achievement motivation*. Academic Press, San Diego, CA, pp. 302–332.

Stranger, M (2002) Student absence from school and juvenile crime project: Draft. National Crime Prevention, Canberra, ACT.

Sullivan, A, Johnson, B, Conway, R, Owens, L & Taddeo, C (2012) *Punish them or engage them? Teachers' views on student behaviours in the classroom*. University of South Australia, Adelaide, SA.

Taylor, C (2012) *Improving alternative provision*. Department for Education, London.

te Riele, K (2006) Youth 'at risk': Further marginalizing the marginalized? *Journal of Education Policy*, 21(2), pp. 129–145.

te Riele, K (2007) Educational alternatives for marginalized youth. *The Australian Educational Researcher*, 34(3), pp. 53–68.

te Riele, K (2008) Are alternative schools the answer? *New Transitions: Re-Engagement Edition*, 12(1), pp. 1–6.

te Riele, K (2012) *Learning choices: A map for the future*. Dusseldorp Skills Forum, Victoria University, Melbourne, VIC.

te Riele, K (2014) *Putting the jigsaw together: Flexible learning in Australia*. Dusseldorp Skills Forum, Victoria University, Melbourne, VIC.

Thomson, P (2002) *Schooling the rustbelt kids: Making a difference in changing times.* Allen & Unwin, Crows Nest, NSW.

Tsai, S-F & Cheney, D (2012) The impact of the adult–child relationship on school adjustment for children at risk of serious behavior problems. *Journal of Emotional and Behavioral Disorders*, 20(2), pp. 105–114.

Wang, M & Eccles, J (2012) Social support matters: Longitudinal effects of social support on three dimensions of school engagement from middle to high school. *Child Development*, 83(3), pp. 877–895.

Wentzel, K (2009) Students' relationships with teachers as motivational contexts. In K Wentzel & A Wigfield (eds), *Handbook of motivation at school*. Routledge, New York, NY, pp. 301–322.

Wentzel, K & Caldwell, K (1997) Friendships, peer acceptance, and group membership: Relations to academic achievement in middle school. *Child Development*, 68(6), pp. 1198–1209.

Wentzel, KR, Battle, A, Russell, SL & Looney, LB (2010) Social supports from teachers and peers as predictors of academic and social motivation. *Contemporary Educational Psychology*, 35(3), pp. 193–202.

Wigfield, A, Byrnes, J & Eccles, J (2006) Development during early and middle adolescence. In P Alexander & P Winne (eds), *Handbook of educational psychology*, 2nd edn. Lawrence Erlbaum Associates, Mahwah, NJ, pp. 87–113.

Wigfield, A, Eccles, J, Roeser, R & Schiefele, U (2009) Development of achievement motivation. In W Damon & R Lerner (eds), *Developmental psychology: An advanced coursebook*. Wiley, New York, NY, pp. 57–88.

Woolfolk, A & Margetts, K (2013) *Educational psychology*, 3rd edn. Pearson, Frenchs Forest, NSW.

Zweig, JM (2003) *Vulnerable youth: Identifying their need for alternative educational settings*. Urban Institute, Washington, WA.

5

TECHNOLOGY AND WELLBEING

Barbara A. Spears

Cyberbullying

(Excerpts from *High wire act: Cyber-safety and the young* 2014)

I think most children who cyber-bully don't [sic] realise they are doing it, because it is hard to tell what tone something is written in ... for example 'nice pic' could be being nice and giving a good comment or it could be sarcastic and be being mean and only the writer really knows which one, if they meant to be mean or if they were just being nice
(Female aged 14, p. 61)

It depends on how certain teasing comments are taken. Some posts snowball as sometimes about a hundred people all contribute to a discussion which can sometimes include abuse of a person for the opinion they express ... This sort of behaviour is not uncommon

(Female aged 17, pp. 61–62)

My fourteen year old sister is frequently cyber-bullied over both the social networking site Facebook as well as Formspring, as are many of her friends and people she knows. It causes her a lot of distress, largely because she is unable to escape it. It affects her self-esteem and happiness
(Female aged 17, p. 79)

Sexting

(Compiled from actual events reported to the National Children's and Youth Law Centre)
Joanne is 13 years old. A boy her age from school, Mark, sent her some naked pictures of himself which she kept. She wanted him to like her so she sent him a photo of her breasts in

response. Joanne's mum found the photos on her phone and is very concerned. She is now considering taking them to the police. Joanne wants to know if she or Mark could get in trouble because of the photos.

Paul is 16 years old. After meeting Sarah online, she asked him to send some nude photos of himself on Snapchat. Paul didn't really want to do it but he felt pressured so he sent her a photo of his genitals. Sarah is now threatening to post these photos on pornographic websites along with Paul's personal details. Paul wants to know if there is anything he can do to stop this from happening.

Mary is 17 years old. She sent nude photos to a guy from her school, Jack. She has recently discovered that Jack sent these photos to Fiona, another girl in her grade at school. Fiona has shown the photos to a couple of girls in her year. Mary is concerned that Jack and Fiona will show the photos to more people or post them online. Mary is too afraid to tell her parents about this because she feels they would be so ashamed of her. She is also afraid of the punishment her parents would give her for taking the nude photos. Mary wants to know if there is anything she can do to prevent Jack and Fiona from spreading the photos and whether the police could help.

Introduction

> Social media are re-writing how we inter-relate socially, and are forging reconsiderations and reassessments of social boundaries and the relationships which operate within and around them.
>
> *(Spears & Costabile 2012b, p. 1)*

Twenty years ago, being 'online' was unheard of. Since the early 1990s, society has witnessed one of its greatest communication revolutions: the rise of the Internet and contemporary social media. In the space of 20 years, those who were born in 1995, as the Internet was in its infancy, and who could now be emerging as beginning teachers, have already witnessed the shift from basic use of emails and one-dimensional web pages, to the full spectrum of user-centred, fully interactive, user-created and self-published technologies and social media: from Facebook, YouTube and Twitter, to Snap Chat and Instagram, to name but a few.

What does this mean for educators, particularly for wellbeing? Not only do educators have to be skilled in *how* to use and subsequently teach with and about emerging technologies, but as Spears and Costabile (2012b) note above, they also have to be ready to work with young people as they develop. This means: cognitively, socially, and emotionally as they are *surrounded* by constantly changing and evolving technologies, social networking sites and social media. Relationships and connectedness are critical factors in wellbeing, and knowing how young people are responding to technology in and around their relationships is important for contemporary understandings of wellbeing.

There is however, a growing body of evidence which articulates that over-engaging with information, leisure and communication technologies (ITs) is impacting on relationships, and an individual's self-esteem, self-concept and mental health, not to mention physical health through loss of sleep and hunching over keyboards (for example, Campbell, Spears, Slee, Butler & Kift 2012; van Geel, Vedder & Tanilon 2014). At the same time, young people themselves have articulated the importance of these ITs in their social relationships, and the benefits that they derive from them (Spears, Kofoed, Bartolo, Palermiti & Costabile 2012).

Technology, for the purposes of this chapter, is used as an omnibus term to capture the range of information (communication and leisure) technologies (ICTs/ITs). It encompasses all forms of media-related communications across all devices, platforms, and applications. To that end, the term also covers the storage, retrieval, manipulation, transmission or receipt of information electronically, in a digital form.

In Chapter 1 (p. 4) it was argued that wellbeing has been highly debated in the past due to the multiple domains which have an interest in it (e.g. educational, medical and philosophical) and that it comprises more than just an absence of ill health. It includes satisfaction with life and relationships, healthy behaviours and resilience, and notions of sustainability, holism and self-responsibility. Ultimately, however, wellbeing is a personal construct which must be fostered through our connections and relationships with others. Wellbeing, then, is considered a diverse and fluid concept, respectful of individual, family and community beliefs, values, experiences, culture, opportunities and contexts across time and change.

One of those contemporary contexts is schooling, but another is that of the ever-present ITs and social media. In Australia and globally, up to 99 per cent of young people are using the Internet on a daily basis (Burns, Davenport, Christensen, Luscombe, Mendoza, Bresnan, Blanchard & Hickie 2013; Green, Brady, Ólafsson, Hartley & Lumby 2011). Young people's wellbeing therefore no longer exists solely in relation to school and family settings. Nor does it operate in a technological vacuum. As the above scenarios about young people's experiences depict, wellbeing increasingly operates in relation to ever-changing technology though social media and peer contexts, which include such negative online behaviours as cyberbullying and sexting.

This chapter will briefly explore: the notion of 'wicked problems'; the rise of ITs; how Australian governments have responded to this social and communication change in order to support educators; some philosophical and theoretical considerations; and will present findings from two studies to highlight potential impacts on individual wellbeing and mental health and to demonstrate the complexity of the relationship between technology and wellbeing. Implications for educators will also be raised.

Technology and wellbeing: A wicked problem?

How the ubiquitous ITs might *interplay* with wellbeing is thus a question for contemporary educators and policy makers. Technology presents educators, policy makers and society in general with a wellbeing conundrum: it can be both a panacea and a problem, simultaneously creating a tension which needs exploration from both perspectives.

Indeed, the relationship between technology and wellbeing might be considered a 'wicked problem' (Rittel & Webber 1973). Rittel and Webber (1973) outlined that there are two kinds of problems: 'tame' and 'wicked'. Tame problems are not necessarily simple but can be clearly defined and a solution fairly readily identified or worked through. Wicked problems, on the other hand, are complex social or cultural problems, which are interconnected and which cannot be simply solved through any singular approach. According to the *Tackling Wicked Problems* report (Commonwealth of Australia 2007, pp. 3–4) such problems are, by nature, difficult to define, often due to who is asked and the domain they are from; as is the case with wellbeing (see Chapter 1), and there is ongoing debate concerning the causes, extent and solutions. Unforeseen consequences can arise when attempting to address wicked problems as there is not a linear pathway from problem to solution; wicked problems are often not stable, as the environment involved in understanding the problem is often evolving at the same time. This is particularly so for technology which morphs constantly into new platforms, devices, and communication approaches, impacting on the legal, educational and values communities, and providing a virtual moving target for policy makers. It is equally so for the notion of wellbeing.

Wicked problems usually have no clear solutions since there is no definitive, stable, problem; rather there are many interdependencies. Chapter 1 clearly articulates the complexity of defining wellbeing and how it changes in relation to context and discipline (e.g. educational; or medical). This suggests that a focus on 'fixing' or 'solving' may be misplaced, and may need to shift to a focus of 'managing' the issue. How, for example, can you 'solve' bullying, when it morphs into cyberbullying, and impacts on young people's wellbeing on and offline, reaching across and beyond the peer group to the Internet audience at large? Wicked problems are, by nature, socially complex and they do not sit with the responsibility of any one organisation/ domain/system: they require coordinated, interdisciplinary, and whole of community approaches and actions. Technology and wellbeing are clearly interdisciplinary in nature, and whole school/community responses are employed. Finally, some wicked problems are characterised by chronic policy failure, in that, for all the above reasons, they are intractable. Thus, as technology continues to bring new challenges—socially, ethically and technologically—how wellbeing intersects with these changes may well present a wicked problem; one that needs constant revisiting and rethinking.

When used to support young people's relationships and health, technology can be an enabler of young people's wellbeing. Indeed, the Young and Well Cooperative Research Centre (www.youngandwellcrc.org.au) envisions 'A digitally connected world where technologies are used to support young people to feel safe, healthy and resilient'. How technology might be employed to intervene and support young people's wellbeing is a challenge however, for educators, as much of what occurs online falls beyond the educational setting, requiring examination of the wider social, cultural and technological contexts (Spears & Zeederberg 2013).

On the other hand, technology can be seen as a contemporary vehicle which contributes to poorer mental health and wellbeing. As is evident from the sample above of young people's comments on cyberbullying (Joint Select Committee on Cyber-Safety 2011), negative uses of technology and social media, such as cyberbullying and sexting, are common occurrences for many young people and serve to exacerbate traditional forms of bullying already occurring in schools. Such negative experiences have significant implications for contemporary young people's wellbeing, as their relationships are now enacted across both off and online settings, in and out of school, simultaneously and seamlessly.

Spears, Keeley, Bates and Katz (2014) reviewed current Australian and international research and determined that approximately 20 per cent of young people in Australia were at risk of being victimised online in any year. Spears, Taddeo, Daly, Stretton and Karklins (2015c) further report that cyberbullying has the potential to be a public health issue, as research clearly and repeatedly demonstrates that those targeted online experience the following health and wellbeing related problems: more social difficulties; higher levels of anxiety, depression and suicidal ideation than victims of traditional bullying (Campbell et al. 2012; van Geel, Vedder & Tanilon 2014); they also suffer academically, and are twice as likely to attempt suicide than those who have not been cyberbullied (Tokunaga 2010; van Geel, Vedder & Tanilon 2014). Given that cyberbullying is linked with traditional bullying which occurs in schools (Smith 2014), and is driven in part by friendship practices of exclusion and inclusion, the impact on wellbeing is significant, and has not been easily dealt with solely by schools. Luxton, June and Fairall (2012) reported those who had been cyberbullied had greater feelings of isolation, hopelessness and instability. Feeling socially connected with others is a determinant of wellbeing (Jose, Ryan & Pryor 2012), so those experiencing disconnection, loneliness and isolation are at risk of poor social and emotional health. The cyberbullying trajectory then, in terms of mental health and wellbeing, clearly places young people on a downward social and emotional pathway.

Young people are, however, 'connected' through social media, but this does not necessarily mean that they have positive, satisfying relationships with others. They are navigating new, mediated public arenas with seemingly great technical skill, but with the developing brains and flawed decision-making of adolescents, and surrounded by their peers who exercise influence and control over them (Spears & Costabile 2012a).

Knowing how to employ technologies to support wellbeing is therefore important if negative impacts, such as cyberbullying and sexting, are to be avoided or diminished. This is particularly relevant, as young people have determined that the online and offline settings are the same social spaces for them (Spears & Costabile 2012a, p. 206) through which their friendship-driven practices (Ito, Horst, Bittanti, boyd, Herr-Stephenson, Lange, Pascoe & Robinson 2008) operate. That is, contemporary young people's wellbeing is inextricably intertwined with their social relationships, which are also tied to their use of technology and social media.

Whilst many studies have explored the impact of bullying and cyberbullying on young people (see Smith 2014 for a review), this chapter reports briefly on two studies which shed light on the relationship between technology/social media and wellbeing. Study 1 (Spears et al. 2012) explored how young people from different countries (Australia, Italy and Denmark) individually and collectively experienced social networking sites (SNSs), and noted the subsequent positive impacts it had on identify formation, relationships and general wellbeing. Study 2 (Spears, Taddeo, Barnes, Collin, Swirski, Drennan, Scrimgeour & Razzell 2015b; Spears et al. 2015c) examined youth responses to questions about their general health and wellbeing, help-seeking behaviours and cyberbullying experiences, as part of a larger study into youth-centred online social marketing campaigns and their ability to influence attitudes and behaviours in relation to mental health and wellbeing (Safe and Well Online: Young and Well Cooperative Research Centre (http://www.youngandwellcrc.org.au/research/safe-supportive/safe-and-well-online/).

Together, these studies highlight that social media and technology are influencing attitudes and behaviours which impact upon and support wellbeing, both in and out of school settings. The challenge then, for contemporary schooling and society in general, is how to harness the positive, and reduce the negative impacts of technology so that young people's wellbeing is enhanced, and that technology itself is an enabler for their social and emotional development, rather than an inhibitor.

Historical context: The rise of the Internet and social media

In order to position this discussion, however, a brief acknowledgement of the history of the Internet is pertinent. The following snapshot is drawn from Curtis (2013) and serves to provide a basis from which to consider the impact of this enormous and rapid technological change on young people, their social and mental health and wellbeing.

Whilst the first email was sent in the 1970s, and the word 'Internet' was first used in 1982, Tim Berners-Lee, a British engineer, began work for CERN (European Organization for Nuclear Research) in 1989 developing a new technique for distributing information on the Internet, which he called the World Wide Web (WWW). In 1991, the WWW 'opened' to the public with the release of the source code to the public domain, and the first web pages were subsequently well in use by 1993. By 1994, the WWW was known as the 'information super-highway', and was commercialised for public use in 1995, when it began to weave its way into everything we do: business, schools and families.

By 1997, there were already one million websites; Hotmail was open for business (1996); blogging had begun (1998) and Blackboard was established as an online course management system for educators and learners. Google arrived in 1998; Wikipedia emerged in 2001; with Friendster (2002) and MySpace (2003) commencing as 'social networking sites'. These early iterations were all noted as Web 1.0 environments; basically text-based search engines and static pages, with mainly read-only capabilities. From 2004, the term 'social media' became commonplace with the advent of Facebook, and Web 2.0 became increasingly interactive, with sharing and creating/publishing capabilities.

Since then, an explosion of new ways to communicate online which are increasingly mobile and convergent across platforms and devices were developed: YouTube (2005); Twitter (2006); iPhone and the mobile web, Tumblr (2007); Google Street View and the beginnings of Cloud technology appeared in 2008; Google Docs (2009); and by 2010, Formspring, an anonymous question and answer site evolved, and the iPad was released—it was estimated that over 30 per cent of the global population (1.97 billion) was online. By 2011, social media was accessible virtually anywhere; Facebook reached 1 billion users in 2012; and 2013 had astronauts tweeting from the International Space station. In 2014, new online users were employing more mobile devices than PCs; with 25 per cent of the world's total population using social media, and it was predicted that by 2015, there would be a global population of over four billion Internet users or 60 per cent of the Earth's population.

Young people born around 1995 have only ever known a world that operates in conjunction with the Internet and, most recently, social media. The Internet of the past, however, is making way for the technology trends of the future, all of which will continue to impact on individuals and the ways in which we socially connect, and on educators and the children they will come to teach. Considering the Forbes magazine's list (2015) of the top ten strategic technology trends for 2015, it is apparent that the so-called 'future' is very much here. Relevant items from this list are that: *Computing is Everywhere* with young people generally being mobile-only users; and that wearables means that the computer is no longer in our pocket, but *is* our pocket, our jacket, our fabric; the *Internet of Things* will continue to grow and technology will be embedded everywhere; *3D printing* will continue to get cheaper impacting on everything; *Big Data* will continue to grow as everything is driven by analytics; *Systems will be Context-Aware* and be responsive to their surroundings due to embedded intelligence; *Smart Machines* that can learn for themselves and act accordingly, will continue to evolve; and *Cloud Architecture* will enable simultaneous use across multiple devices. This means that big questions about technological impacts on individuals, their wellbeing, social networks, cognitions and development, need to be posed in ways that capture not only the rapid change occurring around them, but also *how* they are responding to and interacting with that change. Wellbeing can no longer be perceived as operating independently of technology.

Australia's approaches to supporting educators

Given the preceding historical snapshot, it is important to know how governments have responded to support schools and educators deal with the rapid emergence of technological change, as their responses are indicators that that they recognise the seriousness and potential impacts, both positive and negative, of this rapid communication change on young people and their families, and society overall.

In a review of initiatives related to online support, Spears (2012) reported that the Australian government established NetAlert Ltd in 1999, an online guide to provide information to the public about the Internet, to help them navigate it, to learn about it and to be safe when using it. The first reports of cyberbullying were not mentioned in the press in Australia until several years later, however, so this first attempt was as an educative strategy for the whole community.

Importantly, around 2003–2004, it was recognised that teachers in general had little relevant technological knowledge, and schools had few resources or consistency in the ways information about the Internet was being taught. Consequently, a three-phase initiative entitled *CyberSafe Schools,* delivered: (1) resources to every school in the country in 2004, comprising: a wall chart, a quick reference guide, a teacher's guide to the Internet; (2) a primary school focused CD-ROM, *Cyberquoll*; and (3) a secondary school interactive programme, *CyberNetrix.* These approaches reflected the times; they were text-based and largely static resources, in contrast to the already emerging fluid social networking sites where online bullying was already coming to people's attention (Campbell, Spears, Cross & Slee 2010).

This response highlights an ongoing and constant situation; that as soon as an initiative is planned for, funded and implemented, the speed of technological change means that it is probably already out of date. Importantly, these resources were still mainly about providing information.

By 2007, NetAlert had merged with the Australian Communication and Media Authority (ACMA) as part of a national initiative called *Protecting Australian Families Online,* offering various strategies/initiatives such as filters, law enforcement, regulation, supports, education and awareness. It is clear that at this point, there was genuine concern about young people's cybersafety and online activity and possible implications for wellbeing.

As an example of the digital skills divide, however, which was developing between educators, governments and young people, and the well-meaning but misplaced perception that putting up a fence around the Internet would keep young people safe and well, a 16-year-old schoolboy from Victoria, Tom Wood, circumvented the $84 million pornography filter system, developed by the Australian Government for parents to protect their children online. He purportedly took only 30 minutes to override the filter on the day it was released, rendering it 'useless' and 'a waste of money' (see http://www.abc.net.au/news/2007-08-27/teen-hacks-useless-govt-porn-filter/651366). It was clear at this point, that there had to be other ways of managing the online safety and wellbeing of children and families.

A year later a *National Cyber-Safety Plan* was in place and the Consultative Working Group, comprised of industry and education experts was established, and by 2009, finally, a decade after the first initiative, a Youth Advisory Group to the Federal Government had been formed to inform the government of young people's perspectives. The ACMA also assumed responsibility for, *Cybersmart* (www.cybersmart.gov.au), a new educative strategy with an interactive web presence, which continues to evolve in concert with the latest issues and trends faced by young people. *Cybersmart* also now includes outreach programmes to schools and to pre-service teacher education providers.

To inform policy, a *Senate Inquiry into Cybersafety* (Joint Select Committee on Cyber-Safety 2011) surveyed over 33, 751 children aged 12–18 years regarding their online practices; and the *National Safe Schools Framework* (Department of Education 2010) was revised to take account of the importance of the online setting for keeping children and young people safe in schools, and endorsed by all State Ministers of Education. Current policy initiatives to support children and families include *Enhancing Online Safety of Children*, and the establishment of a Children's E-safety Commissioner who will oversee AUD$7.5 million in funding over four years to assist and support schools to access online safety programmes. This initiative acknowledges that schools and families need a coordinated response to help to tackle E-safety issues and thus support students' mental health and wellbeing.

However some gaps emerge in the approaches and supports offered to date. To date, there is no mandated cybersafety subject in the Australian curriculum, in spite of the recognised psycho-socio-emotional impacts of technology on individuals (for example, through cyberbullying), meaning that it is up to the school or individual teachers to determine how, if and when they will support their students' online wellbeing.

School-based interventions aimed at improving young people's social and emotional health and wellbeing, such as *KidsMatter* (http://www.kidsmatter.edu.au/) and *MindMatters* (http://www.mindmatters.edu.au/), have been funded as part of a whole community approach to building social capacity to improve mental health and wellbeing. However, as with any implementation of any new initiative in schools, they run the risk of not being properly implemented. Askell-Williams and Lawson (2013) noted that the World Health Organization (WHO) recommends health promotion activities in school settings, but queried how competent, knowledgeable and skilled teachers were to deliver such interventions, finding that robust ongoing professional development was required. Of importance, is how school-based initiatives such as this, relate to shifts in technology and young people's subsequent wellbeing. There is also little known nationally about pre-service teacher preparation programmes and the emphasis given to learning about cybersafety, bullying, cyberbullying, and wellbeing and strategies for dealing with them (Spears, Campbell, Tangen, Slee & Cross 2015a).

Clearly, the exponential rise in the type and use of communication and social technologies since the inception of the Internet, has had a profound impact—socially, psychologically, economically and educationally—and governments everywhere are attempting to provide resources for young people, families and schools to ensure their wellbeing is supported and maximised. Most recently, the Australian Government has created a one-stop-shop for online safety: the Office of the Children's E-Safety Commissioner, to expressly lead online safety education and to administer a complaints scheme. https://www.esafety.gov.au/.

Philosophical and theoretical considerations: Technology and the child

As most theoretical propositions to explain human behaviour were developed in previous eras, where ITs were not prevalent, it is also necessary to consider how technology might be relevant to understanding them. Theories related to how we learn and develop (social cognitive theory, socio-cultural theories and socio-ecological theories), inter-relate and connect with each other (social network theory), see ourselves in light of others (social comparison theory), value and determine the cost-benefit ratio of relationships (social exchange theory), present ourselves to others (self-verification theory), and how we categorise others as in- or out-group members (social identity theory), require consideration in terms of the influence of technology and social media.

How the child is perceived across eras, in terms of the promotion of wellbeing, is also important as each century has a view that is premised in the social mores and beliefs of the time. The contemporary view is shaped by the adoption of the *Convention on the Rights of the Child* by the United Nations General Assembly (1989), which highlights that children have rights which adults need to uphold. This declaration was significant as it shifted previously held views that children were passive recipients of knowledge, or were little adults in waiting, towards being *active social agents, with knowledge of their own worlds and a right to voice that knowledge.*

It is pertinent to note, however, that the WWW was in its infancy when the UN *Convention on the Rights of the Child* was adopted, and it is necessary to therefore reflect on what the rights of a child in 2015 might mean in terms of technology and wellbeing. The following very brief (and overly simplified) historical view allows us to consider how contemporary technologies might be relevant to a contemporary world-view of children.

Children in early Western societies had little status or rights. They were often considered to be the property of adults, or of economic value to the family or community. Through the emergence of the field of psychology in the twentieth century—and developmental and social psychology in particular—childhood came to be considered as being separate to adulthood; a distinct period of development that was comprised of several unique stages (early, middle, late and adolescence). Slee, Campbell and Spears (2012) noted how adult conceptions of childhood altered over time, in response to social, philosophical and economic upheavals, from Locke's seventeenth-century view of the child at birth as *tabula rasa* (blank slate), through Wesley's *iniquitous (sinful)* child, Rousseau's *virtuous* child, and Elkind's *competent* child.

The *postmodern* child, who is competent and has agency and capacity to act and make free choices, and who reciprocally intersects with the environment, emerged from a new sociological view of childhood which arose in the 1990s (Corsaro 1997; James & Prout 1997). This view draws upon a socio-cultural perspective of childhood; where learning occurs in conjunction with others and their environment. Spears and Kofoed (2013) note that the *postmodern* childhood view emerged just as the Internet arrived in the public domain, and so it is not surprising, that the 'wired' and 'wireless' child view has been proposed in recent times (Slee, Campbell & Spears 2012, p. 26). This view recognises that technology is ubiquitous, that children are directly and indirectly embedded into the online community, and that technology dominates their social interactions (Spears & Kofoed 2013, p. 203). With the increasing mobilisation of technologies, the emergence of the technologically 'mobile' view of childhood seems imminent.

Very young children, under the age of two are using tablets and mobile phones as learning devices, and children under the so-called 'required' age of 13, are signing up to social media and social networks, so the quest for contemporary researchers and educators, is to reflect upon their view of the child, the theories of development, and determine the role that technology plays. These discussions, however, are largely yet to be had. The reader is therefore challenged to consider how these theories might need to evolve in the context of an 'always-on' generation.

In thinking about how technology, social media and wellbeing might intersect, this chapter now considers Bronfenbrenner's socio-ecological model (1977, 1979) as a useful theoretical consideration. This model is comprised of five socially organised sub-systems: *micro, meso, exo, macro* and *chrono* and is often acknowledged as a framework for whole-school approaches to bullying interventions, where there is a multi-faceted approach from the individual level through to the wider social environment (Swearer & Doll 2001). Yet the role that technology and the Internet plays in relation to these five systems, is yet to be fully understood. This is particularly important where social media/social networking technologies are concerned, as they are rapidly emerging and evolving, and are reshaping how we inter-relate socially.

Spears (2011, p. 16) posited that the Internet can be considered simultaneously as both a setting and a system. As a setting the Internet operates as a 'virtual entity', a communication medium and place, for example, an online social networking site (e.g. Facebook) where young people socialise. As a system, however, the Internet operates on a 'virtual plane', encircling Bronfenbrenner's proposed systems, as a 'third dimension', intersecting with individuals, families, schools and workplaces. As with any ideas, empirical testing is required, but as seen below, Johnson (2010b) has begun to explore a similar notion.

Johnson and Puplampu (2008) had earlier proposed a sub-dimension of the microsystem: an ecological techno-subsystem. The microsystem refers to the immediate environment of a child and includes, most notably, home and school interactions. This proposed techno-subsystem includes 'a child's interaction with both living (e.g., peers) and non-living (e.g., hardware) elements of communication, information, and recreation technologies in immediate or direct environments' (Johnson 2010b, p. 178).

Further to this conceptualisation, Johnson (2010b) subsequently measured three constructs which corresponded to three ecological systems: child cognitive development (bio-ecology); indices of the child's use of the Internet at home (techno-subsystem); and family socio-economic characteristics (microsystem), with a sample of Canadian children from first through to sixth grade/year (N=151). Results indicated that family socio-economic characteristics (elements of the microsystem) explained a modest (but significant) amount of the variation in children's cognitive development scores, but that 'indices of home Internet use (elements of the techno-subsystem), in general, were better predictors of children's cognitive development than were family socioeconomic characteristics (elements of the microsystem)' (Johnson 2010b, p. 181).

To put this finding into context, Sirin's (2005) meta-analysis of research on socio-economic impact on academic achievement posited that the impact of socio-economic status on academic achievement, at that time, was gradually being eroded, due in part to the expansion of the middle class, and the increasingly effective impacts of public education, quality child care, early childhood interventions and neonatal programmes. Thus, as Western society has progressively endeavoured to bring social equity through a broadened educative base, the impact of socio-economic status alone on academic outcomes has, according to this meta-analysis, potentially declined. What is notable here, however, is that Sirin's study was conducted on literature published from 1990 to 2000, well before the Internet became sophisticated or ubiquitous for young people, and well before the advent of social media for all. So as the middle classes expanded, and the impact of socio-economic status seemingly declined in response, the explosion of Internet technologies seems well placed to have significant influence as a sub-system; an influence which was certainly not present when Bronfenbrenner first proposed his socio-ecological model (1977, 1979). Johnson (2010a) however, proposed a further addition to the model—a techno-microsystem—where 'a reciprocal, spiralling interaction occurs between a child's characteristics (i.e. the bio-ecology) and use of communication technologies (i.e. the techno-subsystem)' (p. 34).

Given the significant changes that technology and social media have brought to the way we socialise, work, play and live generally—including how we might conceptualise technology in relation to the notion of childhood and theories of relationships and child and adolescent development—the chapter now turns to consider two studies which directly explore the associations between social media, relationships and wellbeing.

Study 1: Positive uses of social networking sites: Youth voice perspectives[1]

Spears and colleagues (2013; 2012) reported that technologies and new devices are important drivers in contemporary socialisation processes for young people as they learn how to navigate their personal relationships and identity formation—including self-branding—in a seemingly time-less and boundary-less space. The challenge is, however, that time and space co-exist through synchronous and asynchronous contexts, and relationships shift rapidly between on and offline settings. This is something which parents of adolescents have not had to contend with in their own relationships when growing up, potentially suggesting that the complexity of young people's relationships operating across both settings could make them more vulnerable to stressors and ill-health than ever before.

The cost-benefit debate concerning use of digital technologies has also sparked a mild 'moral panic' amongst some adults. Rohloff and Wright (2010) and Johannson (2000) explained that moral panic is a sociological concept, where there is an overreaction to a perceived social problem, which is often fuelled by the press/media, distorting and focussing attention on negative events, such as suspected social media-influenced youth suicides and self-harm. Whilst the path to suicide is a complex set of circumstances, bullying and cyberbullying have been identified as playing a contributing part (Hinduja & Patchin 2010; van Geel, Vedder & Tanilon 2014). Clearly, many adults and young people are concerned about how technologies could be misused to arrive at this tragic outcome.

Social networking/social media activities such as: the creation of personal profiles; the visibility of personal relationships through the options of 'liking' 'commenting', or 'sharing'; or the group participation aspects of meeting others, establishing, upholding, changing or dismantling social relationships, means that there is significant interplay between the online and offline environments, potentially impacting on individual and group wellbeing, as young people go about their daily relationship practices/interactions. How young people themselves make sense of their online activities is, therefore, important to know, especially if interventions concerning the appropriate use of technologies are to be successful. Much has been written concerning the negative impacts of technology, such as cyberbullying (Smith 2014), but if environments are to be created where technologies are employed seamlessly and constantly in schools as tools for socialising and learning, greater understanding of young people's views in relation to the positive impacts on them is also needed.

The pilot study discussed here (see Spears et al. 2013; Spears et al. 2012) concerns a multinational (Australia, Italy and Denmark) qualitative exploration of young people's thoughts and views (N=121) of the positive benefits of using social networking sites. It formed part of a larger European/Australian research collaboration exploring cyberbullying (Smith & Steffgen 2013). In particular, this research collective established that using technologies enhanced learning, relationship skill development, curriculum development and pedagogy, as well as online safety and identity development (Spears et al. 2013).

Engaging youth voice ensures that the meanings attached to the use of social networking sites by young people are relevant and authentic and not adult-imposed, which assists in further understanding how young people themselves are making sense of their cyber-social environments (Spears & Kofoed 2013; Spears, Slee, Campbell & Cross 2011). Young people aged 14 to 16 years old from one or more schools from each country were invited to participate in focus groups, of between six to eight individuals. Following transcription, the coding processes were done in the native languages of each country. In the Danish and the Italian cases, quotes and core themes were translated into English for shared analytical purposes. A subsequent face-to-face meeting of the researchers discussed the individual findings and commonalities and differences were determined.

In spite of the adult moral panic which has been associated with young people's use of digital technologies, young people in this study from three different countries reported many positive aspects to being engaged online socially with their peers (Spears et al. 2013, p. 183; Spears et al. 2012, p. 14). These were expressed as the following opportunities:

- Exercising some control

  You have the power to decide [what to say or do]

- Practice social skills

  It opens up communication back at school
  It is easier to tell them some things [embarrassing] you can't do face-to-face

- Taking time to think before you send/upload

  You don't just blurt it out

- Seeking help

  A lot of us open up to our friends on line rather than face-to-face

- Learning and sharing new things

  We had an assignment and we were all talking about it, sharing, proof reading and helping each other

- Being able to test different identities in a public space

  having a virtual public diary … a personal space where I can write and think in freedom and without control of parents, but available for friends

- Feeling less/lower risk when experiencing strong emotions
- Being able to experiment with different kinds of relationships and roles without feeling guilty if they made mistakes or had misunderstandings

Discussion and implications: Study 1

Many of these opportunities relate to identity development, which involves affirming autonomy and identity through the natural separation from parents and the testing of themselves with peers. Until relatively recently, the main influences on a young persons' identity development were offline relationships with peers, parents and significant others. The rise in the importance of social media for young people, however, means that these offline relationships are now supplemented by additional online social networks and virtual communities (Spears et al. 2013). Online networks offer vast opportunities for social comparison and contrast with others who may never have been available for comment in the past, creating both opportunities for positive affirmations, or risk of negative interactions, either way impacting on wellbeing.

Through enabling young people to express themselves creatively and artistically and to make representations of themselves to others through digital images ('selfies'), SNSs also encourage a form of self-branding, i.e. how young people want others to see/perceive them. Image control/management is an important aspect of contemporary adolescent wellbeing, and making deliberate choices—refining and adjusting the image and taking control of impression management—enhances feelings of security and belonging. At the same time, however, there is the potential to lose control over those images, highlighting the volatility of this medium and the potential for negative impacts on wellbeing.

According to boyd (2007, p. 124) SNSs such as Facebook are *networked publics*—spaces which are simultaneously public, networked, and yet perceived of as 'private'. These online spaces are where young people virtually congregate, and they are incredibly dynamic and fluid: it is where they share with each other; manage relationships; declare status; and end friendships.

Indeed, this study on the positive uses of social networking sites demonstrated that the risks, challenges and opportunities of being on social networking sites for young people were intertwined, regardless of where they actually lived (Australia, Italy or Denmark). The researchers identified there was a universal similarity in the friendship-driven practices employed across the cultural contexts, but that the positive uses and impacts were actually 'the flip side of the negative' (Spears et al. 2012, p. 18). Importantly, these young people also reminded adults that 'being on' was more than communicating with a number of contacts, but was more closely linked to accessibility, safety, trust and being part of a community (p. 18). These notions relate strongly to belonging and social connectedness—fundamental components of the human condition—and articulate what it is that keeps them connected.

Allen, Ryan, Gray, McInerney and Waters (2014, p. 18), however, reported mixed findings regarding the role of social media in fostering social connectedness, acknowledging the propensity for both positive and negative outcomes for young people, due to the paradox arising from the ease with which online communities are formed, and the sense of alienation and ostracism which can also be experienced. Thus, whilst the young people in the Spears et al. study (2013) articulated what was positive for them about being on SNSs, and which subsequently contributed to individual and group wellbeing (belonging to a group, sharing and being connected), there is always the flip-side; an undercurrent of negativity which could push them towards a different outcome: exclusion, ostracism, bullying.

For teachers in schools and those preparing to teach, navigating this on and offline peer relationship space is fraught with difficulties. Friendships are important developmentally for young people, increasing in importance as they grow, and SNSs have provided a highly visible way of determining one's place in the social demographic of a peer group. Socialising through this medium is a complex experience for young people, often portrayed by adults as negative. Yet young people found that engaging in SNSs was enabling for them, and provided positive learning and social experiences. The challenge for educators, in terms of student wellbeing, is to recognise the intertwinement of safety and trust issues that exist in these spaces; the risks and opportunities that coexist, where cyberbullying is offset against personal relationship development, and where both represent the two opposite sides of the same 'wellbeing' coin.

Whilst young people report many positive experiences from being online and from social networking, as noted above, there are clearly negative impacts, with cyberbullying being one of those. How positive behaviours such as seeking help and coping might mediate the general health and wellbeing of young people who have been cyberbullied, is therefore important to consider.

Study 2: Help-seeking behaviours, cyberbullying, general health and wellbeing[2]

Cyberbullying, defined as bullying carried out via electronic media—namely mobile phones and the Internet (Smith 2014)—is a complex social relationship issue impacting on mental health and wellbeing, and which requires an equally complex array of responses.

Study 2 reported briefly here, is part of a larger, four-year undertaking to ascertain whether technology can be used to support the mental health and wellbeing of young people (see Young and Well Cooperative Research Centre 2013b). The cyberbullying experiences and wellbeing profiles of 2,338 young people in Australia, aged 12–18 years were examined as part of a social marketing campaign concerned with the promotion of positive messaging, called: *Appreciate A Mate* (see Young and Well Cooperative Research Centre 2013a). An App allowed users to generate customisable, highly crafted messages of appreciation and then pass them on via Tumblr, Twitter, Facebook, Instagram and SMS. In the first few months (January–June 2013) over 26,000 messages were created (see http://www.appreciateamate.com/; http://www.campaignbrief.com/2014/01/young-and-well-crc-launches-ap.html).

The relationship between cyberbullying, help-seeking and wellbeing is complex. Those being targeted are known to avoid reporting incidents and to seek help (Dooley, Gradinger, Strohmeier, Cross & Spiel 2010; Smith, Mahdavi, Carvalho, Fisher, Russell & Tippett 2008), often for fear of further persecution or loss of access to the technology. There is also a self-perception amongst some young people that they should be able to deal with the issue on their own (Murray-Harvey, Skrzypiec & Slee 2012). A review of recent Australian studies estimated that approximately 20 per cent of young people had been cyberbullied in the previous year (Spears et al. 2014). International prevalence figures range from 10 to 40 per cent (Kowalski, Giumetti, Schroeder & Lattanner 2014), highlighting that this is indeed a problem confronting young people and their wellbeing today. It is known, for example, that not only those being victimised suffer, but so too do those who bully, and those who witness it (Smith 2014). In effect, this means that this is everyone's problem, and everyone's wellbeing is put at risk.

Most anti-bullying and cyberbullying interventions are conducted within the education sector, and many have been implemented at the whole school level, involving everyone in the solution. Providing individuals with the skills, knowledge and the tools to deal with bullying and cyberbullying is one component of this approach. Early studies of bullying explored the role of the individuals within the peer group, and identified that peers are usually present 85 per cent of the time (Pepler & Craig 1995). Salmivalli and colleagues (1996) further identified the roles that individuals play in a bullying situation, separating the bystanders out into ringleaders, followers, reinforcers, defenders and outsiders who actively or passively contributed to the situation. Smith (2014, p. 82) notes however, that the roles in cyberbullying situations appear more complex and the bystander might: (1) be with the perpetrator when the act is sent/posted online; (2) be with the victim when it is received; or (3) is with neither, but receives it from another or visits the relevant site online. Enhancing the moral engagement of bystanders to intervene is also considered an individual intervention pathway (e.g. Hymel, Rocke-Henderson & Bonanno 2005; Price, Green, Spears, Scrimgeour, Barnes, Geer & Johnson 2014).

Surprisingly, however, little attention has been given to building capacity in young people to safely reach out to others for help and support in a timely manner, particularly when online. Children who have proactively sought help have been found to develop systematic problem-solving skills, as well as demonstrate more mature interactions with others (Nelson-LeGall 1981), and those who seek help in classrooms have been found to have better learning strategies and outcomes (Newman 1990). All of these contribute towards positive sense of self, and subsequently wellbeing. The barriers to help-seeking, however, are anathema to wellbeing and include stigma, fears regarding confidentiality, embarrassment and lack of appropriate youth-friendly services, as well as a fear of retaliation from bullies (Rickwood 2012).

Help-seeking options comprise formal (seeking out professionals such as teachers, or counsellors) and informal (using personal networks, such as friends and family) strategies. In recent times, with the advent of communication and leisure technologies and social media, the notion of online self-help has emerged, whereby a person can seek help from online and computer-mediated sources (Rickwood & Thomas 2012). Online options now also include both formal and informal sources, but young people have been slow to engage with the sources of help currently available to them (Rickwood 2012), and Ellis and colleagues (2013) report that only 13 per cent of young men and 31 per cent of young women actually seek help at all when needed.

Furthermore, Ivancic et al. (2014, p. 7) noted that over 60 per cent of young Australians aged 15–19 with a probable serious mental health condition were uncomfortable seeking information, advice or support from professional services, such as phone hotlines, online counselling and/or community agencies, but *were* comfortable accessing friends and the Internet for information, advice or support. Glasheen and Campbell (2012), however, found promising results in their trial of an online counselling service *in* schools. This study reported that boys were the main users, and most users followed up with a face-to-face consultation with the counsellor, and in addition, students with disabilities appeared to be less inhibited online. It would seem that the dual opportunity of anonymous online help-seeking, followed by trust in a face-to-face encounter within the school setting, is one that needs ongoing consideration and exploration.

Changing attitudes and behaviours relating to this reluctance to seek help is therefore important if we are to ameliorate the damaging effects of cyberbullying, and improve wellbeing for these young people in schools.

In order to obtain a comprehensive wellbeing profile of young people in this study, several reliable and valid measures were employed to examine: mental health; general wellbeing; depression, anxiety and stress; social connectedness; and help-seeking (Spears et al. 2015b; Spears et al. 2015c). A summary of the (statistically significant) findings related to the online practices and general health and wellbeing of this cohort of young people, aged 12 to 18 is outlined below (see Spears et al. 2015c for further detail).

This snapshot indicates that most young people in this study were well, and that technology was not a significant negative issue in their lives, but for those experiencing cyberbullying or being online late at night, it is clear that some intervention is required in terms of supporting their wellbeing. The complexity of the interplay between wellbeing, technology, intention to seek help and cyberbullying is evident from the findings italicised below. In summary, young people in this study reported:

- They spent considerable amount of time online:

  ○ 44 per cent (n=975) spent time online after 11 pm, most of these in the older age group, with almost half being online after 11 pm at least four times a week;

  ○ 12 year olds were less likely than all other age groups to use a mobile phone to go online, but more likely to use a Tablet or iPad to do so;

  ○ online gaming is one of the top three uses of the Internet, with four in five young people playing games online; and

  ○ a small number of young people gambled online, however, their associated mental health and cyberbullying issues were vastly above the norm.

- Generally, they experienced positive mental health and wellbeing, and those who did were more likely to:

  ○ appreciate the social norms around helping others to feel good about themselves;

  ○ be positively oriented towards helping others; and

  ○ they felt they had the control, desire and intent to help others to feel good about themselves and be affirming of others.

- Those who used the Internet after 11 pm however, had poorer mental health than those who did not and were:

  ○ less likely to be socially connected;

  ○ more likely to have negative attitudes and perceptions regarding helping others to feel good about themselves;

  ○ less likely to have the control, desire or intent to help others to feel good about themselves; and

  ○ less likely to be helping others to feel good about themselves

- Girls were found to be significantly more depressed, anxious and stressed than males overall.

This study also found that there was a consistent pattern in terms of the mental health and wellbeing profile of young people when examined by cyberbullying status (Spears et al. 2015b; Spears et al. 2015c). Those who were both cyberbullied and cybervictimised (cyberbully victims) reported poorer mental health, lower levels of social connectedness, and greater stress, anxiety and depression. Further profiling of this group also demonstrated that they were accessing the Internet after 11 pm, yet were unlikely to access help online, but a quarter preferred to seek help first from friends.

Discussion and implications: Study 2

Pleasingly, most young people reported being well and technology, whilst omnipresent, was not a negative influence in their lives. Those who engaged late at night, who were gambling online or were cybervictimised, however, had a different story and were compromised in terms of their mental health and wellbeing. Clearly, technology in these instances has a negative impact. The vulnerability of those identified as cyberbully victims, warrants ongoing consideration, for there is also a multiplier effect on wellbeing, when the overlap of traditional bullying is also considered. Indeed, Landstedt and Persson (2014) found that the combination of traditional (in real life) bullying and cyberbullying was particularly negative for mental health, and Messias, Kindrick and Castro (2014) found that reports of sadness and suicidality were highest amongst those reporting both forms of bullying, followed by those reporting cyberbullying only. However, Van Geel, Vedder and Tanilon (2014) found that cyberbullying was more strongly related to suicidal ideation compared with traditional bullying. The wellbeing of these young people is at risk, and so strategies which not only deal with traditional bullying need consideration, but also those which serve to ameliorate the impact of cyberbullying. Reaching out safely to others for help is one such strategy.

In terms of young people who did seek help in this study, informal networks comprising parents and friends, were the key providers of support for young people. Young people were unlikely to employ more formal sources of help (either on or offline), but older youth were more likely to seek help from a boyfriend/girlfriend, or access online sources. This is to be expected in terms of turning to the closest relationships for support as one develops intimate partnerships, but it also suggests that there is increasing awareness and/or trust in accessing online resources. However, it was concerning that the oldest group in this cohort was least likely to seek help from anyone. This could however, reflect the perception that they can and should be able to deal with it themselves. Clearly building capacity in seeking help is one strategy for ameliorating the impacts of cyberbullying, but developmental trends have to be taken into account, so that the most effective and appropriate network is available for the young person when help is needed. Knowing that help is available, and how to access that help would seem to be a supportive mechanism for young people's wellbeing.

Taken together, these findings highlight key aspects relevant to young people's health and wellbeing (see Spears et al. 2015c for the full report). In brief: parents and friends (informal networks) remain the key support for young people's wellbeing; Internet use after 11 pm is important and is linked with vulnerability to victimisation; cyberbully victims are particularly vulnerable to poor mental health outcomes; social connectedness matters for health and wellbeing; and potential avenues of help-seeking need to be considered in line with young people's developmental, social and emotional needs.

As educators, we need to be asking: what is within the realms of possibility, as individuals, and collectively, to support the health and wellbeing of students, when they are seamlessly shifting their social activity between on and offline, in a 24/7 environment.

Technology is an integral part of young people's lives and this study has demonstrated that it is not impacting negatively on most. For those whose wellbeing is being challenged, urgent and special focus needs to be given, so as to assist them to find ways of dealing with it. Perhaps encouraging young people to overcome the barriers to seeking help might be a good place to start.

Conclusions and implications

This chapter highlights the paradox and tension between use of technology/social media and wellbeing; simultaneously a panacea and a problem. What this means for educators, is that they have to become skilled in not only how it is used, but in how to use it to support young people. Employing technologies as part of the solution is important, as is understanding young people's views and uses of emerging technologies, as they are the active agents in this rapidly changing space. Paying heed to the rights of the child to participate fully, and to be heard and valued, is critical if adults are to fully comprehend the positive role that technology plays in young people's lives—socially and educationally. Considering how technology interplays with the socio-cultural system is therefore also highly relevant, as is educators' own world view of the child in the twenty-first century.

One clear message which resonates from the voices of young people reported in this chapter, is that the risks, challenges and opportunities arising from using ITs and social media are closely intertwined; where positive experiences are deemed to be the 'flip side' to the negative, and where they are simply deemed to be 'different sides to the same (relationship) coin' (Spears et al. 2013, p. 193). In many ways, technology and wellbeing really do present us with a wicked problem of complex and rapidly changing constructs. But perhaps that means that we need to be interdisciplinary in our approaches, be creative in how we address it, and be mindful that young people have the best voice to be listened to in this space.

Wellbeing follow-up activities

The following reflective challenges are designed to connect you with the content of this chapter; to position yourself in terms of the start of the IT revolution, and to ascertain your understanding of the relationship between technology and wellbeing as an educator. I would welcome your responses to any of these activities at barbara.spears@unisa.edu.au.

1. Where were you when the Internet was first available? How, when and where did you first engage with it?
2. When did you first join a social networking site? Which one? Why did you join? Reflect on your engagement with it: are you always 'checking' what others are up to? What does this mean for your wellbeing? What is your world view of technology/social media: panacea or problem? Does this change when you think about young people?
3. What would you need to support your wellbeing? How similar or different is that for young people?
4. How can we use technology to engage young people in the work of wellbeing? What is out there already that we can point them to?
5. Think of a child born today, who will attend school for the first time in 2020. What do you think the wellbeing and technology challenges might be for him/her and the school? (You might want to revisit the Forbes List noted earlier)
6. Think about your pre-service teacher education and/or any in-service teacher professional development: How equipped are you to support young people's wellbeing through technology? How equipped are you to deal with the negative aspects of being online: cyberbullying and sexting?
7. What does your school setting have in place to support you and your wellbeing as you go about your work in these areas?

Some resources for exploration and consideration

There is an exponential growth in self-help apps and technologies, which are always on, always accessible and easily worn and represent the intersection between digital technologies and intelligent thinking. Game-ifying health and wellbeing for young people through smartphone applications may be one avenue for consideration, where bio-feedback mechanisms or cognitive behavioural therapies operate in synch with the individual at a moment's notice, as distinct from visiting an online support service or a face-to-face practitioner weekly or monthly.

Self-knowledge through *self-tracking* is not new, but with new technologies, hard data can be accumulated by the individual, which can be used to modify patterns of behaviours. Making young people not only aware of these options, but also that they can reach out for help at any time, is an important step in supporting their wellbeing.

But first you have to become acquainted with what is available. This relates to the two points made at the beginning of the chapter, i.e. that not only do educators have to be skilled in how to use and subsequently teach with and about emerging technologies, but educators also need to be ready to work with young people as they develop cognitively, socially, and emotionally, surrounded by constantly changing and evolving technologies, social networking sites and social media.

This requires you to think about the theories which underpin your pedagogies in light of what technology has to offer, to consider your world view of children in the twenty-first century, and to reflect on what research can tell us about practice.

The following are some online programmes/apps for consideration. These are created, designed and supported by leading mental health organisations across Australia and this is not an exhaustive list. To be current, please go to the major mental health and wellbeing organisations such as Reachout.Com (please check for current links when reading this, as later versions may be available).

Resources for educators

The Young and Well Wellbeing Policy: a guide to being safe, healthy and resilient in the workplace. Use this to consider your own workplace policy. http://www.youngandwellcrc.org.au/wp-content/uploads/2014/12/Young-and-Well-CRC_Wellbeing-Policy_Final.pdf

The *Mobile Application Rating Scale*: a multi-dimensional tool for determining quality of health-related apps.
http://www.youngandwellcrc.org.au/mobile-application-rating-scale-mars-new-tool-assessing-quality-health-apps/

Building Resiliency in Young People: a resource linked to the General Capabilities of the Australian Curriculum.
http://au.professionals.reachout.com/-/media/pdf/professionals/teachers/building resiliencyinyoungpeopleprintdownload/buildingresiliencyinyoungpeopleprintdownload.pdf

Reachout.com Professional Development for teachers: a link to webinars and resources. http://au.professionals.reachout.com/professional-development/teachers

The *Mood Assessment Program* (MAP) (*not* self–help), from the Black Dog Institute: a computerised assessment and diagnostic tool for mood disorders. This app is used by health professionals and is not available as a self-help mechanism, but is an example of how technology is also supporting the professions to help young people.
http://www.blackdoginstitute.org.au/healthprofessionals/map/overview.cfm

Cybersmart: a national cybersafety and cybersecurity education programme managed by the Australian Communications and Media Authority (ACMA), as part of the Australian Government's commitment to cybersafety. The programme is specifically designed to meet the needs of its target audiences of children, young people, parents, teachers and library staff.
http://www.cybersmart.gov.au/

http://www.cybersmart.gov.au/Parents/Cyber%20issues/Sexting.aspx
http://www.cybersmart.gov.au/Parents.aspx

Resources for young people

e-Headspace: online counselling for young people and their families.
https://www.eheadspace.org.au/

KidsHelpline: online/web counselling, one-on-one for young people.
http://www.kidshelp.com.au/teens/get-help/web-counselling/

Smiling Mind: modern meditation for young people and is designed to give clarity, calm and contentment. Developed by psychologists with expertise in youth development and therapy, it enables young people to begin the journey towards better mental health in a non-threatening, private way.
http://smilingmind.com.au/

The *Talking Anxiety* app from Sane Australia: brings together eight short videos from people who have 'been there and done that'; they have learnt to manage their anxiety in successful ways. The app provides tips, information and quizzes and a daily tip can be sent to your iPad/iPhone.
https://itunes.apple.com/au/app/talking-anxiety/id542101737?mt=8

The *Recharge Sleep* app: offers a personalised six-week programme focused on improving mood, energy and wellbeing by putting in place good sleep/wake patterns.
http://au.reachout.com/recharge-sleep-app)

MoodKit: designed by clinical psychologists, is an app created to help you apply effective strategies of professional psychology to your everyday life. It engages you in mood-enhancing activities, identifies and changes unhealthy thinking, rates and charts mood across time, and enables the creation of journal entries using custom templates designed to promote well-being.
https://itunes.apple.com/us/app/moodkit-mood-improvement-tools/id427064987?mt=8

The Sorter, recommended for those aged 17+: the Sorter is the compass to guide you through whatever obstacle comes your way.
http://au.reachout.com/thesorter

The Line: enjoy healthy and respectful relationships and recognise behaviour that 'crosses the line'.
http://theline.org.au/

Resources for everyone

MoodGYM: a free online programme that aims to reduce mild to moderate symptoms of depression in adults by teaching them the principles of cognitive behaviour therapy. The programme is made up of modules, an interactive game, assessments, a downloadable relaxation audio file, an online workbook and a feedback assessment.
https://moodgym.anu.edu.au/welcome

The Desk: a free online programme aimed at providing Australian tertiary students with strategies and skills for success and wellbeing during their time at university or TAFE (technical and further education).

http://www.youthbeyondblue.com/do-something-about-it/keeping-well/thedesk

Tips for Communicating
http://au.reachout.com/tips-for-communicating

Preventing Harm from Alcohol
http://www.vichealth.vic.gov.au/Programs-and-Projects/Alcohol-Misuse.aspx

Changing Your Relationship with Alcohol
https://www.hellosundaymorning.org/

Notes

1 This study was undertaken as part of the Co-operation of Science and Technology (COST) Action ISO801: *Cyberbullying: coping with negative and enhancing positive uses of new technologies, in relationships in educational settings.*
2 This study was supported by the Young and Well Cooperative Research Centre (CRC), an Australia-based, international research centre that unites young people with researchers, practitioners, innovators and policy makers from over 70 partner organisations. The Young and Well CRC is established under the Australian Government's Cooperative Research Centres Program.

References

Allen, K, Ryan, T, Gray, D, McInerney, D & Waters, L (2014) Social media use and social connectedness in adolescents: The positives and the potential pitfalls. *The Australian Educational and Developmental Psychologist*, 31(1), pp. 18–31.

Askell-Williams, H & Lawson, M (2013) Teachers' knowledge and confidence for promoting positive mental health in primary school communities. *Asia-Pacific Journal of Teacher Education*, 41(2), pp. 126–143.

boyd, d (2007) Why youth (heart) social network sites: The role of networked publics in teenage social life. In D Buckingham (ed), *Youth, identity, and digital media*. The MIT Press, Cambridge, MA, pp. 119–142.

Bronfenbrenner, U (1977) Toward an experimental ecology of human development. *American Psychologist*, 32(7), pp. 513–531.

Bronfenbrenner, U (1979) *The ecology of human development: Experiments by nature and design*. Harvard University Press, Cambridge, MA.

Burns, J, Davenport, T, Christensen, H, Luscombe, GM, Mendoza, JA, Bresnan, A, Blanchard, ME & Hickie, IB (2013) *Game on: Exploring the impact of technologies on young men's mental health and wellbeing. Findings from the first Young and Well National Survey*. Young and Well Cooperative Research Centre, Melbourne, VIC.

Campbell, M, Spears, B, Cross, D & Phillip, S (2010) Cyberbullying in Australia. In JA Mora-Merchan & T Jager (eds), *Cyberbullying: A cross-national comparison*. Verlag Empirische Pädagogik, Landau, pp. 232–244.

Campbell, M, Spears, B, Slee, P, Butler, D & Kift, S (2012) Victims' perceptions of traditional and cyber-bullying, and the psychosocial correlates of their victimisation. *Emotional and Behavioural Difficulties*, 17(3–4), pp. 389–401.

Commonwealth of Australia (2007) *Tackling wicked problems: A public policy perspective*. Australian Public Service Commission, Canberra, ACT.

Corsaro, WA (1997) *The sociology of childhood*. Pine Forge Press, London.

Curtis, A (2013) *A brief history of social media*, Mass Communication Dept., University of North Carolina at Pembroke. Viewed 10 January, available from http://www2.uncp.edu/home/acurtis/NewMedia/SocialMedia/SocialMediaHistory.html.

Department of Education (2010) *The National Safe Schools Framework.* Australian Government.Viewed 11 November, 2014, available from https://www.education.gov.au/national-safe-schools-framework-0.

Dooley, JJ, Gradinger, P, Strohmeier, D, Cross, D & Spiel, C (2010) Cyber-victimisation:The association between help-seeking behaviours and self-reported emotional symptoms in Australia and Austria. *Australian Journal of Guidance and Counselling,* 20(2), pp. 194–209.

Ellis, LA, Collin, P, Hurley, PJ, Davenport,TA, Burns, JM & Hickie, IB (2013) Young men's attitudes and behaviour in relation to mental health and technology: Implications for the development of online mental health services. *BMC Psychiatry,* 13(1), p. 119.

Forbes (2015) *Top 10 strategic technology trends for 2015.* Forbes, Inc.Viewed 21 January 2015, available from http://www.forbes.com/pictures/fgjd45eldm/1-computing-everywhere-2/.

Glasheen, K & Campbell, M (2012) Online counselling for enhancing relationships. In A Costabile & B Spears (eds), *The impact of technology on relationships in educational settings.* Routledge, New York, NY, pp. 128–136.

Green, L, Brady, D, Ólafsson, K, Hartley, J & Lumby, C (2011) Risks and safety for Australian children on the internet. *Cultural Science,* 4(1), pp. 1–73.

Hinduja, S & Patchin, JW (2010) Bullying, cyberbullying, and suicide. *Archives of Suicide Research,* 14(3), pp. 206–221.

Hymel, S, Rocke-Henderson, N & Bonanno, RA (2005) Moral disengagement: A framework for understanding bullying among adolescents. *Journal of Social Sciences,* 8(1), pp. 1–11.

Ito, M, Horst, H, Bittanti, M, boyd, d, Herr-Stephenson, B, Lange, PG, Pascoe, C & Robinson, L (2008) *Living and learning with new media: Summary of findings from the Digital Youth Project (John D. and Catherine T. MacArthur Foundation reports on digital media and learning).* MIT Press, Cambridge, MA.

Ivancic, L, Perrens, B, Fildes, J, Perry, Y & Christensen, H (2014) *Youth mental health report.* Mission Australia and Black Dog Institute, Australia.

James, A & Prout, A (eds) (1997) *Constructing and reconstructing childhood: Contemporary issues in the socio-logical study of childhood.* Psychology Press, East Sussex.

Johansson, T (2000) Moral panics revisited. *Young,* 8(1), pp. 22–35.

Johnson, G & Puplampu, P (2008) A conceptual framework for understanding the effect of the Internet on child development:The ecological techno-subsystem. *Canadian Journal of Learning and Technology,* 34(1), pp. 19–28.

Johnson, GM (2010a) Internet use and child development: The techno-microsystem. *Australian Journal of Educational & Developmental Psychology,* 10, pp. 32–43.

Johnson, GM (2010b) Internet use and child development:Validation of the ecological techno-subsystem. *Educational Technology & Society,* 13(1), pp. 176–185.

Joint Select Committee on Cyber-Safety (2011) *High-wire act: Cyber-safety and the young. Interim report.* Parliament of the Commonwealth of Australia, Canberra, ACT.

Jose, PE, Ryan, N & Pryor, J (2012) Does social connectedness promote a greater sense of well-being in adolescence over time? *Journal of Research on Adolescence,* 22(2), pp. 235–251.

Kowalski, RM, Giumetti, GW, Schroeder, AN & Lattanner, MR (2014) Bullying in the digital age: A critical review and meta-analysis of cyberbullying research among youth. *Psychological Bulletin,* 140(4), pp. 1073–1137.

Landstedt, E & Persson, S (2014) Bullying, cyberbullying, and mental health in young people. *Scandinavian Journal of Public Health,* 42(4), pp. 393–399.

Luxton, DD, June, JD & Fairall, JM (2012) Social media and suicide: A public health perspective. *American Journal of Public Health,* 102(S2), pp. S195–S200.

Messias, E, Kindrick, K & Castro, J (2014) School bullying, cyberbullying, or both: Correlates of teen suicidality in the 2011 CDC Youth Risk Behavior Survey. *Comprehensive Psychiatry,* 55(5), pp. 1063–1068.

Murray-Harvey, R, Skrzypiec, G & Slee, PT (2012) Effective and ineffective coping with bullying strat-egies as assessed by informed professionals and their use by victimised students. *Australian Journal of Guidance and Counselling,* 22(1), pp. 122–138.

Nelson-LeGall, S (1981) Help-seeking: An understudied problem-solving skill in children. *Developmental Review*, 1(3), pp. 224–246.

Newman, RS (1990) Children's help-seeking in the classroom: The role of motivational factors and attitudes. *Journal of Educational Psychology*, 82(1), pp. 71–80.

Pepler, DJ & Craig, WM (1995) A peek behind the fence: Naturalistic observations of aggressive children with remote audiovisual recording. *Developmental Psychology*, 31(4), pp. 548–553.

Price, D, Green, D, Spears, B, Scrimgeour, M, Barnes, A, Geer, R & Johnson, B (2014) A qualitative exploration of cyber-bystanders and moral engagement. *Australian Journal of Guidance and Counselling*, 24(1), pp. 1–17.

Rickwood, D (2012) Entering the e-spectrum: An examination of new interventions for youth mental health. *Youth Studies Australia*, 31(4), pp. 18–27.

Rickwood, D & Thomas, K (2012) Conceptual measurement framework for help-seeking for mental health problems. *Psychology Research and Behavior Management*, 5, pp. 173–183.

Rittel, H & Webber, M (1973) Dilemmas in a general theory of planning. *Policy Sciences*, 4(2), pp. 155–169.

Rohloff, A & Wright, S (2010) Moral panic and social theory beyond the heuristic. *Current Sociology*, 58(3), pp. 403–419.

Salmivalli, C, Lagerspetz, K, Björkqvist, K, Österman, K & Kaukiainen, A (1996) Bullying as a group process: Participant roles and their relations to social status within the group. *Aggressive Behavior*, 22(1), pp. 1–15.

Sirin, SR (2005) Socioeconomic status and academic achievement: A meta-analytic review of research. *Review of Educational Research*, 75(3), pp. 417–453.

Slee, P, Campbell, M & Spears, B (2012) *Child, adolescent and family development*. 3rd edn, Cambridge University Press, UK.

Smith, PK (2014) *Understanding school bullying: Its nature and prevention strategies*. SAGE, London.

Smith, PK, Mahdavi, J, Carvalho, M, Fisher, S, Russell, S & Tippett, N (2008) Cyberbullying: Its nature and impact in secondary school pupils. *Journal of Child Psychology and Psychiatry*, 49(4), pp. 376–385.

Smith, PK & Steffgen, G (2013) *Cyberbullying through the new media: Findings from an international network*. Psychology Press, Hove, UK.

Spears, B (2011) Cyberchat: Using technology to enhance wellbeing. *Education Technology Solutions*, 40, p. 16.

Spears, B (2012) A review of initiatives using technology to promote cyber-safety and digital citizenship. In A Costabile & B Spears (eds), *The impact of technology on relationships in educational settings*. Routledge, London, pp. 188–203.

Spears, B, Campbell, M, Tangen, D, Slee, P & Cross, D (2015a forthcoming) Australian pre-service teachers' knowledge and understanding of cyberbullying: Implications for school climate. *Les Dossiers des Sciences de l'Éducation* 30.

Spears, B & Costabile, A (2012a) Conclusion. In A Costabile & B Spears (eds), *The impact of technology on relationships in educational settings*. Routledge, London, pp. 204–207.

Spears, B & Costabile, A (2012b) Introduction. In A Costabile & B Spears (eds), *The impact of technology on relationships in educational settings*. Routledge, London, pp. 1–5.

Spears, B, Costabile, A, Brighi, A, Del Rey, R, Pörhölä, M, Sanchez, V, Spiel, C & Thompson, F (2013) Positive uses of new technologies, in relationships in educational settings. In P Smitt & G Steffgen (eds), *Cyberbullying through the new media: Findings from an international network*. Psychology Press, London, pp. 178–201.

Spears, B, Keeley, M, Bates, S & Katz, I (2014) *Research on youth exposure to, and management of, cyberbullying incidents in Australia: Part A. Literature review on the estimated prevalence of cyberbullying involving Australian minors (SPRC Report 9/2014*. Social Policy Research Centre, University of New South Wales, Sydney, NSW.

Spears, B & Kofoed, J (2013) Transgressing research binaries: Youth as knowledge brokers in cyberbully-ing research. In P Smith & G Steffgen (eds), *Cyberbullying through the new media: Findings from an international network*. Psychology Press, London, pp. 201–221.

Spears, B, Kofoed, J, Bartolo, M, Palermiti, A & Costabile, A (2012) Positive uses of social networking sites: Youth voice perspectives. In A Costabile & B Spears (eds), *The impact of technology on relationships in educational settings*. Routledge, London, pp. 7–21.

Spears, B, Slee, P, Campbell, MA & Cross, D (2011) *Educational change and youth voice: Informing school action on cyberbullying*. Centre for Strategic Education Seminar Series (No. 208), Centre for Strategic Education, VIC.

Spears, B, Taddeo, C, Barnes, A, Collin, P, Swirski, T, Drennan, J, Scrimgeour, M & Razzell, M (2015b) *@ppreciateamate: Positive messaging. Safe and Well online: A report on the methodology and find-ings of research to develop and evaluate digital campaigns for youth safety and wellbeing.* Young and Well Cooperative Research Centre, Melbourne, VIC.

Spears, BA, Taddeo, CM, Daly, AL, Stretton, A & Karklins, LT (2015c) Cyberbullying, help-seeking and mental health in young Australians: Implications for public health. *International Journal of Public Health*, 60, pp. 219–226.

Spears, B & Zeederberg, M (2013) Emerging methodological strategies to address cyberbullying: Online social marketing and young people as co-researchers. In S Bauman, D Cross & J Walker (eds), *Principles of cyberbullying research: Definitions, measures and method*. Routledge, New York, NY, pp. 273–285.

Swearer, SM & Doll, B (2001) Bullying in schools: An ecological framework. *Journal of Emotional Abuse*, 2(2–3), pp. 7–23.

Third, A, Bellerose, D, Dawkins, U, Keltie, E, & Pihl, K (2014) 'Children's Rights in the Digital Age: A Download from Children Around the World', Young and Well Cooperative Research Centre, Melbourne.

Tokunaga, RS (2010) Following you home from school: A critical review and synthesis of research on cyberbullying victimization. *Computers in Human Behavior*, 26(3), pp. 277–287.

United Nations General Assembly (1989) *Convention on the rights of the child*. United Nations, New York, NY.

van Geel, M, Vedder, P & Tanilon, J (2014) Relationship between peer victimization, cyberbullying, and suicide in children and adolescents: A meta-analysis. *JAMA Pediatrics*, 168(5), pp. 435–442.

Young and Well Cooperative Research Centre (2013a) *Appreciate a mate on National Compliments Day*. Available from http://www.youngandwellcrc.org.au/appreciate-mate-national-compliments-day-3/.

Young and Well Cooperative Research Centre (2013b) *Safe and Well Online*. Available from http://www.youngandwellcrc.org.au/research/safe-supportive/safe-and-well-online/.

6

TEACHER WELLBEING

Faye McCallum and Deborah Price

Don't touch that coffee mug!!

Excitedly I packed my belongings from home and university and I was off. Degree in hand, resources to call upon, umpteen lesson plans, a good pair of sneakers and a hat. What else would I need to survive a new life, living and working in a large town in the rural hinterland? I hadn't been to this spot before but I did do a 'self-help' map which meant I researched the town, community, school and people. I felt assured all was going to be great. The drive was long, dusty and strange. I hadn't lived out of home before so those comforts were behind me, but I have my most treasured belongings from home and I would be fine. Four hours from city life and I arrived and settled in – shopping sorted and I prepared for the next day.

On my first day, I was warmly welcomed by the school principal, met some staff; the kids were great, and the parents awesome. Recess break comes and goes and I get a chance to sit in the staff room at lunch time and meet some colleagues. Invited to have coffee, I grabbed for a mug and was told – 'No, not that one, that's for visitors, you're on staff now'. This took me back to my last practicum experience while a student at university; being shot down for using the teacher's mug, sitting in the wrong place in the staff room, being put down for exciting the children in a mathematics lesson because I used a constructivist approach, being over-planned, getting to school too early, staying too late, getting on with the parents, being male and meeting deadlines.

I nearly lost my desire to teach after that experience but somehow and thanks to my university mentors, I managed to hang in there and finish. I remember being really down but thanks to a final course that focussed on teacher identity and wellbeing, I was able to pick myself up and develop some resilient strategies that helped me to put personal-professional life into perspective and to cope with the ups and downs. How refreshing this will be – I already feel part of this school community and I'm going to stay!

The preceding chapters have focussed predominantly on children and young people's well-being. Throughout the world, researchers, teacher educators, policy writers, curriculum developers and even politicians stress the important role that teachers have in the achievement, satisfaction, and health and wellbeing of children and young people. In Australia, Federal Education Minister Pyne mentioned in his 2013 election speech that 'Nothing drives better outcomes for our children than high quality teaching' (2013). An excellent teacher, he said, is the central ingredient in achieving an excellent education. Yet we find increasing numbers of teachers leaving the profession or 'burning out', many within five years of graduation, due to teaching demands, challenging student behaviour and stress of families/communities (Moon 2007). These demands have short- and long-term effects on teachers and their work, with some choosing to leave the profession. In Western countries, between 25 and 40 per cent of beginning teachers are likely to leave the teaching profession in the first five years (DETE 2005; Ewing & Smith 2003; Moon 2007; Kelly 2004).

The chapter will first situate teacher wellbeing as an important issue in educational settings. This is followed by a discussion about wellbeing education as a central component of initial teacher education. In this context, we share early career teachers' experiences as they transition from the 'safety net' of university or college to the workplace, with a focus on their wellbeing and the issues that are important for the sustainability of teachers in the profession. Here, a specific case study of early career teachers working in a unique isolated environment—a rural location—will be explored in order to promote an understanding of sustainable wellbeing. Finally, a number of practical strategies for teacher wellbeing will be presented.

Why is teacher wellbeing important?

As the opening vignette highlights, the early experiences of a teacher play a crucial role in his or her adaptation to work. Imagine if the vignette had a negative twist … if s/he wasn't as readily accepted into the school by the children, parents/carers, staff and community. For our early career teachers, this is unfortunately the case in too many of our schools and educational sites. And as teachers continue their work over the span of a career, some also have negative experiences of people and places, and this affects their satisfaction and sustainability. The vignette also highlights the sometimes negative experiences our pre-service teachers have as they complete the professional experiences associated with their qualifying degrees. We know that pre-service teachers are excited about undertaking their professional experience placements, but many teacher educators hear about the less-than-positive stories that sometimes filter back to the university classroom. We argue that the focus ahead needs to be positive for both initial teacher education and teacher employers as we aim for all teachers to be 'well' and 'fit' throughout fulfilling careers.

Increasingly the demands of teaching are becoming self-evident, particularly the emotional side of teachers' work. Sometimes, where there is little acknowledgement from parents/carers, the media or general society for the dedicated, hard and emotive work that teachers perform, both early and mid-career teachers leave the profession. Data across the English-speaking world is consistent: 20 per cent of teachers leave education in their first three years and 50 per cent within five years (House of Commons Education and Skills Committee 2004; Roffey 2012). A significant body of research supports the proposition that workplace-based stress is a strong factor influencing teacher attrition, which implies that stress levels have significant implications for educators' physical and mental health (Carson, Baumgartner, Matthews & Tsouloupas 2010;

Kyriacou 2001; Sass, Seal & Martin 2011). This finding is not unique to any single region; according to Skaalvik and Skaalvik (2011), 'the high rate of teacher attrition is reported not only in the U.S., but also in other countries around the world regardless of differences in their educational system, for instance in Australia, China, and England' (p. 1029). In Australia, 'accurate ... figures are difficult to obtain because each state and territory education department gathers its own exit statistics and there is often a reticence to publicly reveal the data, in particular, concerning the number of years of service of those leaving the profession' (Buchanan, Prescott, Schuck, Aubusson, Burke & Louviere 2013, p. 8).

Yong and Yue (2007) claim that teachers have one of the most stressful occupations: 'Long-term work stress may lead to burnout, which gravely affects teachers' physical and mental health, lowers the quality of their work, and, in turn, impairs their students' physical and mental health and development and imperils the sound development of education' (p. 78). It appears the work is highly complex and demanding, accountability is increasing, and changes in policy, curricula or political agendas impose additional burdens and time constraints on schools and their workers. Furthermore, teachers cite increased behavioural issues in classrooms, lack of respect and even violence towards them. Teacher status and identity with regard to community standing has declined and the complex demands arising from their work are increasing (e.g. Committee for the Review of Teaching and Teacher Education 2003; MCEETYA 2003; Australian Parliament, Senate Employment, Education and Training References Committee 1998).

The challenges of early career teaching are well documented. These include: the increasing battering of teachers by the media and some community members; isolation; increased workload and accountability; post-university 'reality shock' when faced with the demands of employment; increased parent/carer demands; student misbehaviour; poor or minimal induction and professional development; sub-standard working conditions compared to other professions; and the high degree of casualisation of the teaching workforce. In Australia, these challenges contribute to a teacher attrition rate of greater than 20 per cent in the first five years of teaching. Studies of teacher attrition highlight that induction and mentoring programmes, while useful, are not sufficient to address this problem (Kelly, Reushle, Chakrabarty & Kinnane 2014).

A recent study to assess the stress and wellbeing of the Australian population has indicated that, compared with previous years, Australians currently have significantly lower levels of wellbeing and significantly higher levels of stress and distress, and depressive and anxiety symptoms (Casey 2013, p. 4). In this survey Casey reports that:

- working Australians reported significantly lower overall workplace wellbeing in 2013 (as measured by the Workplace subscale of the UK wellbeing scale) compared with findings in 2012 and 2011;
- working Australians reported significantly lower levels of job satisfaction compared with previous years;
- working Australians reported significantly lower levels of interest in their job compared with 2012; and
- similar to previous years' findings, almost half of working Australians rated issues in the workplace as a source of stress (Casey 2013, p. 6).

Although these survey findings are not specific to teachers, there are nevertheless comparable significant implications for educators. If individuals are already experiencing lowered wellbeing, then the additional stress of teaching can be expected to compound this. Workplace stress and reduced wellbeing is a major reason identified by those teachers that leave the profession.

Whilst teachers are considered the biggest in-school influence on student achievement, rather than being seen as an asset, they are often blamed for student poor performance (Dinham 2013). Teacher quality, confirmed as one of the most influential factors in relation to student achievement (e.g. Darling-Hammond 1999, 2003; Santiago 2002) around the world shows that the most important factor in determining how well children do is the quality of teachers and teaching. Thus, as in other professions, teachers need to be 'well' in order to ensure they can sustain their quality work and to be there for the next generation. If, as a society, we expect our children and young people to grow up 'well', skilled to contribute to society, able to gain employment, be physically fit and have healthy social-emotional capacities, then we must ensure that teaching is a 'well' and sustainable profession. Simply put, without teachers' wellbeing it is hard to build up students' wellbeing (Konu, Viitanen & Lintonen 2010, p. 44).

Wellbeing in initial teacher education

A national review of curriculum content conducted in 2014 related specifically to teacher wellbeing within initial teacher education programmes across Australia found no content that specifically addressed the causes of wellbeing or strategies to be well. There is generic reference to teacher wellbeing during professional experience courses when students are on practicum, but no explicit teaching material was located in this review. Table 6.1 shows the overall content covered from the survey of programmes in 31 universities in Australia that offer initial teacher education.

Table 6.1 shows that most wellbeing content in relevant courses/units has a health, physical education, or psychological perspective. In Chapter 1, we characterised wellbeing as 'diverse and fluid, respecting individual, family and community beliefs, values, experiences, culture, opportunities and contexts across time and change. It encompasses intertwined individual, collective and environmental elements which continually interact across the lifespan'. Given this, initial teacher education programmes are encouraged to broaden their wellbeing educational philosophies to include such relational, contextual and fluid notions.

Of further note, within the university programmes that were reviewed, only two indicated a minor focus on teacher wellbeing as indicated by these content statements:

> In this subject students explore, develop and reflect on their attitudes and behaviours towards their own and other people's health and wellbeing. Students explore aspects of wellbeing and sustainable living in order to gain a greater awareness of, and take responsibility for their wellbeing so they are prepared for the demands of tertiary study and of their future profession.

And,

> This subject explores the concept of wellness and wellbeing for staff and children in early childhood services.

Initial teacher preparation programmes, globally, are concerned with preparing teachers for a sustained and fulfilling career in education. However, it appears that strategies to achieve this

TABLE 6.1 Wellbeing content in Australian initial teacher education programmes (n=31)

Bachelor of Education/Teaching – early childhood (n=11)

Examples of content related to wellbeing:
Concept of wellness and wellbeing in early childhood services; a health model of wellness and wellbeing is used related to the development and care of young children; examines social and emotional, linguistic, and cognitive development of children from birth to eight years; health, wellbeing, nutrition and safety of children from infancy; syllabus content associated with the personal development, health and physical education (PDHPE) key learning area with particular focus on the safe living, personal health choices, and growth and development strands.

Bachelor of Education/Teaching – primary (n=12)

Examples of content related to wellbeing:
Develop students' understanding of the issues that impact on student wellbeing; physical, personal and social learning; the domains of health and physical education, interpersonal development, personal learning and civics and citizenship; understandings of health information, a knowledge of the nature of health and a positive attitude towards being healthy; student wellbeing, relationships and sexuality, nutrition, and outdoor education will be explored; role of primary schools in working to promote children's health and wellbeing.

Bachelor of Education/Teaching – secondary (n=6)

Examples of content related to wellbeing:
Provide students with an understanding of young people and their wellbeing, contemporary policy contexts, as well as skills in developing supportive classroom strategies and practices; examine the concept of mental health; aspects of wellbeing and sustainable living; psychosocial dimensions of health as major contributors to wellbeing in contemporary society; socio-cultural factors influencing mental health.

Post graduate (e.g. Graduate Certificate or Master of Education) (n=2)

Examples of content related to wellbeing:
The development of skills and knowledge essential for developing healthy and inclusive school communities; theoretical perspectives and current research on wellbeing and inclusive schooling and strategies for integrating learning into practice in school communities; teachers to develop and enhance knowledge and skills to promote student wellbeing in schools at the individual and organisational level.

are not yet explicitly taught during teacher preparation. For this to be successfully achieved, higher education systems can learn from proactive and positive initial teacher education wellbeing models. One such example follows.

Case study: Wellbeing curriculum in higher education

In Australia, Wellbeing Education within initial teacher education is not awarded the highest priority given an overcrowded curriculum and National Standards that determine prescribed content and evidence to be achieved by pre-service teachers for graduation and registration. In fact, at the 2014 European Education Research Association conference in Porto, Portugal, following a presentation by the authors, an American participant from the audience commented: 'Yes. It's important but how can you do that [focus on wellbeing] when we have philosophy, sociology, psychology, discipline content knowledge, literacy and numeracy requirements and all that to do. There just isn't room for that stuff.' This resonates with the vignette presented in Chapter 1, reinforcing the barriers to a wellbeing curriculum as it competes with traditional and core learning areas.

The review of Australian teacher wellbeing content in initial teacher education (Table 6.1) shows that a focus on teacher wellbeing is not given sufficient allocation in programmes compared to the wellbeing emphasis exemplified in this case study. This core course, Constructions of Wellbeing and Identity, is included in the final semester of an undergraduate education degree, just prior to a final professional experience practicum and subsequent graduation. So this course is timely and aims to equip graduating students with the awareness, knowledge and strategies needed to promote their wellbeing and that of their learners. The interrelationship between teacher wellbeing and learner wellbeing is foundational within this course, that is 'well teachers, well students' (McCallum & Price 2010). It is anticipated that a proactive focus on teacher wellbeing at this stage of the programme will have positive results in terms of retaining these prospective teachers in the profession. This premise is currently being evaluated.

The wellbeing curriculum comprises five modules:

1. Constructions/theories of wellbeing and identity
2. Holistic learner wellbeing/implications for curriculum, pedagogy and assessment
3. Proactive educational practices to promote learner wellbeing
4. Community approaches to wellbeing
5. Sustainable educator wellbeing and identity

The course extends students' expertise as cutting-edge professionals, through their multidisciplinary engagement in critical analysis of the dynamic and interconnected wellbeing issues and priorities influencing education. The modules build student capacity to lead the development of knowledge, engagement, research and ethical professional practice for sustained school community wellbeing.

A 'communities of practice' methodology connects and engages students, academics, educators and community in contemporary wellbeing curriculum, pedagogy and practice. This multidisciplinary research-informed curriculum enhances the student experience through: supporting the transition to the workplace by participation in place-based community connections; developing problem-solving capacities to address wellbeing issues that influence sustained learner and teacher wellbeing; and improving one's wellbeing.

Wellbeing education is central to the preparation of early career teachers as they transition to employment. The course begins by challenging the definitions and understandings of wellbeing which we know is a contentious and unresolved issue (see Chapter 1 and, particularly, Figure 1.1). Within the course, the concept of wellbeing is promoted as a positive personal and physical state which incorporates a sense of belonging. This enables young people to become empowered by viewing the world critically, experiencing it physically and then acting independently, cooperatively and responsibly. We integrate critical analysis across wellbeing dimensions including holistic, multidimensional (DECS 2007), psychological, relational, sociocultural and health perspectives (Wyn 2009). Contemporary practices of teaching and learning within the course:

> *What is your definition of wellbeing?*
>
> *How will you know the wellbeing of each individual in your care?*
>
> *As an educator, how can you make a difference and be a champion of wellbeing?*

FIGURE 6.1 Introductory wellbeing activity

- explores how young peoples' wellbeing can be enhanced through developing positive identities, relationships, purpose (hope), empowerment, success and safety within a complex system where multiple literacies and thinking skills are essential; and,
- challenges prospective teachers to work together to know and understand young people in their care, and to employ powerful pedagogical strategies to extend them within supportive environments.

The course promotes student-centred learner and teacher wellbeing through engaging, ethical, purposeful and contextual curriculum and pedagogy. Embedded in course assessment tasks, students apply action-based research collaboratively with community projects such as the *School of Education Aspirations Project* (which involves networks of schools and academic staff working together on action research driven, professional development projects). Wellbeing principles are scaffolded in the course through a teach–research–practice approach. The teaching encourages critical thinking and analysis of: wellbeing constructions related to achievement; potential wellbeing barriers; and protective strategies. Students are influenced, motivated and inspired by the course material. The students embark on wellbeing action research which explores a sensitive and personal issue: their own wellbeing. They research enabling and protective factors associated with wellbeing issues and apply these in authentic and practical ways. This approach provides purposeful learning and research-informed teaching practice through the modelling of a Communities of Practice approach. For example, students collect authentic and contextual wellbeing data on their own issues in class activities, focus on setting group norms around social learning environments, designing wellbeing teacher resources (Figure 6.2) and conducting collegial presentations.

The preliminary research task involves a self-survey design with wellbeing self-reports covering cognitive, social, emotional, physical and spiritual dimensions, and using empirical tools such as the Happiness Scale (Emotions survey) (Fordyce 1988) and Futures Perspective (Hope Scale) (Snyder, Hoza, Pelham, Rapoff, L, Danovsky, Highberger, Rubinstein & Stahl 1997). A Narrative Reflective Writing assessment includes literature and survey data to inform their views of wellbeing. The focus on both teacher and learner wellbeing equips these students for their final capstone professional experience placement of significant 'boundary crossing', practitioner inquiries, conference presentation and specialised teaching. The enterprise of wellbeing is promoted through mutual engagement and diverse strategies including: our facilitator role; modelling strategies that initiate and build community; and forming group norms using child protection curriculum methodology. The social learning environment is addressed through group critique of *what does wellbeing mean for us?* Generation and sharing of knowledge are promoted (see Figure 6.3), learning is embedded in practice, connections are made with others, a space is created for creativity, there is joint enterprise, and trusting relationships and a sense of belonging are developed. Additionally, Circles of Influence were implemented to inform safe networks.

FIGURE 6.2 Example of a student resource to address sensitive issues in the course

The online course offering ensured that strategies to support wellbeing were accessible to all students including remote, rural, full-time workers, caregivers etc. It ensured teacher quality and responsiveness by broadening the knowledge, skills and capacities of future educators to address youth wellbeing issues, such as those as identified in a recent Australian survey (Mission Australia 2013). The five modules have been developed for students to work through at their

Learning Objective: To identify the positive wellbeing characteristics of our young people as well as the areas to improve.

Two Stars and a Wish: After reading the first three core readings for the course, identify two areas of young people's wellbeing that you believe are faring well, give them a gold star.

For example:

 Many young people are becoming more independent and confident in their ability to access help when needed

 The message of smoking being harmful must be having an increased impact because less are smoking

Then identify one *wish* that you have to improve an area of wellbeing that has been identified in the readings.

For example:

 I wish that as an educator I could understand more about steps to reduce student anxiety and stress.

Once you have identified your two stars and a wish, proceed to the discussion board and post them. Look at other postings and provide feedback to your peers.

FIGURE 6.3 Online activity to promote wellbeing

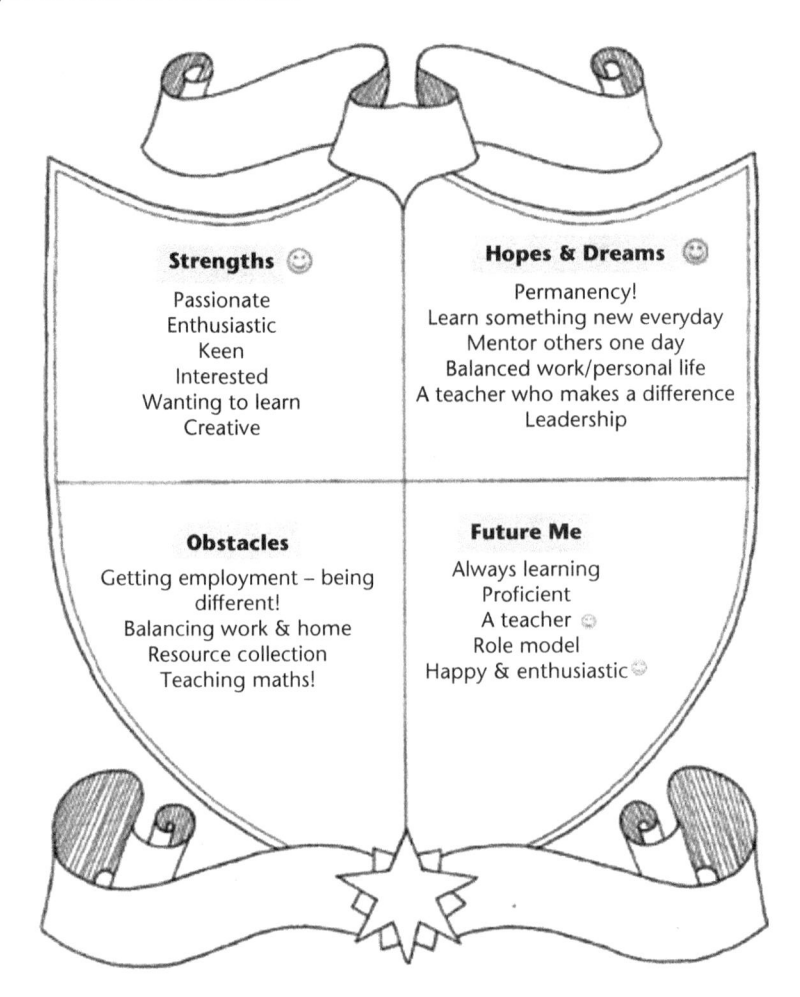

FIGURE 6.4 Coat of Arms activity

own pace, connecting with peers and the course coordinator in innovative platforms including picture galleries, graffiti boards, concept mapping, and discussion forums.

Personalised student-centred learning was achieved through the sharing of personal wellbeing artefacts. A Coat of Arms resource (Figure 6.4) provided reflective and futures oriented perspectives on the themes of Hopes and Dreams, Strengths, Obstacles and a Future Me. These innovative approaches to teaching motivated students to examine teacher wellbeing simultaneously; that is, wellbeing approaches directed at learner wellbeing were interconnected with personal teacher wellbeing. Mutual engagement was achieved through promoting group identity, a sense of belonging and shared enterprise working for common goals.

Student feedback from the course consolidated the value of course content and the teaching approaches used. For example:

> *[The lecturers] passionately mentored me in my initial teaching in this course. Their knowledge of*
> *Wellbeing research and innovative pedagogical design was enthusiastically embraced by me and the*

other students and we were challenged to explore extremely contextual and contemporary Wellbeing issues. [The lecturers] modelled Communities of Practice in their approach to the course, and embedded research as central to course design.

An evaluative survey was conducted with the graduates from the 2014 class and on this quote captures the learning links by one participant:

the key principle I learnt is ensuring that the learner wellbeing is paramount to the teaching content and that it is a foundation for learning ... It is important to understand that teacher wellbeing affects learner wellbeing therefore I ensure my wellbeing is optimum for my students' sake.

This example of one approach to embedding teacher wellbeing in initial teacher education shows that explicit learner and teacher wellbeing curriculum can have an impact on sustainable wellbeing for early career teachers. Discuss what are the implications for transferring knowledge, skills and behaviours in the transition to the workplace?

Early career teachers: The move from university to work

Global research identifies that early career teachers can struggle in their transition from university to work, and the unexpected demands and stresses of teachers' work challenges their resilience (McCallum & Price 2010; Reese 2004). Johnson and colleagues (2010) declare that it is a tough time to be a teacher. According to Anderson and Stillman (2013), factors affecting teachers' work come at a time when there is popular outcry about: educational inequity; widespread belief in teacher quality as the core lever for improving student achievement; tenuous debate about how to define, ensure, and reward quality teaching; and a policy climate marked by sweeping curricular reform, unprecedented scrutiny of teaching and learning, and expanding market-based initiatives that seek to privatise public education and deregulate teacher preparation. McCallum and Price (2014) acknowledge that teaching is a highly socialised and interactive profession, yet teachers often feel their work is more complex and demanding than others perceive. Shann and colleagues (2014) summarise some of the extensive demands entailed in teaching: dealing with difficult students; building a healthy classroom culture; accommodating the needs of diverse student groups; planning outcomes-based lessons; teaching students with special needs; scaffolding the required literacies on which to build knowledge; engaging with fellow staff members; collecting required evidence that address professional standards; using new technologies to a level that engages students in the digital world; and navigating their way out of confusing and challenging classroom events (p. 90). And all these aspects are magnified for early career teachers who are still learning the job.

As indicated earlier in the chapter, retaining beginning teachers in the profession is a challenge faced across all Western countries. The problem of maintaining a sustainable teacher workforce is compounded as the profession ages. Shortages are created through retirement—with increased numbers leaving the profession prematurely—and fewer applicants are entering teacher training (McCallum & Price 2010, p. 19). Some argue that many teachers in the current workforce are unable to relate to contemporary students. So, we feel it is timely to focus on the problem and ask ourselves: why is it that teachers' feel so overworked and undervalued?

What can be done to retain early career teachers beyond a five-year period? And, what place does a focus on teacher wellbeing have here?

Numerous studies (Johnson et al. 2010; McCallum & Price 2008; McCallum & Price 2010, 2012; Price & McCallum 2014) have focussed on the early career teacher in an attempt to understand these issues and sometimes argue for proactive measures. The factors which affect the performance of early career teachers, or which influence their decisions to leave, are both personal and professional. These factors include: poor induction or lack of professional development; isolation from friends or family; increased workload compared to their pre-service teaching experiences; lack of support from school leadership or structures; and pre-service programmes that do not sufficiently prepare them for the realities of the classroom. Using an ecological perspective, Price and McCallum (2014) discuss these personal and professional factors in detail. Four ecological levels are identified: the microsystem (individual and collective capacities); mesosystem (interrelationships between contexts); exosystem (organisational); and macrosystem (societal and legislative influences)—all of which are compounded by the influence of time at the chronosystem level. These multi-level ecological influences impact on teacher wellbeing and ability to be 'fit' for sustained performance.

In an earlier study, McCallum and Price (2008) discuss the protective factors that teachers can employ to help keep themselves well. The early career teachers involved in the study shared strategies in each of the five dimensions of wellbeing: social, emotional, physical, cognitive and spiritual. The research participants deemed a balance between these dimensions to be important rather than achieving wellness in each dimension because wellbeing is an individual trait. In a subsequent 2010 study, early career teachers expressed the view that the multidimensional nature of a wide range of wellbeing strategies would contribute to their retention in teaching (p. 31). A summary of useful teacher strategies drawn from these studies is shared in Table 6.2, arranged according to the wellbeing dimensions addressed.

In addition, Jones, Bailey and Jacob (2014) stress that teachers must use their own social-emotional skills to establish high-quality relationships with students. Providing teachers—and especially new teachers—with concrete social-emotional strategies, can enhance their capacity for positive interactions and effective communication with students (p. 21). Their study focussed on the relationship between social and emotional learning and classroom management, finding that if all members of the school community used the similar coping strategies, then issues that challenge one's wellbeing become more predictable and manageable. They identify a number of interconnected strategies (i.e. professional development and support, classroom lessons that focus on wellbeing, and daily structures and routines that promote calm operations) within a positive framework that develops a 'community of self-regulated learners' and aims to build and sustain adult and child skills that support learning (p. 21).

A study was carried out by Johnson and colleagues (2010) with 59 primary and secondary early career teachers across Western and South Australia. The data enabled the researchers to identify conditions that supported early career teacher resilience. These conditions were grouped into five major domains: (a) relationships; (b) school culture; (c) teacher identity; (d) teachers' work; and (e) system policies and practices. Table 6.3 identifies some of the important strategies identified in that study.

These studies provide a number of useful strategies to promote the wellbeing of early career teachers, and which are equally applicable to all teachers. In addition, the concept of schools as learning organisations is important as many of these strategies can be fostered across schools and sites. Learning organisations have given way to the idea of *communities of practice*

TABLE 6.2 Examples of teacher wellbeing strategies

Dimensions	Examples of teacher strategies
Physical	Minimise voice disorder by eliminating causes (e.g. smoking), seeking early detection and treatment, restricting speaking; avoiding caffeine, increasing water intake, reduce alcohol; addressing problems with sleep, exercise, diet, illness or unhealthy lifestyle; align furniture to avoid accidents, ensure good airflow and sunlight, keep classroom hygienic and reduce dust; nutrition and healthy eating; keeping fit; participating in 'down time' activities to relax and reinvigorate; balanced diet so that energy and alertness levels are maintained; breakfast is important as are regular meals; regular physical activity, either alone or in a group; watch breathing and weight control, these help to reduce risks associated with injury and illness; regular health screening checks.
Emotional	Walking away your blues—by finding a quiet and relaxing place after a tough day/ week and walking at a leisurely pace; concentrating on deep breathing; 'me time', i.e. massage, meditation, Tai Chi, beach walks, music, yoga, quiet time, sleep, taking a bath, positive thinking, reading and counselling; seeking out colleagues to debrief and give/ receive support; having harmonious workplace relationships, build up relationships with staff and students.
Social	Organised social activities in the workplace and outside of school; contact with others, including professional groups; conversations with family, friends and colleagues; debriefing; build in leisure time; relax with dogs or pets, maintain contact with friends; go to movies, concerts etc.; walk in groups; in rural areas need to mix with other teachers and locals, attend country fairs, sport and events, become part of the community; network on social media sites; stay connected.
Cognitive	Maintain professional development; be prepared; have good organisation; put thought and effort into your lessons and your job; observe other teachers; seek feedback on your own practice; know school policies; be mentored; seek support if needed; recognise your own and others' achievements; respect and trust leadership; be involved in democratic decision-making; conduct collaborative inquiry; establish mutually supportive relationships with likeminded colleagues; have a culture of inquiry; reflect daily; use reflective questioning with self and others; be willing to learn; establish daily routines and good habits early; plan short- and long-term goals.
Spiritual	Religious involvement; listen to music; sketching; bush walking; writing a journal; poetry; relaxation; establishing a positive classroom environment (with plants, music, calm relaxing voices, being uncluttered); promote school values; constantly evaluate what is important; have positive relationships both inside and out of the work environment where personal values and beliefs can be shared; finding or confirming one's sense of purpose and spiritual self.

(Lave & Wenger 1991; Wenger 1998) whereby schools and other organisations are linked in their learning through mutual interest and benefit. Perhaps we need a new concept of global communities of practice?

Case study of an at-risk group: Teachers in rural areas

In Australia, as is the case in countries around the world with a large hinterland, the biggest shortfall of teachers, and the highest levels of staff turnover occur in rural and remote school-ing, posing a major challenge to employing authorities, schools, and rural communities.

TABLE 6.3 Supporting early career teacher resilience (from Johnson, Down, Le Cornu, Peters, Sullivan, Pearce & Hunter 2010)

Domains	Supportive conditions
Relationships	Promote a sense of belonging, acceptance and wellbeing; foster pedagogical and professional growth; promote collective ownership and responsibility.
School culture	Promote a sense of belongingness and social competence; develop educative, democratic and empowering processes; provide formal and informal transition/induction processes; develop a professional learning community.
Teacher identity	Understand the discursive nature of personal and professional identities; be reflexive; enable the development of a strong sense of agency, efficacy and self-worth.
Teachers' work	Acknowledge the complex, intense and unpredictable nature of teachers' work; develop teachers' curriculum and pedagogical knowledge and strategies; provide support to create engaging learning environments; ensure access to appropriate ongoing support, resources and learning opportunities.
System policies and practices	Provide relevant, rigorous and responsive pre-service preparation for the profession; creative and innovative partnerships and initiatives that assist smooth transitions to the workforce; implement transparent, fair and responsive employment processes.

In Australia, rural school students, along with those from low socio-economic backgrounds, form the major proportion of students who show poor achievement in literacy, numeracy, problem-solving and science, according to the Program for International Student Assessment (PISA) tests in literacy, numeracy, problem-solving and science testing (McGaw 2006). Thus, while Australia is among the top-ten countries in achievement in those areas, its rural populations are at a significant disadvantage. In fact, it is well known that, compared with their peers in urban communities, students who attend rural schools in Australia have lower educational outcomes, lower high school retention rates, are less likely to complete year 12, less likely to attend university, and have lower results on standardised tests of academic performance (Sullivan, Perry & McConney 2014, p. 522). Few rural students attend universities despite higher education institutions in Australia aspiring to enrol up to 25 per cent of rural students. Rural students' life satisfaction, health and wellbeing are also reported to be more at risk than children growing up in urban areas. In a study that examined indicators of rural children's subjective wellbeing and predictive wellbeing indicators, Newland and colleagues (2014) found that the strongest predictors of both life satisfaction and mental health were school satisfaction, family, teacher and peer relationships. Again, we argue teachers and schools play central roles and are of the utmost importance in optimising student achievement and wellbeing.

In this context we share this anonymous poem that highlights an emotional response from one child living in such an environment:

> *Forgotten Child*
>
> *I am a forgotten child*
> *Who lives together with a snow-capped mountain*
> *Who walks together with the rain*
> *Who moves with the wind*

City people only think of city children
And only in the city can they be found
I am a child forgotten
Who lives at the foot of the most sacred, snowy mountain, Ausangate
Even living at the foot of Ausangate
I am equal to the children of the city
I eat, cry and also feel pain
But I am equal to the people of the city
Even living at the foot of Ausangate, the most sacred of the mountains.

(Anonymous child)

(This poem was on display in a child's orphanage in Cusco and the author is not known. Ausangate is a mountain of the Willkanuta mountain range in the Andes of Peru. With an elevation of 6,384 metres it is situated around 100 kilometres southeast of Cusco. The mountain has significance in Incan mythology.)

High quality teachers are critical in developing and maintaining student achievement yet some rural schools struggle to attract and retain teachers. Often early career teachers begin their careers in rural settings, but, as discussed earlier in this chapter, there are additional stressors on this group. Australia's remote, rural and regional schools are frequently staffed with young, inexperienced teachers with high teacher turnover (Roberts 2005). The wellbeing of students, their families and the rural community is critical to the wellbeing of the teachers employed there. Teachers, like doctors and other professionals, are not often attracted to rural areas for employment despite many lifestyle, early career progression and economic advantages. And of those professionals that do seek employment in rural areas early in their careers, few stay beyond three to five years as they see it as a short-term arrangement.

Significant research in Australia (Boylan 2008; Cuervo 2012; Green 2008; Sharplin 2010; White, Green, Reid, Lock, Hastings & Cooper 2008), and in Alaska, Scotland, Canada and the US, highlight these difficulties, identifying that early career teaching in rural areas is challenging. Morrison (2013) points out that the transition from pre-service to early career teaching is a precarious experience which is heightened by contextual factors of teaching within rural and remote schools (p. 116), a finding also supported by White and colleagues (2011). Morrison's study of a teacher working in a rural school in the first year of teaching found that her experiences included issues of acute personal and professional isolation, absence of professional and personal dialogue and support, and a seeming lack of acknowledgement of the implications of deteriorating personal and professional wellbeing (p. 116). A current Australian Research Council (ARC) Linkage Grant *Renewing the teaching profession in regional areas through community partnerships* (Brennan, McCallum & Simons 2011–2014) argues that developing a sense of 'community' in a regional location helps teachers to settle in; this assists greatly in enhancing their sense of belonging and initial feelings of wellbeing. In this study, community groups (i.e. Economic Boards, Councils, Young Professional Networks etc.) worked in partnership with teacher educators from an Australian university to welcome, orientate and support early career teachers to experience living and working in rural communities. Other studies also advocate this approach. For example, White reframes the preparation of teachers away from a *classroom only* focus to include the broader key components of preparing teachers to be *community ready*, *school ready* and *classroom ready* (White et al. 2011).

Burnout of beginning teachers in rural communities was common which O'Brien, Goodard and Keeffe (2007) state is '... has a devastating influence on the personal lives of beginning teachers and their families but the associated attrition also negatively impinges on the entire teaching profession'. The isolation and sometimes the weather, the isolation felt because of large distances from family, and also lifestyle services like inadequate shopping or housing were also reported by Collins (1999) as reasons teachers gave for leaving rural areas. Halsey (2006) has explored the pre-service teachers who undertake a rural practicum and adds that the 'social and economic costs' impacted negatively on their experience. And Sharplin (2002) who has examined pre-service teachers' perceptions of taking up a rural career found that many feared the anticipated isolation, lack of access to resources and cultural differences, and consequently it influenced future career decisions not to teach in a rural area. Hudson and Hudson add to these findings (2008) which result in rural staffing shortages. They found that 'Younger teachers point to issues such as overwork, pay structures, being put on contract without assurance of permanency, community expectations, student management and lack of social status' (p. 67). Starr and White (2008) add that access to professional learning and support, and a lack of available teaching resources exacerbates feelings of loneliness as teachers are often expected to teach in areas where they are not trained, or are promoted to greater areas of responsibility early in their careers.

This leaves early career teachers feeling unprepared for their work and points to initial teacher education to better prepare them for work in rural areas. Halsey (2006) has even suggested that policies need to be developed and others have advocated for a curriculum approach. The attraction, recruitment and sustainability of teachers for rural areas remains a critical issue in Australia and globally particularly in Canada, Alaska and Scotland. Extensive work in an Australian Learning and Teaching Council (ALTC) funded project, *Renewing Rural and Regional Teacher Education Curriculum* (RRRTEC) has attempted to address the issue to better prepare teachers for rural and regional work (White & Kline 2012, p. iii). Their work asks teacher educators to re-think the way teachers are prepared for rural work during their degrees. Many initial teacher education programmes support students to undertake a practicum or professional experience placement in a rural location. However, this is only one aspect of teacher education and does not adequately prepare teachers holistically for living and working in a rural environment for a sustained period of time, nor does this strategy address teacher and staffing shortages. White and colleagues (2008) highlight that rural communities will benefit from having better prepared teachers in them. And, teachers will be happier and more settled if they are better prepared for their work which will contribute to a more sustainable rural workforce. Figure 6.5 shows one strategy used to prepare pre-service teachers for teaching in regional locations. As part of their coursework, pre-service teachers were asked to build a 'self-help' map (after Halsey 2006) for a specific rural or regional location. It is anticipated that, once embarking on their professional career, a real-world 'self-help' map would help initial teachers develop a sense of place and assist in their transition to a new community.

Effective skills for teaching in rural schools are needed. These may include:

- knowledge about different school structures compared to city schools, i.e. multi-age and graded classes;
- understanding rural and regional students' funds of knowledge (Moll, Amanti, Neff & Gonzalez 1992);

Task:

Build a *self-help map* (Halsey 2006) to support your situating process and to help understand the students in the schools you will be teaching.

Learning Outcomes:

Research the demographics and community resources of a rural area to get to know it better. Learn about the cultural groups of a specific rural area and consider the impact of this on your role as a teacher.

Reflect on the knowledge gained to consider applying for a teaching position in a rural area.

Notes:

Understanding the town, the people and families who live there will give you background information in order to understand the students you will be teaching. This understanding supports you in designing a curriculum which is connected and relevant, and helps your transition to being a professional in a rural area. There are several strategies you can employ to achieve a successful move to rural teaching.

Suggested Procedure:

Select a town and work through the following strategies. As you go, you will build a self-help map.

Strategy 1 – Getting to know community demographics

Investigate the community and school in which you will be working by completing a search using Google and/or other search engines or sites such as My School, Australian Early Development Index, Australian Bureau of Statistics, so that you have current background knowledge of the school and community. You need to consider issues of social space so that you can bring/prepare appropriate place-based teaching resources. Consider issues in the rural sector that impact on schools – shearing, planting harvest time, climate?

Explore:

- How far (kms) from your home is the rural town/school? What is the geographical location (i.e. coastal or inland) and context?

- How many schools are in the town/area? What types of schools are there? What is the context of the school you have chosen to the others?

- School website – what does this tell you about the school and the values and focus for learning? How many students, how are the year levels structured, what are the curriculum priorities?

- How many staff are there and what is the structure of the leadership team? What are the staffing priorities?

Strategy 2 – Getting to know community resources and services

Investigate accommodation, banking, retail options that might be available to you if you gain employment in this location.

What influences may affect your understanding of the students:

- **Geographic/environmental implications:** rainfall, terrain, temperature? How may this be an influence?

- **Historical:** What is the history of the town and how may this influence families or give you contextual understanding? Is there local tourism?`

- **Diversity:** What is the population breakdown represented in the town and therefore school?

- **Culture:** What cultural groups are present in this town? What sports and recreational activities are played in the town? What are the recreation activities?

FIGURE 6.5   An exercise in developing a self-help map (adapted from Halsey 2006)

- **Economic:** What is the main industry/business in the town or local area? What are the implications for the families? What other services exist in the area?

- **Political:** Are there political agendas in the town? Is there a local council and what are the key issues on the council agenda at the moment which may have implications for the students you will be teaching?

Strategy 3 – Preparing to build relationships
While you have attended to many pragmatic issues to support a successful transition, you also need to have effective workplace relationships skills. Consider the following as you prepare for your rural experience:

- Effective communication skills for a range of audiences

- Life experience, news, study, common sense

- My School: http://www.myschool.edu.au/

- Australian Bureau of Statistics http://www.abs.gov.au/

- Population social atlas:
  http://www.publichealth.gov.au/interactive_mapping/sa_education_2009/IRSD_scores.pdf

- School homepage

- Local infrastructure and services, i.e. regional office, Tourism Board, Economic Development Board, local business

What cultural annual events, tourist festivals or highlights are key in the area?
How might a school be involved?

FIGURE 6.5 (Continued)

- awareness of students' virtual school bags, which teachers need to unpack (Thomson 2002) which might mean understanding social, cultural, geographical, historical and political differences; and
- an understanding and appreciation of place (Gruenewald 2003) and skills to develop place-based or place-conscious curriculum that connects students to their communities.

What has arisen from the research conducted in this area and from the dedicated ALTC, RRRTEC and ARC projects is that, to ensure the wellbeing of teachers in rural locations, initial teacher education should include: professional experience placements in rural areas; dedicated 'rural preparation' as core content in coursework; an embedded and inclusive approach to teaching and living in a unique location; and a pedagogical approach that utilises some of the points made above, i.e. 'sense of place' and community focus.

Conclusion

This chapter has highlighted the importance of teacher' wellbeing and the correlation between their wellbeing and that of learners in schools and all educational sites. Educator and learner wellbeing is an individual, collective and community responsibility. It is evident that wellbeing as a concept has a place in initial teacher education to ensure that early career teachers are retained in the profession alongside seasoned teachers in all hard-to-staff locations across the globe. It has also been established that there is a clear link between teachers' wellbeing, their role in the classroom and school community, and the success and satisfaction of children and young people while in the educational years. It is hoped that if these years are positive and productive ones, in which learners and staff experience a positive school ecology, then students will complete their schooling well and will be positive about their futures. This aspiration resonates with the book title *From little things big things grow*, and this common old African proverb:

It takes a village to raise a child!

Wellbeing follow-up activities

1. Decide whether you would like to make a classroom for early childhood, primary or secondary school students. Create your ideal classroom or learning space, one that establishes, promotes and sustains positive wellbeing. You can draw it, make a diorama or decorate an actual room and take photos. Write a 1,000 word reflective essay or poem telling us about your space and why it would be a positive learning environment for students and teachers.
2. *Two stars and a wish* (refer to Figure 6.3). Identify two areas of your wellbeing that you believe are faring well, give yourself a gold *star*. Identify one *wish* that you have to improve an area of wellbeing and identify strategies to achieve this. Share with colleagues.
3. What artefact represents wellbeing to you? It could be an object, drawing, photo, poem or song. Share with a colleague.
4. Ask yourself *what's the worst that can happen?* Make a list of your own strengths and accomplishments and refer to it to boost confidence. Don't waste energy worrying. Take action on what you can control and minimise risks for what you can't.

Identify warning signs: These vary from person to person, but might include things like tensing your jaw, grinding your teeth, getting headaches, or feeling irritable and short tempered.

Identify triggers: There are often known triggers which raise our stress levels and make it more difficult for us to manage. If you know what the likely triggers are, you can aim to anticipate them and practise calming yourself down beforehand, or even find ways of removing the trigger. Triggers might include late nights, deadlines, seeing particular people, hunger or over-tired children.

Establish routines: Having predictable rhythms and routines in your day, or over a week, such as regular times for exercise and relaxation, meal times, waking and bedtimes, can be very calming and reassuring, and can help you to manage your stress.

Spend time with people who care: Spending time with people you care about, and who care about you, is an important part of managing ongoing stress in your life. Share your thoughts and feelings with others when opportunities arise. Don't 'bottle up' your feelings.

Look after your health: Make sure you are eating healthy food and getting regular exercise. Take time to do activities you find calming or uplifting, such as listening to music, walking or dancing. Avoid using alcohol, tobacco or other drugs to cope.

Notice your 'self-talk': When we are stressed we sometimes say things in our head, over and over, that just add to our stress. This unhelpful self-talk might include things like: 'I can't cope', or 'I'm too busy', or 'I'm so tired', or 'It's not fair'. Try more helpful self-talk like 'I'm coping well given what's on my plate', or 'Calm down', or 'Breathe easy'.

Practise relaxation: Make time to practise relaxation. This will help your body and nervous system to settle and readjust. Consider learning a formal relaxation technique such as progressive muscle relaxation, meditation or yoga; or make time to absorb yourself in a relaxing activity such as gardening or listening to music.

FIGURE 6.6 Tips on managing inhibitors to your wellbeing (from Casey 2013, p. 59)

5. A strategy to help your wellbeing as you transition to a rural or any new school environment to teach is to consider if you are 'community ready', 'school ready' and 'classroom ready'. In a table list your relative strengths and weaknesses with respect to these three areas. This is a good strategy to help you identify the resources you need to help in your preparation.

'community ready'		'school ready'		'classroom ready'	
strengths	weaknesses	strengths	weaknesses	strengths	weaknesses

6. Consider Tables 6.2 and 6.3 and Figure 6.6. List the strategies you will employ in each of the five dimensions of wellbeing to ensure that you remain fit and well to teach for a very long and satisfying career.

References

Anderson, LM & Stillman, JA (2013) Student teaching's contribution to preservice teacher development: A review of research focused on the preparation of teachers for urban and high-needs contexts. *Review of Educational Research*, 83(1), pp. 3–69.

Australian Parliament, Senate Employment, Education and Training References Committee, *A Class Act: Inquiry into the Status of the Teaching Profession*, Canberra, 1998.

Boylan, C (2008) Rural teacher education: A literature review. In B Green (ed), *Spaces & places: The NSW Rural (Teacher) Education Project*. Centre for Information Studies, Charles Sturt University, Wagga Wagga, NSW, pp. 27–60.

Brennan, M, McCallum, F & Simons, M (2011–2014) *Renewing the teaching profession in regional areas through community partnerships (LP100200499)*. Australian Research Council, Canberra, ACT.

Buchanan, J, Prescott, A, Schuck, S, Aubusson, P, Burke, P & Louviere, J (2013) Teacher retention and attrition: Views of early career teachers. *Australian Journal of Teacher Education*, 38(3), article 8.

Carson, RL, Baumgartner, JJ, Matthews, RA & Tsouloupas, CN (2010) Emotional exhaustion, absenteeism, and turnover intentions in childcare teachers examining the impact of physical activity behaviors. *Journal of Health Psychology*, 15(6), pp. 905–914.

Casey, L (2013) *Stress and wellbeing in Australia survey 2013*. The Australian Psychological Society, Melbourne, VIC.

Collins, T (1999) *Attracting and retaining teachers in rural areas*. ERIC Clearinghouse on Rural Education and Small Schools, Charleston, WV.

Committee for the Review of Teaching and Teacher Education (2003) *Australia's teachers: Australia's future. Advancing innovation, science, technology and mathematics*. Department of Education, Science and Training, Canberra, ACT.

Cuervo, H (2012) Enlarging the social justice agenda in education: An analysis of rural teachers' narratives beyond the distributive dimension. *Asia-Pacific Journal of Teacher Education*, 40(2), pp. 83–95.

Darling-Hammond, L (1999) *Teacher quality and student achievement: A review of state policy evidence*. Center for the Study of Teaching and Policy, University of Washington, Seattle, WA.

Darling-Hammond, L (2003) The effects of initial teacher education on teacher quality. Paper presented at the *ACER Conference: Building Teacher Quality: What does the research tell us?*, Melbourne, 19–21 October 2003.

DECS (2007) *DECS Learner Wellbeing Framework for birth to year 12*. Department of Education and Children's Services, Adelaide, SA.

DETE (2005) *Submission to the House of Representatives Standing Committee on the Education and Vocational Training Inquiry into Teacher Education*. Department of Education, Training and Employment, Brisbane, QLD.

Dinham, S (2013) The quality teaching movement in Australia encounters difficult terrain: A personal perspective. *Australian Journal of Education*, 57(2), pp. 91–106.

Ewing, R & Smith, D (2003) Retaining quality beginning teachers in the profession. *English Teaching: Practice and Critique*, 2(1), pp. 15–32.

Fordyce, M (1988) A review of research on the happiness measures: A sixty second index of happiness and mental health. *Social Indicators Research*, 20(4), pp. 355–381.

Green, B (ed) (2008) *Spaces & places: The NSW Rural (Teacher) Education Project*. Centre for Information Studies, Charles Sturt University, Wagga Wagga, NSW.

Gruenewald, DA (2003) Foundations of place: A multidisciplinary framework for place-conscious education. *American Educational Research Journal*, 40(3), pp. 619–654.

Halsey, JR (2006) Towards a spatial 'self-help' map for teaching and living in a rural context. *International Education Journal*, 7(4), pp. 490–498.

House of Commons Education and Skills Committee (2004) *Secondary education: Teacher retention and recruitment*. HMSO, London.

Hudson, P & Hudson, S (2008) Changing preservice teachers' attitudes for teaching in rural schools. *Australian Journal of Teacher Education*, 33(4), pp. 66–77.

Johnson, B, Down, B, Le Cornu, R, Peters, J, Sullivan, A, Pearce, J & Hunter, J (2010) Conditions that support early career teacher resilience. Paper presented at the Australian Teacher Education Association Conference, Townsville, Queensland, 4–7 July 2010.

Jones, SM, Bailey, R & Jacob, R (2014) Social-emotional learning is essential to classroom management. *Phi Delta Kappan*, 96(2), pp. 19–24.

Kelly, N, Reushle, S, Chakrabarty, S & Kinnane, A (2014) Beginning teacher support in Australia: Towards an online community to augment current support. *Australian Journal of Teacher Education*, 39(4), pp. 68–82.

Kelly, S (2004) An event history analysis of teacher attrition: Salary, teacher tracking, and socially disadvantaged schools. *Journal of Experimental Education*, 72, 195–220.

Konu, A, Viitanen, E & Lintonen, T (2010) Teachers' wellbeing and perceptions of leadership practices. *International Journal of Workplace Health Management*, 3(1), pp. 44–57.

Kyriacou, C (2001) Teacher stress: Directions for future research. *Educational Review*, 53(1), pp. 27–35.

Lave, J & Wenger, E (1991) *Situated learning: Legitimate peripheral participation*. Cambridge University Press, Cambridge.

McCallum, F & Price, D (2008) Beginning teacher perspectives on wellbeing: The transition to teaching. *Education Connect*, 11, pp. 6–9.

McCallum, F & Price, D (2010) Well teachers, well students. *Journal of Student Wellbeing*, 4(1), pp. 19–34.

McCallum, F & Price, D (2012) Keeping teacher wellbeing on the agenda. *Professional Educator*, 11(2), pp. 4–7.

McCallum, F & Price, D (2014) Redressing teacher quality: Pre-service teachers' perceptions of their wellbeing in an initial teacher education program. Paper presented at the European Educational Research Association Conference, Porto, Portugal, 2–5 September 2014.

MCEETYA (2003) *Demand and supply of primary and secondary school teachers in Australia*. Ministerial Council for Education Employment Training and Youth Affairs, Melbourne, VIC.

McGaw, B (2006) *Achieving quality and equity education. Occasional address for the Bob Hawke Prime Ministerial Centre. University of South Australia, August 2006*. Available from http://w3.unisa.edu.au/hawkecentre/events/2006events/barrymcgaw_presentation_aug06.pdf.

Mission Australia (2013) *Youth Survey 2013*. Mission Australia, Sydney, NSW.

Moll, LC, Amanti, C, Neff, D & Gonzalez, N (1992) Funds of knowledge for teaching: Using a qualitative approach to connect homes and classrooms. *Theory Into Practice*, 31(2), pp. 132–141.

Moon, B (2007) *Research analysis: Attracting, developing and retaining effective teachers: A global overview of current policies and practices (working paper)*. UNESCO, Paris.

Morrison, CM (2013) Slipping through the cracks: One early career teacher's experiences of rural teaching and the subsequent impact on her personal and professional identities. *Australian Journal of Teacher Education*, 38(6), article 8.

Newland, LA, Giger, JT, Lawler, MJ, Carr, ER, Dykstra, EA & Roh, S (2014) Subjective well-being for children in a rural community. *Journal of Social Service Research*, 40(5), pp. 642–661.

O'Brien, P, Goddard, R & Keeffe, M (2007) Burnout confirmed as a viable explanation for beginning teacher attrition. Paper presented at the AARE Conference: Research Impacts-Proving or Improving?, Fremantle, WA, 25–29 November 2007.

Price, D & McCallum, F (2015) Ecological influences on teachers' well-being and 'fitness'. *Asia-Pacific Journal of Teacher Education,* 43(3), pp. 195–209.

Pyne, C (2013) *Nothing drives better outcomes for our children than high quality teaching*, Retrieved 9 November 2014 from www.pyneonline.com.au/media/speeches-nothing-drivesbetter-outcomes-for-our-children-than-high-quality-teaching.

Reese, R (2004) The bottom line: Strategies for reducing teacher stress-and protecting your investment in new teachers. *American School Board Journal*, 191(8), pp. 26–27.

Roberts (2005) *Staffing the empty schoolhouse: Attracting and retaining teachers in rural, remote and isolated communities*. NSW Teachers Federation, Surry Hills, NSW.

Roffey, S (2012) Pupil wellbeing—teacher wellbeing: Two sides of the same coin? *Educational and Child Psychology*, 29(4), pp. 8–17.

Santiago, P (2002) *Teacher demand and supply: Improving teaching quality and addressing teacher shortages.* OECD, Paris.

Sass, DA, Seal, AK & Martin, NK (2011) Predicting teacher retention using stress and support variables. *Journal of Educational Administration*, 49(2), pp. 200–215.

Shann, S, Germantse, H, Pittard, L & Cunneen, R (2014) Community and conversation: Tackling beginning teacher doubt and disillusion. *Asia-Pacific Journal of Teacher Education*, 42(1), pp. 82–97.

Sharplin, E (2002) Rural retreat or outback hell: Expectations of rural and remote teaching. *Issues in Educational Research*, 12(1), pp. 49–63.

Sharplin, E (2010) A taste of country: A pre-service teacher rural field trip. *Education in Rural Australia*, 20(1), pp. 17–27.

Skaalvik, E & Skaalvik, S (2011) Teacher job satisfaction and motivation to leave the teaching profession: Relations with school context, feeling of belonging, and emotional exhaustion. *Teaching and Teacher Education*, 27(6), pp. 1029–1038.

Snyder, C, Hoza, B, Pelham, W, Rapoff, M, L, W, Danovsky, M, Highberger, L, Rubinstein, H & Stahl, K (1997) The development and validation of the Children's Hope Scale. *Journal of Paediatric Psychology*, 22(3), pp. 399–421.

Starr, K & White, S (2008) The small rural school principalship: Key challenges and cross-school responses. *Journal of Research in Rural Education*, 23(5), pp. 1–12.

Sullivan, K, Perry, LB & McConney, A (2014) How do school learning environments differ across Australia's rural, regional and metropolitan communities? *The Australian Educational Researcher*, 41, pp. 521–540.

Thomson, P (2002) *Schooling the rustbelt kids: Making a difference in changing times.* Allen & Unwin, Crows Nest, NSW.

Wenger, E (1998) *Communities of practice: Learning, meaning, and identity*. Cambridge University Press, UK.

White, S, Green, B, Reid, J, Lock, G, Hastings, W & Cooper, M (2008) Teacher education for rural communities: A focus on 'incentives'. Paper presented at the Australian Teacher Education Association Conference, Sunshine Coast, QLD, 8–11 July 2008.

White, S & Kline, J (2012) *Renewing rural and regional teacher education curriculum – Final report.* Department of Industry, Innovation, Science, Research and Tertiary Education (Office for Learning and Teaching), Sydney, NSW.

White, S, Kline, J, Hastings, W & Lock, G (2011) *Renewing rural and regional teacher education curriculum [online resource]*. Australian Teaching and Learning Council, Melbourne, VIC. Available from http://www.rrrtec.net.au.

Wyn, J (2009) *Youth health and welfare: The cultural politics of education and wellbeing*. Oxford University Press, South Melbourne, VIC.

Yong, Z & Yue, Y (2007) Cause for burnout among secondary and elementary school teachers and preventive strategies. *Chinese Education and Society*, 40(5), pp. 78–85.

7

LEADING AND EMPOWERING LIFELONG WELLBEING

Well educators, well learners, well communities

Deborah Price and Faye McCallum

> *... the habits we form from childhood make no small difference, but rather they make all the difference.*
>
> (Aristotle)

When I feel my wellbeing is being addressed and in the state I feel comfortable with, I am so better positioned to provide for the learners in my care both academically and, equally as important, their wellbeing. But moving beyond this, experiencing wellbeing leadership within educational settings which prioritises empowering individual learners, staff and the broader community in wellbeing initiatives, forges a collective wellbeing enterprise which contributes to improved societal productivity and quality life experiences.

As an experienced educator in a lower socio-economic mainstream secondary educational setting, I have been privileged to experience first-hand the power of school leadership, committed firstly to addressing learner wellbeing as core business in enhancing their engagement to the educational setting and strengthening social connections with peers and staff. Such quality leadership integrated whole school wellbeing policies and principles negotiated by the school community members, empowered staff through professional development, resourcing through time to collegially plan and research and valued staff expertise and innovation in meeting the needs of highly complex needs of learners and their broader contextual influences. Such resourcing and trust elicited by school leadership, enhanced my wellbeing as an educator, building a sense of value, respect and empowerment which then filtered through to my energy and commitment to planning and building the wellbeing and academic achievement of my students.

The strengthening of relationships with my students as a result of this, created a deeper understanding of the virtual schoolbags students come to school with, their unique complexities of life experiences and most importantly, the qualities, strengths and aspirations that every learner possesses which may be highly visible for some or hidden just awaiting to be discovered. As I worked with these students taking the focus away from analysing and assessing individual achievements and redirected their energies into community wellbeing initiatives,

(Continued)

(Continued)

what emerged were strong, highly knowledgeable, skilful, empathetic and highly communicative learners whose self-concept was strengthened by servicing the community. For example, working in the local nursing home, students taught residents new technological skills through using iPads, mobile phones, laptops, iPods which contributed to both the learner wellbeing and the nursing home staff and residents' wellbeing. For one resident, they were able to use google maps to zoom in on their childhood home in the UK to show the street view, aerial view and neighbourhood pictures. As an educator, the power of these relationships and reciprocal benefits for wellbeing, significantly influenced my wellbeing as an educator… and this was only possible by leadership valuing wellbeing.

(Stephen, Year 9/10 teacher)

Stephen's vignette highlights an individual educator's effort to support learner wellbeing and academic achievement, as well as attempting to sustain his own wellbeing. This identifies that teacher wellbeing can be significantly advanced through quality leadership both within the educational site and also through broader macrosystem influences including policy, legislation and curriculum design. Later in the chapter we will return to this vignette and outline how Stephen and his colleague, who were working with a challenging and diverse class of young people, involved their school leader to tackle the wellbeing of both teachers and learners. But first, we start this chapter by summing up the key themes presented throughout in an attempt to bind together the important points that must be raised to nurture wellbeing in education.

The preceding chapters have established that both learner and educator wellbeing influence learner achievement, and social and emotional development. In addition, the role of leaders in school and education sites and indeed the whole educational community have a significant role and responsibility when it comes to ensuring the wellbeing of all. Central within this complex interplay between wellbeing and learning, is that all individuals and communities have a fundamental right to wellbeing according to differentiated needs, aspirations, beliefs and contexts. To achieve educator, learner and community wellbeing, we propose that leadership and empowerment are key to initiate, sustain and advance wellbeing initiatives both at individual and collective levels. Being empowered, as an individual and within a community, positions educators, learners and community members as active agents in their own wellbeing and in that of others. This involves having a lifelong wellbeing perspective, empathy and respect for others, being responsive to change and creatively putting deliberate and considered measures in place to advance wellbeing.

In this final chapter we will reflect on the key messages from each of the preceding chapters and highlight our position for leading the empowerment of the wellbeing of ourselves and others. We will do this by drawing on the learning work of Banks and colleagues (2007), relating the theoretical framework to the concept of wellbeing. This final discussion will promote the importance of *Nurturing wellbeing development in education* which is reflected in diagrams that portray the key aspects of teaching and research, which have been presented in this book. Integrating wellbeing as central within learner, educator and community educational initiatives from the outset, sews wellbeing and learning seeds given the notion how … *from little things, big things grow.*

Key findings/implications

In acknowledging in Chapter 1 the complex notion of wellbeing, and its varied definitions and applications within the educational field, we presented our definition which encompasses individualised wellbeing.

> Wellbeing is diverse and fluid respecting individual, family and community beliefs, values, experiences, culture, opportunities and contexts across time and change. It encompasses intertwined individual, collective and environmental elements which continually interact across the lifespan. Wellbeing is something we all aim for, underpinned by positive notions, yet is unique to each of us and provides us with a sense of who we are which needs to be respected. Our role with wellbeing education is to provide the opportunity, access, choices, resources and capacities for individuals and communities to aspire to their unique sense of wellbeing, whilst contributing to a sense of community wellbeing.

This definition challenges learners, educators, researchers, and policy and curriculum developers to be mindful of divergent wellbeing notions which can be fluid across one's lifespan. Underpinning such a definition is the recognition that *Wellbeing Education is for all* community members and an integral contributor to academic learning and achievement (see Figure 7.1).

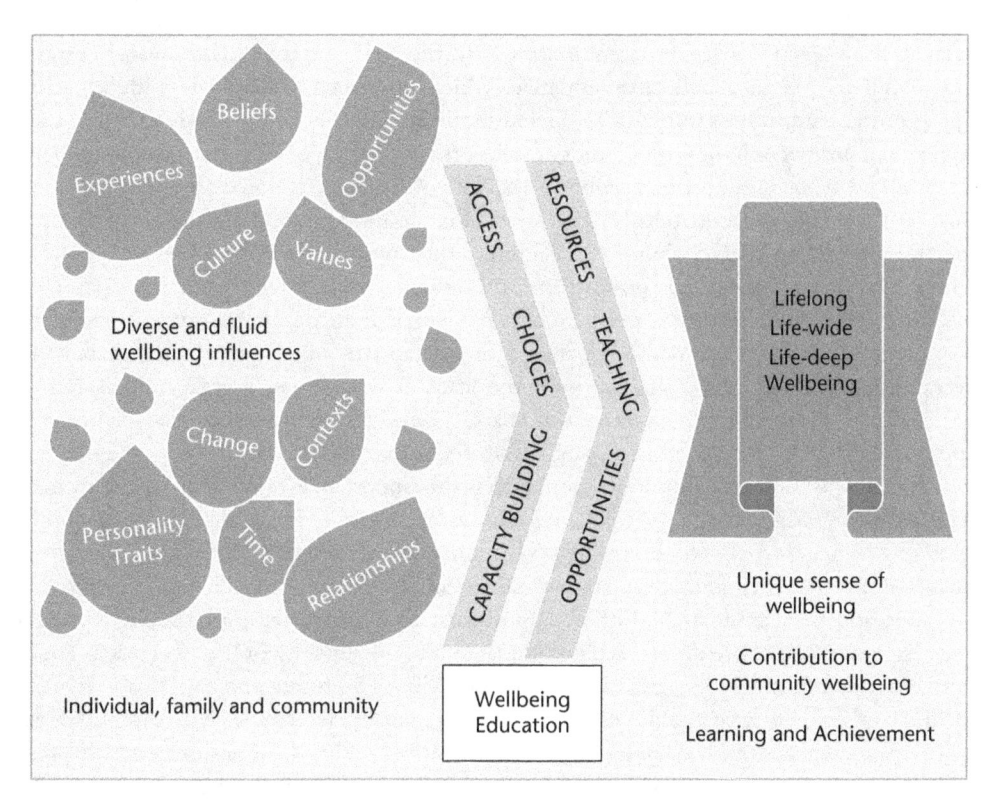

FIGURE 7.1 Wellbeing education

Within Chapter 1, the increasing emphasis on providing Wellbeing Education (inclusive of education *about* wellbeing and education *for* wellbeing dimensions) were outlined spanning a range of holistic, multidimensional, positive psychology, resilience, mental health, social and emotional learning, health, physical, relational, community and school ecology approaches. Whilst these initiatives are by no means exhaustive, they have emerged due to increasing evidence of the interplay between wellbeing, learning, academic achievement and quality of life. Given our diverse and fluid definition of wellbeing, we challenge educators, researchers, community members and stakeholders to authentically monitor, assess and measure learner and educator wellbeing, through a range of holistic and multidimensional quantitative and qualitative approaches. This is imperative to ensure inclusivity in valuing individual and community wellbeing. In respecting diversity, we also contend that, for a range of reasons, individual and community wellbeing can be placed at risk. Therefore, in alignment with this book's aim, we argue that deliberate and considered wellbeing education initiatives are an integral component in not just reacting to adverse experiences and events, but to empower individuals and communities with capacity, resources, attitudes and choices to sustain and/or advance their wellbeing.

Chapter 2, *Wellbeing for all,* provided a positive school ecology model whereby the whole school community are charged with responsibility for promoting wellbeing as well as academic learning. Within this model, hope, happiness and belonging were central elements needed for wellbeing to flourish. We identified seven critical factors that influence hope, happiness and belonging: student voice; resilience and coping; flexible thinking; individual student perceptions and interpretations; sense of community; positive thinking; and being friendly. We suggest that genuine commitment to the wellbeing of all educational community members lies in a collective initiative, which empowers individuals with capacities, opportunities and futures thinking to operate both individually and as a united community. Applying a positive school ecology model values the wellbeing of all community members.

Given everyone's foundational right to wellbeing, Chapter 3 explored an often overlooked theme of wellbeing and disability. A key message is the need to ascertain the voice and perspectives of students with disabilities in relation to their wellbeing needs, desires and priorities. This is in contrast to seemingly positive and well-intentioned wellbeing initiatives undertaken by others including educators, peers, policy and curriculum developers, parents/caregivers and community members which are based on their own judgements, values, beliefs and assumptions, without fully engaging with the learners themselves. To fully understand the wellbeing of students with disabilities, this chapter identifies the need for creative alternative approaches such as visual ethnography, arts-based programmes and assistive technologies which facilitate students' communication. Given the importance of relationships with peers, staff and the wider community, wellbeing education initiatives for students with disabilities need to advance the opportunities, accessibility and communication tools which promote the initiation, maintenance and advancing of interactions with others. Wellbeing is inclusive of everyone and their contexts, and offers opportunity to flourish, belong, be resilient, experience happiness and contentment, which ultimately provides quality of life. And just as educational curriculum and pedagogies require differentiation, adjustment and negotiation which is inclusive of students with disabilities, their wellbeing equally deserves such accommodations.

In advancing positive wellbeing education initiatives inclusive of all learners, Chapter 4 addressed an issue under-represented in the literature, that of the wellbeing of learners within alternative educational settings. A key argument presented was that learner wellbeing is paramount to meaningful learning and educational engagement whereby wellbeing is influenced through the educational and social environments and interactions in which learners are immersed. Alternative education plays a major role in supporting the academic, social, behavioural and emotional wellbeing of students who are marginalised through, and by, mainstream school settings. In particular, the interactions that students have with both peers and teachers have a significant impact on an individual's wellbeing and educational trajectory. This chapter highlighted the ways in which we can actively include students and, conversely, the ways in which we actively exclude them. For these students who have been marginalised by, or through, education, we were alerted to the fact that they make conscious decisions regarding educational opportunities including investing little effort, or holding little expectation to succeed, based on the experiences that these students have encountered. To counteract deficit models, which attribute educational marginalisation to factors *within students* (Faubert 2012; Quinn et al. 2006; Riordan 2006; te Riele 2006, 2012), acknowledgement that causal, external factors *within educational contexts*, such as school processes, achievement-related experiences and social interactions, influence learner wellbeing and educational marginalisation (Faubert 2012; Riordan 2006). Educators, educational communities and policy makers need to increase their responsibility for providing earlier intervention within mainstream education as well as respectful alternative education options by:

- reassessing how school rules and expectations are enacted;
- listening to students, including them, asking questions, checking for understanding and providing assistance in positive and productive ways, thus making them active participants in the decision-making process;
- designing respectful curriculum founded on rigour, relevance and high expectations for student outcomes;
- developing educational policies which include learner perspectives regarding what they learn, how they learn and with whom, and integrate an emphasis on both wellbeing and academic outcomes; and
- increasing educational motivation and engagement by promoting a sense of belonging and connectedness via interaction with positive peers who are supportive and academically oriented.

We contend that such efforts will proactively engage learners who may have been traditionally deemed at risk within mainstream education as well as reconnect learners within alternative education through applying a wellbeing educational approach.

As a counterpoint to exploring wellbeing within school systems, Chapter 5 highlighted the significance of the *technology/social media* revolution on young people's wellbeing. It drew attention to the paradox inherent in contemporary social media and communication/leisure technologies that they can simultaneously provide positive and negative experiences, which can enhance wellbeing, or serve to diminish it. As young people themselves noted, the positive impacts were the 'flip side of the negative', raising the importance of listening to young people, and acknowledging their rights to participate and be heard.

Importantly, young people identified that they learn from, and benefit from engaging with social media and social networking sites, countering the adult 'moral panic' view that social media and social networking is a necessarily negative experience. Young peoples' wellbeing profiles also demonstrated that they were also, on the whole, 'well'.

However, negative acts, such as cyberbullying, which usually occur outside the school setting, nevertheless impact most on the social relationships within school subsequently affecting all young people's health and wellbeing. Cyberbullying contributes to poorer academic outcomes, increased stress, anxiety and depression, lower levels of social connectedness and increased social difficulties for those involved, but particularly for those who are both targets and perpetrators—*cyber bully-victims*. These are the most at-risk individuals in school classrooms—at risk socially, emotionally, and academically.

One important, yet largely under-researched finding relates to the time of night young people are involved online. Those who were on late at night (after 11 pm) were more often vulnerable to the negative impacts of social media, yet even though they were online, were unlikely to access help from that setting. How communities deal with cyberbullying then, is critical if young people are to feel safe and supported, and well enough to learn and fulfil their social, emotional and academic potential. Mandating cyber-safety lessons within the curriculum is one approach to consider, but so is harnessing contemporary technology as part of the solution: to assist and support young people to reach out for help in a timely manner, especially when they are online and parents and friends are not present.

Young people's relationships, and the friendship-driven practices which underpin, sustain and influence them are enacted seamlessly across both online and offline settings. To consider young people's wellbeing without understanding the role that technology plays in that social dynamic, is to fail to recognise the 'third dimension' which encircles all components of their lives: family, school and community.

Undeniably, within the educational realm, learner wellbeing and academic achievement would be the highest priorities for educators. However, as identified in Chapter 6, the significance of teacher/educator wellbeing needs a higher profile across the teaching career, and especially during initial teacher education and transition to the workforce. Ever-changing roles and responsibilities are associated with the education profession. These include teacher quality, professional teacher standards, increasing learner outcomes, differentiation of curriculum and pedagogy inclusive of student diversity, technological advances, national curriculum agendas and supporting learner wellbeing, educational policy, leadership and resourcing. Such elements require an increasing focus on supporting teachers and educators' wellbeing for sustained and productive careers. This chapter deliberately challenged this increasing focus through initiatives such as:

- integrating explicit wellbeing education curriculum within higher education (initial teacher education);
- specifically training teachers for diverse teaching experiences inclusive of: professional experience placements (e.g. rural areas); a dedicated curriculum (e.g. rural) included as core in coursework; an embedded and inclusive approach to teaching and living in a unique location, and a pedagogical approach adaptive to location;
- advocating teacher wellbeing models, e.g. think well, act well, be well; ecological systems influences; multidimensional;
- adopting a 'communities of practice' methodological approach which connects students, academics, educators and community in contemporary wellbeing curriculum, pedagogy and practice;
- analysing constructions/theories of wellbeing and identity;

- scaffolding educator understanding of holistic learner wellbeing philosophy and examine implications for curriculum, pedagogy and assessment;
- advocating proactive educational practices to promote learner wellbeing and community approaches to wellbeing;
- self-assessing wellbeing, e.g. multidimensional; resilience; life graphs; self-help mapping; self-talk; and
- explicitly planning for the transition to diverse contexts (i.e. remote, rural location) by investigating protective and risk factors, circles of influence, support networks, future hopes, aspirations, demographic research.

In much the same way that learner wellbeing requires a dedicated curriculum, explicit teacher/educator wellbeing initiatives from the outset of initial teacher education are essential. One cannot assume that teacher wellbeing naturally occurs; rather, deliberate and considered education is required to support smooth transitions to the workplace and sustained careers which ultimately promote learner wellbeing and academic achievement.

Nurturing wellbeing education through a lifelong philosophy requires effective leadership which empowers individuals and communities, as identified in this final chapter. Empowering all stakeholders to take responsibility for both their own wellbeing and that of others promotes learner wellbeing, educator wellbeing and community wellbeing.

Wellbeing is lifelong, life-wide and life-deep

We have established that wellbeing is central to learning. In fact, we acknowledge that wellbeing both within and outside of educational sites is lifelong, life-wide and life-deep (Banks et al. 2007). Wellbeing is everyone's business to ensure children and young people, educators and leaders, and the whole school/educational community remain *well*. Globalisation, the digital world, adversity, environmental degradation and worldwide disasters make it imperative for educators to be well and active for a sustained career to ensure good outcomes for children and young people as they travel through their schooling/educational years and transition to further study, work or other purposeful contributions to society. An overarching tenet of this book is that educators can increase the academic achievement and life satisfaction for young people through a collective wellbeing approach. Learning occurs in formal and informal environments with most happening across the lifespan in informal settings. However, the formal environment of a school or educational site is an ideal place in which to instil effective and sustainable wellbeing attitudes and strategies.

Lifelong wellbeing refers to the acquisition of fundamental behaviours and real information; it's about engaging one's body and mind together in wellbeing. As defined by Banks and colleagues—who modelled this concept on learning, we consider lifelong wellbeing to extend from birth to old age which includes all the ways we manage interpersonal sociability, reflecting on our belief systems, and orienting us to new experiences (adapted from Banks et al. 2007). To acquire lifelong wellbeing, specific kinds of information and awareness are needed and these relate to the daily ways in which we go about life. If motivated to do so and if exposed to wellbeing as a holistic way of life from an early age, then our interests, curiosity, pleasure and sense will support a move toward lifelong wellbeing even in the face of adversity. Orientation to observing, trying, testing and finding wellbeing will become lifelong. This wellbeing can be present from an early age through play, physical activity, sport, and other opportunities to work alone and in teams.

Life-wide wellbeing involves a breadth of experiences, guides, and locations and includes core issues such as adversity, comfort, and support in our lives. This wellbeing takes individuals through adaptation to new situations. Bell (2013) refers to the 'learning across settings' phenomena as the 'life-wide' dimension (p. 95). In relation to wellbeing this is the dimension where people circulate from moments of family life, compulsory schooling, participation in online communities, or other patterned routines of daily practice. Experiences of ourselves and others, of time and space, of unexpected circumstances, events or crises, helps us to adapt, to transfer skills and knowledge gained in one situation to another and to transform experiences into strategies and tactics for future use (Banks et al. 2007). Amongst the challenges life brings, if someone cannot take care of issues alone, they at least need to know how to find someone they can trust to help them.

Life-deep wellbeing embraces religious, moral, ethical and social values that guide what we believe, how we act and how we judge ourselves and others (Banks et al. 2007, p. 12). Developing life-deep wellbeing is influenced by how young people grow and develop, through constant interactions with their families, the communities that surround them and larger societal institutions like schools which predominantly serve as spaces for engaging in cognitive activities (Banks et al. 2007). To be well on the inside, cognitively and emotionally, to be able to express to ourselves and to others how we feel and what we believe, is important in one's overall balance and perspective on life.

To facilitate lifelong, life-wide, and life-deep wellbeing educators and leaders in education should draw on the cultural capital students bring from their homes and communities (adapted from Banks et al. 2007). In response we have identified four principles related to informal and formal wellbeing that we can use to enhance the wellbeing of all children and young people. The principles are based on research, teaching within schools and settings, extensive experience in initial teacher education and our work with educators over several decades. These are:

1. It is everyone's responsibility, including our own, to ensure the wellbeing of all, in or out of schools or educational sites, and inclusive of diversity or historical cultural backgrounds or circumstances.
2. Modelling, observing, teaching, monitoring and leading wellbeing is our core business.
3. Nurturing a sense of wellbeing as early as possible in a young person's life is central in promoting a lifelong, life-wide and life-deep wellbeing perspective.
4. Respectful wellbeing is unique, diverse and fluid reflecting individual, family and community beliefs, values, experiences, culture, opportunities and contexts across time and change.

In this book we have presented an argument for the development and sustainability of well children, young people, educators, and communities. In this technological advanced world of consistent and challenging ups and downs we must remind all that productive, successful citizens can only be realised if we are in fact *well*. We have presented new concepts to assist in the development of positive structures, frameworks, and strategies that can help us in this forward mission, to achieve lifelong, life-wide and life-deep wellbeing. However, in achieving this, commitment to wellbeing education from educational leadership, both within sites and across the broader education stakeholder community, is deemed as critical.

Lifelong wellbeing leadership and empowerment

As evidenced by Stephen's vignette at the outset of this chapter, the effort to support learner wellbeing and academic achievement, as well as one's own teacher wellbeing was significantly advanced through quality leadership at the school site and through broader macrosystem influences including policy, legislation and curriculum design. As Roffey (2012a) identifies:

> School leaders have a critical role in ensuring an effective learning environment for every student – from the most able and compliant to the most disadvantaged and difficult. To do this they need to attend to the quality of their interactions with staff but also ensure that policies within the school are congruent.
>
> *(Roffey 2012a, p. 157)*

Stephen and his colleague Monique were responsible for designing and implementing a Learning in Collaboration (LinC) programme which directly targeted year 9 and 10 students who had for a range of reasons disconnected with the educational system, evidenced by low academic grades, poor student attendance and behavioural issues associated with lack of engagement with the learning programme. Stephen and Monique were particularly concerned about this cohort of students who seemingly were flying under the radar, as they were not officially diagnosed with any learning or behavioural difficulties or disabilities, and therefore did not qualify for funding for any additional support. As a result these teachers engaged their school principal in discussions about how they believed pedagogy and curriculum directly influenced student engagement. Designing pedagogical practices and curriculum based on a wellbeing framework was deemed as essential in shaping the subjectivities and aspirations of young people within their educational site, characterised by socio-economic challenge. What resulted from this conversation was a commitment by school leadership, demonstrated through initiatives such as: timetabling a LinC class of 20 students; funding Stephen and Monique to teach the class; provision of resources for the learning programme; provision of release time for Stephen and Monique to programme and work with university academics in undertaking action research to gather evidence of the programme effectiveness; and providing supportive rationale and communication to the entire school community endorsing the wellbeing curriculum focus. Such trust and support enlisted by the school principal, reinforced Stephen and Monique's professional identity, whilst providing the capacity and empowerment to enact an innovative programme directly connecting to the lifeworlds and contextual needs of the students. As Roffey (2012b) asserts 'the ability to foster positive relationships is at the heart of good leadership. Inspiration and innovation are not enough – true leaders also need emotional and social intelligence to engage workers in co-creating their vision' (p. viii). As an outcome of such supportive leadership was a LinC programme whereby Stephen and Monique genuinely understood, respected, connected and confronted complex student lifeworlds deciding to teach these students, here and now, in this context (Wrench et al. 2013).

Through our engagement in such action, research, and support of educational leaders within educational sites and the broader education community, can prioritise professional development projects in research networks. This enables professional conversations between teachers and academics in an attempt to redesign pedagogy (Noffke & Somekh

2009). Such professional conversations, with support from academic staff as critical friends, enabled Stephen and Monique to challenge curriculum and pedagogy in their aim to unsettle deficit views of students and their communities (Comber & Kamler 2004; Hattam and Prosser 2008). Central within this endeavour were leadership personnel and teachers who *understood* the conceptual notion of wellbeing and *chose* wellbeing as the vehicle to learner achievement and engagement (Wrench et al. 2013). This reinforces the importance of commitment by school leaders, policy developers and curriculum designers to wellbeing education as it cannot solely rest on the educational site alone, but needs to be integrated into a broader community wellbeing enterprise.

Community wellbeing

For Stephen and Monique, the LinC programme focussed on student contextual backgrounds, virtual schoolbags and local community, which directly influenced student engagement in learning, wellbeing and social sustainability. To engage these students at risk of educational disengagement, they had a head set for working differently and being creative and responsive to student contextual needs through designing innovative pedagogy and curriculum focused on community projects. By identifying students' strengths, interests and aspirations, the LinC students worked in nursing homes, gardening initiatives and local kindergarten projects which built relationships across diverse groups, strengthened social and emotional capacities whilst reinforcing their ability to contribute to community wellbeing. In using the term community, the following interpretation has been adopted:

> The word 'community' has a range of connotations. It can refer to those who share a geographical location, who belong to a school or a neighbourhood or who share common knowledge, understandings and values. Active respect among communities that differ but live in the same locality can break down barriers and construct more positive community relationships.
>
> *(McCarthy & Vickers in Roffey 2012b, p. 227)*

They continue:

> The emphasis is on building on the strengths and resilience of people through collaborative endeavours. Established traditional boundaries are breached both by new experiences and by openness to learning—about the self and about 'others'.
>
> *(McCarthy & Vickers in Roffey 2012b, p. 240).*

Banks et al. (2007) suggest that there are many positive benefits from belonging, or feeling like you belong, to a community. Children and young people can receive support and mentoring while learning about a range of perspectives. They can expand their social network and develop forms of social capital; they can develop interests and capacities that serve them well in the future. And, as described by Reid and McCallum (2014), these LinC students developed aspirations for a bright future because of their trusting relationships with the teachers, their peers and because of the connectedness they all felt in their community. But most importantly, holistic wellbeing can be accomplished within and by communities that invest in enabling structures and activities that flourish. Reflect back on the positive social ecology concept presented in Chapter 2 which explained how four domains (Intrapersonal, Environmental, Behavioural and Political) influence factors in the Natural, Information, and Social and Cultural Environments of a community. Although this concept went on to describe what a positive school ecology looked like, schools alone cannot sufficiently enable optimal wellbeing for all.

Final thoughts: Holistic wellbeing

The authors of this book are committed to the belief that child and youth wellbeing is vital for the development of 'well' adults and, ultimately, subsequent generations. Education has a key role to play in this space, as does the wider community.

Educators from all schools, sites and jurisdictions are pivotal adults in the lives of children and young people. They can influence the positive growth and development of young people. This book acknowledges that adverse situations can occur in every child's life, but it also identifies that there are proactive ways to positively influence the future prosperity and health of individuals. We do not want to dwell on adversity but instead place energy in moving on, building and supporting all. We are reminded of this quote from Margaret Mead:

> The solution of adult problems tomorrow depends upon the way we raise our children today. There is no greater insight into the future than recognizing when we save our children, we save ourselves.
>
> *(in Burns 1996, p. vii)*

A guiding framework is provided for the development of evidence-based, preventive and sustainable approaches to improve child and youth wellbeing across Australia and the world. Federal, state and local governments, businesses, schools, non-government agencies, parents and carers, the general community, and children and youth can make a difference if we work collectively toward achieving the changes that are needed. Figure 7.2 presents a Holistic Wellbeing Model. The model situates children at the centre as they are the most important resource in wellbeing. As children grow and develop, their teachers, schools as social institutions and the wider community, can all play a part in each child's development regardless of ability, language, race, socio-economic status or class. Within this framework, the interplay between learner wellbeing, educator wellbeing and community wellbeing needs to be recognised. Reinforcing the positive approach of this book, the issues that influence wellbeing and achievement, and reinforcing the notion *from little things, big things grow*, we identified six strategies for nurturing wellbeing in education and the wider community:

- building and sustaining healthy relationships;
- developing and nurturing individual and group strengths;
- establishing effective and safe communication strategies;
- behaving in a way that welcomes a sense of belonging and connection to others and models positive, peaceful and caring action;
- nurturing emotional health; and
- scaffolding wellbeing through growing leaders with a democratic leadership style.

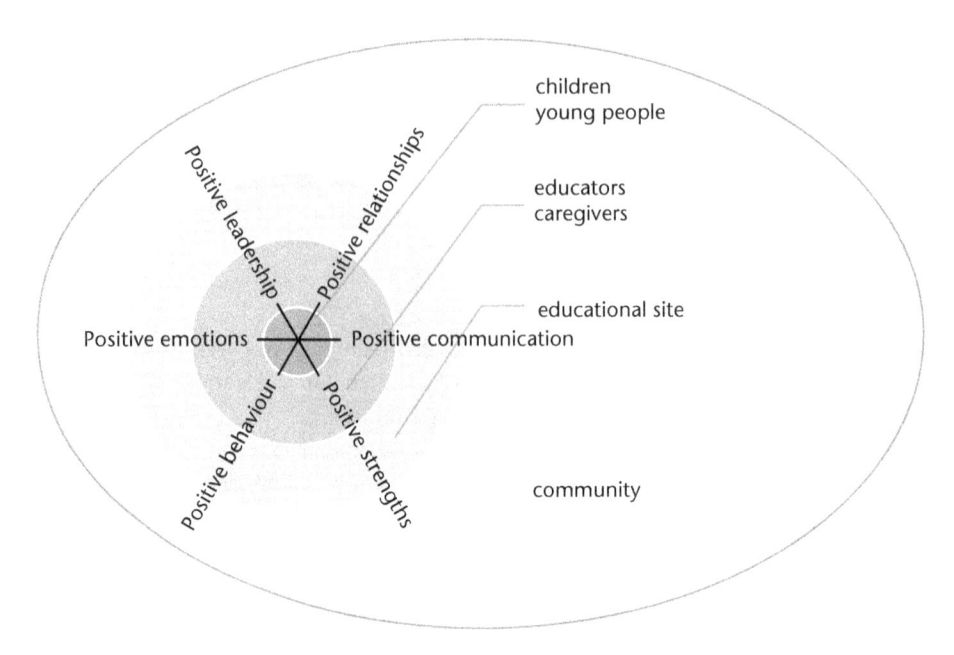

FIGURE 7.2 A model of holistic wellbeing

Wellbeing follow-up activities

1. The following checklist is a tool for educators to use to generate dialogue and be a springboard for discussion and reflection about the principles. There is room to add your specific questions under each key principle; include factors you want to measure in your context/environment.

Principles	How Well are you doing?		
	Not that Well	*Well*	*Really Well*
1. It is everyone's responsibility, including our own, to ensure the wellbeing of everyone, in and out of schools or educational sites, regardless of diversity or historical cultural backgrounds or circumstances.			
a. Who is involved in your wellbeing network? Are everyone's needs being considered?			
b. Are we caring for all groups in our community? Who is 'in', who is left 'out'?			
c.			
d.			
2. Modelling, observing, teaching and evaluating wellbeing is our core business.			
a. How are we doing about actively observing and measuring our wellbeing?			

b.	How effective is our teaching of wellbeing?			
c.	What else can we do?			
d.				
e.				
3.	Instilling a sense of wellbeing as early as possible in a young person's life			
a.	How do we care for and support our very young— emotionally, socially, physically, cognitively and spiritually?			
b.	How do we care for and support all children—emotionally, socially, physically, cognitively and spiritually?			
c.	How do we care for and support the whole community— emotionally, socially, physically, cognitively and spiritually?			
d.				
e.				

References

Banks, J, Au, K, Ball, A, Bell, P, Gordon, E, Gutierrez, K, Heath, S, Lee, C, Lee, Y, Mahiri, N, Valdes, G & Zhou, M (2007) *Learning in and out of school in diverse environments: Life-long, life-wide, life-deep.* The LIFE Center, University of Washington, Stanford University and SRI International.

Bell, P (2013) Introduction: Understanding how and why people learn across settings as an educational equity strategy. In B Bevan et al. (eds), *LOST opportunities.* Springer, Dordrecht, The Netherlands, pp. 95–98.

Burns, T (1996) *From risk to resilience – A journey with heart for our children, our future.* Marco Polo Publishers, Dallas, TX.

Comber, B & Kamler, B (2004) Getting out of deficit: Pedagogies of reconnection. *Teaching Education*, 15(3), pp. 293–310.

Faubert, B (2012) *A literature review of school practices to overcome school failure.* OECD education working papers, No. 68. OECD, Paris, France.

Hattam, R & Prosser, B (2008) Unsettling deficit views of students and their communities. *Australian Educational Researcher*, 35(2), pp. 89–106.

Noffke, S & Somekh, B (eds) 2009, *Handbook of educational action research.* SAGE, London.

Quinn, M, Poirier, J, Faller, S, Gable, R & Tonelson, S (2006) An examination of school climate in effective alternative programs. *Preventing School Failure*, 51(1), pp. 11–17.

Reid, A & McCallum, F (2014) 'Becoming your best': Student perspectives on community in the pursuit of aspirations. *Australian Educational Researcher*, 41(2), pp. 195–207.

Riordan, J (2006) Reducing student 'suspension rates' and engaging students in learning: principal and teacher approaches that work. *Improving Schools*, 9(3), November, pp. 239–250.

Roffey, S (2012a) Developing positive relationships at school. In S Roffey (ed), *Positive relationships: Evidence based practice across the world.* Springer, Dordrecht, The Netherlands., pp. 145–162.

Roffey, S (ed.) 2012b, *Positive relationships: Evidence based practice across the world.* Springer, Dordrecht, The Netherlands.

te Riele, K (2006) Youth 'at risk': Further marginalizing the marginalized? *Journal of Education Policy*, 21(2), pp. 129–145.

te Riele, K (2012) *Learning choices: A map for the future.* Dusseldorp Skills Forum, Victoria University, Melbourne, VIC.

Wrench, A, Hammond, C, McCallum, F & Price, D (2013) Inspire to aspire: Raising aspirational outcomes through a student well-being curricular focus. *International Journal of Inclusive Education*, 17(9), pp. 932–947.

INDEX